INSIGHT GUIDES
SINGAPORE

APA PUBLICATIONS L

Part of the Langenscheidt Publishing Group

HOW TO USE THIS BOOK

This book is carefully structured both to convey an understanding of Singapore and its culture and to guide readers through its attractions and activities:

◆ The Best Of section at the front of the book helps you to prioritise. The first spread contains all the Top Sights, while the Editor's Choice details unique experiences, the best buys or other recommendations.

◆ To understand Singapore, you need to know something of its past. The city's history and culture are described in authoritative essays written by

specialists in their fields who have lived in and documented the city for many years.

◆ The Places section details all the attractions worth seeing. The main places of interest are coordinated by number with the maps.

◆ Each chapter includes lists of recommended shops, restaurants, bars and cafés.

◆ Photographs throughout the book are chosen not only to illustrate geography and buildings, but also to convey the moods of Singapore and the life of its people.

◆ The Travel Tips section includes all the practical information you will need, divided into four key sections: transport, accommodation, activities (including the arts, nightlife, tours and sports) and an A–Z of practical tips. Information may be located quickly by using the index on the back cover flap of the book.

◆ A detailed street atlas is included at the back of the book, with all restaurants, bars, cafés and hotels plotted for your convenience.

PLACES AND SIGHTS

Chapters are **colour-coded** for ease of use. Each neighbourhood has a designated colour corresponding to the orientation map on the inside front cover.

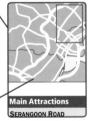

A locator map pinpoints the specific area covered in each chapter.

Margin tips provide extra snippets of information, whether it's a practical tip, a whimsical quote, an historical fact or advice on shopping and eating.

A four-colour map shows the area covered in the chapter, with the main sights and attractions coordinated by number with the text.

PHOTO FEATURES

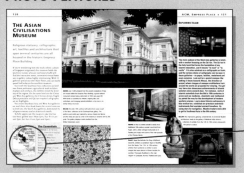

Photo features offer visual coverage of major sights or unusual attractions. Where relevant, there is a map showing the location and essential information on opening times, entrance charges, transport and contact details.

SHOPPING AND RESTAURANT LISTINGS

Shopping listings provide details of the best shops in each area. **Restaurant listings** give the establishment's contact details, opening times and price category, followed by a useful review. Bars and cafés are also covered here. The coloured dot and grid reference refers to the atlas section at the back of the book.

Thai

Thanying
2/F, Amara Hotel, 165 Tanjong Pagar Rd. Tel: 6222-4688. http://singapore.amara hotels.com Open: daily L & D. $$$ 57 p272, B4
Thanying means "Thai noble lady". Indeed, this

TRAVEL TIPS

By Sea

Arriving slowly by sea is a pleasant experience. Most visitors arrive at the **Singapore Cruise Centre** (tel: 6513-2200; www. singaporecruise.com) located at the HarbourFront Centre. The facility is also used by several regional cruise operators, such as Star Cruises, and by many large cruise liners stopping over on their long voyages from around the world.

Travel Tips provide all the practical knowledge you'll need before and during your trip: how to get there, getting around, where to stay and what to do. The A–Z section is a handy summary of practical information, arranged alphabetically.

LEFT: the glittering waterfront.

Maps

THE BEST OF SINGAPORE: TOP SIGHTS

A far cry from its humble beginnings as a fishing village, the Singapore of the 21st century is bursting with brand-new blockbuster-style theme parks, fascinating museums, lush gardens and cultural enclaves

△ **Little India.** Be prepared for a sensory overload. Start at Little India Arcade and walk down Serangoon Road – along the way, pick up a colourful silk sari or tuck into a delicious North or South Indian meal. *See page 163.*

▽ **Chinatown.** Explore Trengganu, Pagoda, Smith and Sago streets and soak in the Singapore of yesteryear. Chinese New Year is the best time to visit this lively and colourful district. *See page 123.*

▽ **Marina Bay Sands.** This "integrated resort" not only has a casino and several top-notch restaurants set up by celebrity chefs, but also a Sky Park perched on the 57th level, an art and science museum, and a superb theatre used for major productions. *See page 138.*

◁ **Singapore Botanic Gardens.** Singapore's oldest national park, set up in 1859, is known as a living museum of tropical plants. The National Orchid Garden is brimming with over 1,000 species of orchid. *See page 154.*

▷ **Universal Studios.** Experience the world's first Madagascar theme park ride; trace the past in Ancient Egypt, then fast forward to the future at Sci-Fi City. *See page 182.*

▽ **National Museum.** The Singapore History Gallery exhibits 11 national treasures, and the Singapore Living Galleries celebrate the creativity of Singaporeans through the themes of food, fashion, film and photography. *See page 108.*

▽ **Singapore Zoo.** This is the place to come face to face with a variety of wildlife. The open-air enclosures present animals in their natural environment, captive breeding of endangered species, and attractive landscaping. A unique activity is breakfast with wildlife. *See page 224.*

◁ **Jurong Bird Park.** This well-known bird park is known its commitment to avian conservation. Beautifully created habitats include four walk-in free-flight aviaries. *See page 200.*

▽ **Singapore Flyer.** Stunning views of the city skyline can be enjoyed from the Singapore Flyer, the world's tallest observation wheel. The "Full Butler Sky Dining" experience is the first of its kind in the world. *See page 103.*

▽ **Night Safari.** The world's first night wildlife park, the Night Safari is home to 115 nocturnal species. There are eight zones, including the Indian subcontinent, Himalayan foothills and African plains. *See page 225.*

THE BEST OF SINGAPORE: EDITOR'S CHOICE

Setting priorities, saving money, unique attractions... here, at a glance, are our recommendations, plus some tips and tricks even locals don't always know

BEST FOR FAMILIES

- **DUCKtours**. An amphibious craft transports you around the Civic District before splashing into the Singapore River. *See pages 103.*
- **Escape Theme Park** and **Wild Wild Wet**. Thrilling adrenalin-pumping rides for the fearless and young at heart. *See page 214.*
- **Jurong Bird Park**. The region's leading bird park has some 380 species of birds. Don't miss the four walk-in free-flight aviaries. *See page 200.*

- **Night Safari**. Clever lighting and realistic habitats make you feel as though you're in a tropical jungle at night. *See page 225.*
- **Singapore Science Centre**. Everything you need to know about science is found here in its 1,000-plus exhibits. Kids will have fun with the interactive galleries. *See page 199.*
- **Singapore Zoo**. More than 300 species of wildlife are presented in their natural environments. Not to be missed are the animal shows, animal feedings and Rainforest Kidzworld. *See page 224.*
- **Sentosa**. An island retreat that has everything for the family: the Universal Studio theme park, Underwater World, an old fort, beaches and more. Plan to spend a full day. *See page 181.*
- **East Coast Park**. Kayak out to sea, frolic by the beach or rent bikes or roller blades. *See pages 210.*
- **Singapore Botanic Gardens**. Jacob Ballas Children's Garden is Asia's first children's garden, where kids under 12 can appreciate plants and nature through play and exploration. *See pages 154.*

ABOVE: the Fountain of Wealth at Suntec City.
BELOW LEFT: kids are well catered for at Sentosa.
BELOW: a Sentosa funfair.

Left: Indian performers at the Chingay Parade. **Above:** Chinese fans in Chinatown; the area is full of interesting shops.

BEST FESTIVALS AND EVENTS

- **Chingay Parade.** Celebrated as part of Chinese New Year, the city's biggest street procession sees decorated floats and acrobats parading down the street. January or February. *See page 56.*
- **Great Singapore Sale.** A retail blowout that offers steep discounts all over the island. From late May until early July. *See page 57.*
- **Singapore Arts Festival.** Three weeks of dance, music and theatre by some of the world's most innovative performers. Late May and June. *See page 57.*
- **Singapore Food Festival.** This month-long festival celebrates Singaporeans'

favourite pastime with food tours and food-related events. July. *See page 58.*
- **Thaipusam.** Male devotees bear the *kavadi*, a heavy metal arch with spikes on a procession between two temples. Usually takes place in January. *See page 56.*
- **Thimithi.** Hindu devotees demonstrate their faith, courage and endurance by walking across a bed of burning coals at the Sri Mariamman Temple. Usually in October or November. *See page 59.*
- **World Gourmet Summit.** Some of the world's best chefs cook up a storm at top restaurants during this two-week event. Mid-April. *See page 57.*

BEST MARKETS

- **Campbell Lane.** Fresh produce, jasmine garlands, aromatic incense, Bollywood CDs and statues of Hindu gods are all found here. It becomes especially lively in the evening. *See page 166.*
- **Tekka Centre.** Some of the freshest seafood and herbs are sold in this bustling market. Stallholders are friendly and knowledgeable about their produce. *See page 165.*

- **Chinatown Complex.** Start early in the morning and head to the basement to see a "wet" produce market. The fishmongers at work make for great photography. *See page 128.*
- **Chinatown Night Market.** Every evening Trengganu, Pagoda and Sago streets close to traffic and vendors set up carts selling souvenirs and gifts. *See page 127.*

Below: a Hindu penitent, spiked and skewered with steel rods and carrying a *kavadi*, at the annual Thaipusam festival.

10

Above: worshippers at Kong Meng San Phor Kark Temple.
Left: barman in action at Fullerton Hotel's Post Bar.

Best Bars and Clubs

- **Attica/Attica Too.** This ultra-hip multi-venue bar/lounge/club at Clarke Quay is one of the city's hottest night-spots. *See pages 67 and 248.*

- **Ice-Cold Beer.** This wildly popular bar at Emerald Hill continues to draw regulars and expats thanks to its chill-out ambience and, yes, plenty of chilled beer and excellent pub grub. *See pages 68 and 159.*

- **St James Power Station.** The city's largest party venue, with nine entertainment spots – pick from Latin, house, jazz and more – under one roof. *See pages 67 and 249.*
- **New Asia Bar.** The drinks are easily overshadowed by the stunning floor-to-ceiling views of the city from its 71st-floor perch at the Swissôtel The Stamford hotel. *See pages 68, 119 and 249.*
- **Post Bar.** Elegant pre-dinner spot at The Fullerton hotel. *See pages 68, 100 and 119.*
- **Zouk.** Where serious clubbers head to for cutting-edge dance music and a wild party atmosphere. High on the "be-seen" scale. *See pages 67, 115 and 249.*

Top Parks

- **Bukit Timah Nature Reserve.** The number of plant species here exceeds that found in the whole of North America. *See page 223.*
- **MacRitchie Reservoir Park.** Several trails, taking from one to five hours, offer a good workout; signboards in the reserve offer an insight into its flora and fauna. *See page 222.*
- **Pulau Ubin.** The last bastion of rural Singapore has flora and fauna aplenty. Explore

the island on a rented bike. *See page 214.*
- **Singapore Botanic Gardens.** Singapore's oldest national park is a living museum of tropical plants. Picnickers, t'ai chi and yoga practitioners are a common sight. *See page 154.*
- **Sungei Buloh Wetland Reserve.** Noted for its diversity of bird life, the park has hides to allow you to birdwatch. Don't miss the walk through the mangrove forest. *See page 227.*

Most Important Places of Worship

- **Kong Meng San Phor Kark See Temple.** Singapore's largest (and busiest) Buddhist temple is also an important Vesak Day place of worship. *See page 221.*
- **Sri Mariamman Temple.** The city's oldest Hindu temple is dedicated to the Goddess Mariamman, who cures people of serious illnesses. *See page 125.*
- **Srinivasa Perumal Temple.** This Hindu temple in the heart of Little India is a hive of activity on most days. Its busiest time of the year, however, is during the annual Thaipusam festival. *See page 168.*

- **Sultan Mosque.** Singapore's largest mosque, with its striking golden dome, is a familar landmark in the Malay-dominated enclave of Kampung Glam. *See page 171.*
- **St Andrew's Cathedral.** This colonial-era monument, completed in 1862, is where Singapore's Anglican community worships. *See page 104.*
- **Thian Hock Keng Temple.** Dedicated to Ma Cho Po, Goddess of the Sea, this ornate temple, dating back to 1842, is always thronged with devotees burning joss sticks. *See page 134.*

Below: bronze sculpture at the Singapore Botanic Gardens.

- **Museums**. The Asian Civilisations Museum and Singapore Art Museum have half-price and free admission respectively on Fri evenings, while the NUS Museum are free from Mon to Sat. *See pages 98 and 108.*
- **Music**. Head to the Outdoor Theatre at Esplanade – Theatres on the Bay on Fri–Sun evenings for free music performances. Singapore Botanic Gardens has outdoor concerts at least once a month. *See pages 101 and 154.*
- **Nature Reserves**. Entry to most nature reserves – Bukit Timah, Pierce, Seletar and MacRitchie – is free. *See pages 222–4.*
- **Newspapers and Magazines**. Pick up the free *Today* tabloid from MRT and bus stations. Get free *I-S* and *Where* magazines with the latest on dining and clubbing, at some eateries and bars.
- **Temples**. Entry to all churches, temples and mosques is free.

ABOVE: woven baskets of every shape and size at Arab Street.
LEFT: statue at the Asian Civilisations Museum, Empress Place.
BELOW LEFT: live music at Esplanade – Theatres on the Bay.

BEST SHOPPING EXPERIENCES

- **Serangoon Road**. This main Little India street, and side streets leading off it, are lined with shops selling incense, silks, flowers, jewellery and arts and crafts. *See page 163.*
- **Funan DigitaLife Mall**. Computer and electronics buffs will find everything they need at this specialist mall. *See page 114.*
- **Ngee Ann City**. Japanese retailer Takashimaya and Singapore's largest bookstore, Kinokuniya, are here. *See pages 152 and 154.*
- **Tanglin Shopping Centre**. Asian furniture, antiques, rare prints and Persian carpets are the mainstays of this mall. *See page 154.*
- **Tangs**. This home-grown department store has slick electronic gadgets for the home and top local fashion labels. *See pages 152 and 154.*
- **VivoCity**. The city's largest shopping mall offers a mind-boggling array of retail and dining options. There is also a huge Cineplex. *See page 192.*

MONEY-SAVING TIPS

Discounted Tickets. Avoid watching movies on Fridays and weekends when ticket prices are highest. Similarly, at the theatre, watch a matinee instead of an evening performance. Save with a ParkHopper ticket that gives access to three attractions – Singapore Zoo, Night Safari and the Jurong Bird Park.

Admission to museums. The Asian Civilisations Museum has discounted admission every Friday, 7–9pm. Singapore Art Museum is free to enter on major public holidays, on weekdays between noon and 2pm and on Fridays 6–9pm.

Save on GST. If you plan to shop, be sure to claim your GST refund, which amounts to 7 percent off your total cost. See page 261. The best time to shop is during the annual Great Singapore Sale from the end of May to early July (www.singaporesale.com.sg).

Cheap Drinks. Import taxes on alcohol are high, so a Martini at a top-end bar can cost as much as S$18 a pop. Savvy drinkers can get their money's worth during "happy hour", when prices can be discounted by 50 percent. Happy hour can extend from 3 to 9pm.

Pay What You Want. Unbelievable but true. At Annalakshmi, an Indian restaurant serving vegetarian meals, you pay what you want after your meal. See page 141. At some Buddhist temples, vegetarian meals on the 1st and 15th of every month are free; it's polite to give a small donation.

SAVVY SINGAPORE

A surprising transformation is taking place in what was once regarded as the blandest city in Southeast Asia. Singapore is learning to have fun, and everywhere you go there are exciting things to do and see

Who would have thought that this city-state, famous for its draconian rules and chewing gum ban, would become hip and happening? Singapore is undergoing a renaissance of epic proportions. A new financial district and a revitalised waterfront has given it an extra boost, and tourism looks set to shine with a glut of new big-ticket attractions, including two mega-casinos and a Universal Studios theme park.

Arts in the city

Singapore's economy is being liberalised, whizz-kid foreigners are being hired as top management in Singapore companies, home-grown entrepreneurs are aiming to become world-class names, and technology is alive and kicking. Censorship laws have been eased to pave the way for greater artistic freedom.

Films that would previously have been banned are given a Restricted (Artistic) rating, allowing even full frontal nudity. Actors on stage are showing more skin than ever, shedding their clothes, along with other inhibitions, without a qualm. Not only was the local gay play *Asian Boys Trilogy* given the nod by the usually strait-laced censors, its sequel went on to win the Best Script prize.

When the Esplanade – Theatres on the Bay was unveiled, the authorities unashamedly proclaimed Singapore's intention to be the region's arts hub. Detractors may argue that the Esplanade has some way to go before it becomes Asia's answer to Sydney's Opera House, but no one can deny it has created some ripples in international arts circles.

This liberalisation is not confined to the arts alone. The call for an open society saw former prime minister Goh Chok Tong announce that

PRECEDING PAGES: Singapore skyline from the Marina Promenade; pastel-hued shophouses on Koon Seng Road. **LEFT:** Chinatown Night Market at New Year. **ABOVE LEFT:** patriotic girl. **ABOVE RIGHT:** view from the pool at Marina Bay Sands.

homosexuals would be accepted in the civil service. Embracing diversity was no longer confined to religion and race. Singapore is swinging today: nubile young things routinely clamber onto bar tops to dance, and gay bars make no bones about whom they court – all sanctioned by the authorities, of course.

Smart orderliness

On a map of any scale, Singapore is just a dot at the tip of peninsular Malaysia, yet this tiny 699-sq-km (267-sq-mile) island has blossomed into one of Asia's success stories. Much of this has to do with its obsession with cleanliness, orderliness and a healthy *kiasu* ("afraid to lose" in the Hokkien dialect) attitude. Not content with consistently bagging the world's best airport, port and airline titles, and as if to compensate for its lack of size, Singapore relentlessly builds the biggest and tallest something. Singapore has the world's biggest fountain (at Suntec City), and the Singapore Flyer has superseded the London Eye as the world's highest observation wheel. And no one can deny that the Marina Bay Sands complex is an architectural sight unlike any other. Its three lofty towers, their shape inspired by a stack of cards, are linked by a 0.4-hectare (1-acre) sky park.

Singaporeans are laughably methodical, even when it comes to fun and leisurely pursuits. Afraid of the less than desirable effects gambling could bring, the government promptly set up the National Council on Problem Gambling in 2006, right after they awarded the licence for the city's first casino. Sanitised Chinatown is ironically trying to recreate its former bustle

with the street markets it was once famous for (but without the attendant chaos). Contrived as it may be, many have to come appreciate how everything works with a systematic clockwork precision.

A melting pot

Asian and Western cultures and values mesh here, giving rise to eclectic lifestyles, a heavenly range of cuisines and a funky, but still wholesome, nightlife scene. The lingua franca is English, but on the streets you will see Chinese, Malay, Indian, Eurasian and Caucasian faces.

The island-state may appear Western in its outlook, but in reality, Confucian precepts still temper ideals of personal freedom, and respect for one's elders ranks high. Society and public discourse are kept on a tight rein, and there are fines for littering, spitting and other social misdemeanours. Overall, though, Singapore is Asia with all its exotica and colour but without the slog sometimes associated with travelling in the region. It is, as its tourism advertising has claimed, Uniquely Singapore. ❑

ABOVE LEFT: playing draughts in Chinatown. **ABOVE RIGHT:** National Day. **RIGHT:** Palawan Beach on Sentosa.

A NATION OF CULTURES

Ethnically diverse but racially tolerant, Singaporeans have managed to combine time-honoured traditions with modern ways of life. Their traditional Asian hospitality, too, has helped to create a multicultural society that is both gracious and warm

Framed against a backdrop of skyscrapers, a Singaporean in shirtsleeves and tie steps out of his Mercedes, phone plugged to his ear. Likely as not, he's on the line with his stockbroker, checking the latest share market gyrations as he heads for his favourite lunch spot, a tiny noodle stall in Chinatown.

In another vignette of tradition amid modernity, a *feng shui* (geomancy) expert is called in when things do not go well at a luxury hotel on Orchard Road. He recommends that the main doors be re-angled, and profits magically soar. Why? Because the cashier's desk was previously placed opposite the main door, so money and luck had "flown out into the streets".

These two faces of Singapore are no contradiction. A Singaporean may be sophisticated and completely at home with Western ways, but he is not above hedging his bets with the

Singaporeans seem to have no difficulty reconciling Western pragmatism with Asian tradition – they may work for a multinational corporation yet practise feng shui.

gods of fortune. A Hindu penitent may walk on glowing coals in supplication to his god, and a Chinese may light paper effigies of household

items, intended for a deceased relative in the expectation of reciprocity.

Singapore's Asian aspect manifests itself in other ways as well. Agreeing with elders and superiors is important to help preserve "face", and the government's paternalistic rule is not as resented as might be expected. There is a sense of practicality behind this: as long as their material welfare remains secure, few question the role of the government in their private lives.

Singaporean imperatives

A multiethnic melting pot of Chinese, Malays, Indians, Eurasians and Caucasians, Singaporeans have been socialised over the years by

LEFT: Singaporeans are encouraged to be courteous to each other and to visitors. **RIGHT:** culturally diverse Singaporeans on Sentosa Island.

official policies of multiracialism and meritocracy to think of themselves as Singaporeans first. There are four official languages: English, Mandarin, Malay and Tamil. The language of administration is English, which is also the lingua franca.

It would certainly be myopic to take the view that the different races live together as one big happy family. There are underlying tensions which may not be noticeable to the first-time visitor *(see also page 172)*. The Muslim community, for instance, like elsewhere in the world has suffered following 9/11. An Al-Qaeda-linked plot by a group of local Muslims to bomb the US embassy was uncovered in January 2002, leading to some tension among the different communities. A few months later, four Muslim schoolgirls who insisted on wearing the *tudung* (headscarf) to school were suspended. The government's line is that schools need to maintain a certain uniformity in dress.

Likewise, some Malays and Indians feel that

THE PERANAKAN PEOPLE

Singapore's Chinese population has an interesting subgroup known as the Peranakans. They are the descendants of intermarriages between Chinese men and Malay women that took place from the 17th century onwards in the Malayan Straits Settlement colonies of Melaka, Penang and Singapore.

Male Peranakans are called *baba* and the women *nonya*. Their lingua franca is a Chinese-Malay patois. "Inside Chinese, outside Malay" was one description applied to the Peranakans, although increasingly they are becoming less distinct as a racial group, having intermarried with other races. The Peranakans were the first locals to speak English and to adopt Western customs. In fact,

their loyalty to the British led some to describe them cynically as the "King's Chinese".

The often wealthy Peranakan families in Singapore, at Emerald Hill *(see pages 150–1)* and also in Katong *(see pages 207–8)* on the east coast, left behind a rich culinary heritage blending Malay and Chinese cooking styles and ingredients, clothing and also quaint houses with a distinctive architectural style. To learn more about the Peranakan culture, visit these two areas as well as the Peranakan Museum *(see page 110)* and Baba House *(see page 131)*. See also the website of the Peranakan Association at www.peranakan.org.sg.

It's all about Youth.!

they are disadvantaged, especially when they seek employment in Chinese-dominated companies. Racial differences do remain under a veneer of modernism, but tolerance is always the watchword. Most people, if cornered and asked, would place their nationality first and their ethnic identity second.

Locals tend to be reserved in conversation, but they will immediately ask "How much you pay, ah?" when you've bought anything from a new BMW to a bowl of noodles. Part of this stems from the money-driven society they live in, and visitors should not see this as an intrusion of privacy. It's just the way Singaporeans are.

The one thing which unites Singaporeans, Chinese and Malay, old and young, is food (see page 71). Talk to a Singaporean about culinary matters and you're on the right track. Singaporeans put in long hours at the office, but unless exceptionally hard-pressed, they'd prefer a decent cooked meal (even if served on styrofoam) to grabbing a sandwich at the desk.

Many Singaporeans are tech-savvy and as adept with computers and the internet as any Silicon Valley whizz-kid.

Constantly urged to strive for excellence, Singaporeans are only happy with straight "A"s. They have become afraid to lose out to the next fellow. This trait is now humorously termed the "*kiasu* syndrome" (see page 24) and is often the subject of social comment. For example, parents, anxious not to lose out in their children's education, queue up overnight to get them into a school of choice. It's common for children to have extra tuition after school hours to keep their grades up and help them do better than their fellow classmates. Getting a bargain is more than mere monetary satisfaction for the Singaporean, it is almost a moral victory.

That they can laugh about all this is a refreshing thing. Satirical and even critical books written by locals are nudging for space where once they were proscribed, and censorship has been eased. Things are changing slowly, paving the way for more original thought and a more open society.

Increasingly, racial differences are submerged beneath shared experiences and Western

---

Left: an upmarket store in an Orchard Road mall.
Top: at the Singtel Singapore Grand Prix concert.
Above: family outing on Orchard Road.
Above Right: an outdoor party after Chingay Parade.

influence. Young singles want their own apartments, and married couples (an increasing number of which are inter-racial) prefer not to live with their in-laws. Marriage and starting a family have taken a back seat as getting ahead in one's career takes priority. Yet family ties remain strong, and it is not unusual for married offspring to visit their parents every weekend.

Singaporeans have left their immigrant and post-colonial struggles behind and are finding their place in the international community. Sandwiched between East and West, they attempt to combine the best of both worlds.

The Chinese

The Chinese comprise 74.1 percent of Singapore's 5.08 million population (Census of Population 2010). This is no recent phenomenon. When Stamford Raffles founded modern Singapore in 1819, Chinese planters, pirates, fishermen and traders were already present. Five years after its establishment, Singapore had 3,000 Chinese and more were arriving weekly. Most were traders from southern and eastern China fleeing the turmoil and corruption of 19th-century Chinese politics. By 1836 Chinese were the numerical majority, a pattern of racial

demographics that exists to this day.

Singapore's Chinese population can be broken down into several linguistic groups. Hokkiens from the southern Fujian province form the largest subgroup (42 percent), followed by Teochews (23 percent) from the Shantou region in Guangdong, Cantonese (17 percent), who hailed from Hong Kong and the lowlands of central Guangdong, Hakkas (7 percent) from central China and Hainanese (6 percent) from Hainan Island.

KIASU-ISM

Kiasu is a common Singlish word made popular through the army and taken from two Chinese Hokkien dialect words, *kia* (afraid) and *su* (to lose). Its early usage in the army was innocent enough: a recruit over-zealously putting in an extra minute or doing a centimetre more was guilty of being *kiasu*. But in the last decade, *kiasu* has become a Singaporean preoccupation.

Fuelled by global recognition in just about every quarter, Best Airport, Best Airline, Best Economy, Best Students, Best Hotel – you name it, Singapore bests it. Once a term used of a person, "Why are you so *kiasu*?", it is now tagged to the nation: "Singapore is so *kiasu*."

The Chinese speak a variety of dialects, but their common link is Mandarin, or *huayu*, the language of the Beijing area, which is taught in Singapore schools as the official mother tongue of the Chinese. The long-standing Speak Mandarin Campaign, held annually, is an attempt to promote the use of Mandarin in place of native Chinese dialects.

A further unifying bond between many Chinese is a belief in superstition. Fortune tellers and geomancers figure largely in the Chinese world, their advice meticulously followed to bring luck and prosperity. The older generation also place their trust in the old ways, eschewing modern medicine for herbal cures. Acupuncture is popular too.

Food occupies a pre-eminent place in Chinese culture. A minister once quipped: "If a Chinese sees a snake in the grass, he'll think of a way to eat it." Not surprisingly, restaurants offering every conceivable Chinese dish are found in Singapore.

The Malays

Like the Chinese and Indians, Singapore's Malays are largely descendants of immigrants, although their arrival most certainly pre-dates that of the other ethnic groups. For this reason the Malays are considered the indigenous people of Singapore. Today, they make up 13.4 percent of Singaporeans, and comprise several

sub-ethnic groups who trace their origins to the Javanese, Sumatrans, Bugis, Boyanese, Arabs and local Malays, among others.

Singapore's Malay origins are enshrined in the symbolic trappings of statehood – the national anthem is sung in Malay, one of the national languages is Malay and the island's first president after independence was a Malay. Today, despite Singapore's dominant Chinese population, it retains in many ways its Malay core: graceful *baju-kurung*-clad girls, or the more traditional *tudung*-attired females, are as much a part of the cityscape as their Western-attired compatriots; the *surau*, or community mosque, lies at the heart of every Malay neighbourhood; and *satay* – skewered pieces of grilled meat dipped in spicy peanut sauce – is as much a symbol of Singapore as Hokkien noodles.

Until as late as the 1970s, everyday Malay life centred on the *kampung*, or village – with wooden slat houses built on stilts and where food was grown to feed the community. Such *kampung* are now almost non-existent, as most Malays have moved to government apartments and adapted to high-rise living. Having imbibed the government's ambitious approach, a good number have merged into the landscape as professionals and entrepreneurs.

Historically, however, the Malay community has always been socio-economically weaker than the Chinese and Indians. This is partly because of

FAR LEFT: Chinese family at Lian Shan Shuang Lin. **TOP LEFT:** visiting Jurong Bird Park. **LEFT:** children are well catered for. **ABOVE:** at the Asia Fashion Exchange. **RIGHT:** around 15 percent of Singaporeans are Muslim.

its rural roots and partly due to Malay education, which closely follows a religious syllabus and has a reputation of lagging behind the English school system. The government, aware of the social and educational problems of the Malay community – including drug abuse and school dropouts – set up a self-help organisation called Mendaki to promote the progress of the Malay community. Today, Malay youths are successfully entering the mainstream, slowly improving the negative perceptions attached to their community.

The Malays are deeply religious and follow Islam. Orthodox Malays save hard for holy pilgrimages to Mecca, as their status increases with the title Haji and the use of the white skullcap earned from a pilgrimage.

The Indians

Although Indians constitute only 9.2 percent of the population, they are a vital component of Singapore. Their documented habitation of the island goes back to the days of the arrival of Singapore's founder, Sir Stamford Raffles, in 1819, when he was accompanied by sepoys (soldiers) from the East India Company brought along to guard Britain's imperial interests. This trickle soon enlarged to include Indian merchants, with a larger flow arriving in the 1820s in the form of convicts from Britain's penal colony in Bencoolen.

These Indians were a polyglot mix, and came from all over India and Sri Lanka. Reflective of the original inflow, Singapore's Indian population today consists of numerous sub-ethnic and ethnic divisions, ranging from Tamils, Malayalees and Bengalis to Punjabis, Telegus, Gujaratis and Sindhis. The majority (60 percent) are Tamils, with Malayalees the next largest group (8 percent). Religion-wise, they comprise a colourful mix of Hindus (55 percent), Muslims (26 percent), Christians (12 percent) and Buddhists (1 percent), as well as smaller groups of Sikhs, Jains and Parsis.

The Indian population of early Singapore tended to group together according to region of origin, religion and occupation type. Today, certain traditional Indian trades still occupy specific locations in Singapore. Sindhi, Sikh and Gujarati textile and electronic goods merchants are still located along High Street, while the Tamil Muslims still predominate in the money-changing trade, in areas such as Arab, Chulia and Market streets.

Although the first-generation Indians who settled in Singapore in search of a better life still maintain sentimental ties to their homeland, their offspring lack such attachments and consider themselves Singaporeans first.

Nevertheless, in the late 1980s and early 90s, a significant number of well-educated Indians

left Singapore for greener pastures in Australia, Canada and the US. This outflow from the professional class was partly due to an unease over state policies promoting the Chinese culture and language in Singapore, and uncertainty over equal opportunities in the job market.

Like the Malays, the Indians have a socially and educationally disadvantaged segment that has been left behind in the rush to progress. The Singapore Indian Development Association (SINDA) was set up in 1990 to help these elements re-enter the mainstream.

Singapore's foreign workers often congregate in their particular communities on Sundays, for example Filipinos at Lucky Plaza, Indians in Little India, and Thais and Burmese at Golden Mile Tower.

LEFT: Sri Veeramakaliamman Temple.
TOP AND ABOVE: Indians make up around 9.2 percent of Singapore's population. **ABOVE RIGHT:** Hindu at Sri Veeramakaliamman temple during the Diwali festival.

Other races

Singapore's census shows an enigmatic category called "Others", which includes all those who are not Chinese, Malay and Indian. The most numerous "Others" are the Eurasians, who form less than 1 percent of Singaporeans. Most are the offspring of mixed marriages, dating back to the times when the region was occupied by the Portuguese and Dutch. Eurasians are often half English, half Dutch or half Portuguese. Some are immigrant Eurasians who came from Indonesia, Malaysia, Thailand and other parts of Asia. The Eurasians often carry family names such as D'Souza or Pereira (Portuguese), Westerhout (Dutch), Scully (Irish) or Young (British). Many are also part Filipino, Chinese, Malay, Indian, Sri Lankan or Thai.

Although a sense of alienation in the 1970s caused sizeable numbers to migrate, Eurasians today fit well into the society. They are a close-knit group, and there is even a Eurasian Association to promote the interests of the community. Patois Portuguese (or Cristão) is still spoken among the older generation. Many Eurasians still profess a sentimental attachment to Katong in the eastern part of Singapore, as the community congregated in this area before

urban development caused habitation patterns to shift.

There are very few Armenian families remaining in Singapore. The Jews, once a thriving community that occupied the Sophia Road, Queen Street, Wilkie Road and Waterloo Street areas, are now scattered through urban renewal; only the old Hebrew lettering on some of the shophouses in these localities bears testimony to their once vibrant presence.

Foreigners

More than a million people living in Singapore are foreigners, many of whom have acquired Permanent Residency status. They come from all corners of the world. In the past, expatriates were mainly Westerners, often sent to Singapore by their home companies to oversee local or regional operations. They mostly came on expatriate packages that included a generous salary, a fairly luxurious residence, company car and maid. Today that picture has undergone a transformation. Expatriates are as likely to hail from India and China as from the West, and most are offered employment packages that are no different from those given to local workers.

Referred to in the local media as "foreign talent", these professionals are mostly employed in the high-tech sectors and finance. Their presence is the result of an open-door policy by the Singapore government to recruit qualified workers from abroad to redress the dearth of local talent in high-growth sectors.

Apart from a large pool of expatriates in the white-collar professions, there is a noticeable blue-collar element, made up mostly of South Indians and Southeast Asians, who work in construction and environment maintenance as well as women who work as live-in domestic maids. They generally undertake jobs that hold little appeal for Singaporeans.

Foreign workers are especially visible on Sundays. The Indians and Bangladeshis congregate in Little India, the Filipinos at Lucky Plaza, and the Thais and Burmese at Golden Mile Tower at Beach Road. This is their weekly opportunity to catch up on home news and relax in the company of compatriots.   ❑

ABOVE LEFT: shoppers at Tanglin Mall. **TOP:** crowds at the Diwali Festival in Little India. This spectacular festival attracts people from all ethnic groups. **ABOVE:** European families attending a concert at the Botanic Gardens.

Singlish-speak

This unique Singaporean language is a short cut in many ways and, after you've been exposed to it for a while, it's also an endearing one

If ever a language can be described as relaxed and animated, malleable, frank and affectionate, it is Singlish. Singlish is English peculiar to Singapore, hence the term – the concatenation of the "head" of Singapore and the "tail" of English. And, at a wild guess, your Funk & Wagnalls or Oxford English Dictionary is unlikely to have it listed.

Quite simply put – and Singlish says it most simply – it is an oral language that was only given a spelling as recently as 1982.

Once shunned by the print and broadcast authorities as "broken English", which it is not, 21st-century Singlish is no longer a major language issue. It has gained currency islandwide, as evidenced by the occasional spoken or written example in the media. Curiously, having at first won notoriety, it now wins respect as Singapore's unofficial lingua franca.

However, Singlish is not championed in the corridors of academia. Students know not to offer Singlish in their exam papers, just as any white-collar worker knows not to employ it in correspondence. Yet both student and office worker would be likely to use it readily in the canteen and at home. It is at heart a "homey" language that departs from English in structure and syntax, grammar and punctuation, but it is still English, and not broken English at that. Well, maybe a slight fracture – which is not at all helped by the fact that it's often spoken at such breakneck speed that visitors often mistake Singlish for a foreign language altogether.

Singlish is from the gut and to the point, often taking short cuts by losing the article. "Hurry lah!" is "Can you please hurry up?" Sentences often end with the words "lah" or "meh" – derived from the Hokkien dialect – the first to drive a point home, and the second an expression of incredulity.

Singlish is distinct from, say, the pidgin and Creole patois of New Guinea and New Orleans in that it is a patois which has no rank in the social stratum, having taken root among the masses and continued to change with its people.

You know you're in Singapore as a visitor when you try to but cannot understand the following phrases:
• toast bread – toast
• wait first – hold on/later
• check for you – I'll try to find out
• see how – undecided/not sure
• can I hepchew? – can I help you?
• got nets card? – I prefer cash
• any udders? – will there be anything else?

Above: after years of derogatory comments, Singlish is now accepted as part of Singapore's identity.
Right: quirky Singlish on a T-shirt.

DECISIVE DATES

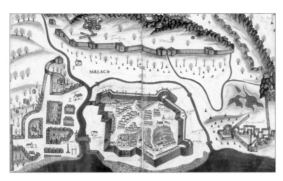

THE EARLY YEARS

3rd century
Chinese are said to have given the island the name P'u Luo Chung.

1292
Marco Polo mentions a large and noble city where Singapore now stands.

1365
The Javanese *Nagarakre-tagama* records a settlement called Temasek – the old name that used to refer to Singapore.

1390s
Temasek is settled by a scion of the Srivijaya empire, Parameswara (also known as Iskandar Shah).

14–15th centuries
Siam (Thailand), followed by Java's Majapahit empire, seizes Temasek but shows little interest in it. Temasek exists as a vassal of the Malay kingdom of Melaka and is governed by a Temenggong (chief) from Johor.

1511
The Portuguese capture Melaka, then an important centre in east–west trade.

17th century
Singapore is forgotten and left to the Orang Laut (sea nomads).

1786–1824
The British East India Company opens a trading post in Penang and assumes possession of Melaka from the Dutch.

BRITISH COLONIAL RULE

1819
Sir Thomas Stamford Raffles arrives in Singapore. He is convinced the island, located at the crossroads of the South China Sea, will become an important port. The Temenggong and Sultan Hussein allow Raffles to open a trading post in Singapore in exchange for money.

1822
Raffles returns to Singapore and draws up plans for the island's development.

1823
Raffles issues regulations outlawing gambling and slavery. Leaves Singapore in June.

1824
The British agree to withdraw from Indonesia, in return for Dutch recognition of British rights over Singapore. Singapore is ceded in perpetuity to the British.

1826
The trading stations at Penang, Melaka and Singapore are named the Straits Settlements, under the control of British India.

1846
Chinese funeral riots. First

major secret society trouble begins.

1851
Straits Settlements placed directly under the rule of the Governor-General of India.

1867
Straits Settlements become a Crown Colony, controlled by Colonial Office in London.

1869
Suez Canal opens and number of ships calling at Singapore increases. Trade flourishes.

1880s
Henry Ridley, director of the Botanical Gardens, succeeds in growing rubber trees. The Malaysian peninsula and Singapore

develop into the world's main rubber exporters.

WORLD WARS

1911
Population of Singapore grows to 250,000 and the census records 48 races on the island, speaking 54 languages.

1920s
The Great Depression's reverberations are felt in Singapore, as prices of commodities such as rubber collapse. But it is still the greatest naval base of the British empire east of Suez.

1923
Singapore is linked to Malaysia by a 1.1-km (¾-mile) causeway.

1941
Japan invades Malaysia, landing at Kota Bahru. Singapore is bombed on 8 December.

1942
British troops surrender to

Japan. The Japanese rename Singapore Syonan, "Light of the South". During their occupation, many civilians, particularly the Chinese, are killed or suffer hardships.

1945
Three-and-a-half years of Japanese rule end in August, with the landing of Allied troops. The British declare Singapore a Crown Colony.

INDEPENDENCE AND FEDERATION

1948
The British allow limited elections to the Legislative Council. A state of emergency is declared in June following the Communist Party of Malaya's uprising against imperialism.

1951
Legislative Council election. Singapore formally proclaimed a city with a royal charter.

FAR LEFT: the Portuguese capture Melaka, 1511. LEFT: Sir Thomas Stamford Raffles. ABOVE: the harbour with Fort Canning in the distance, c.1840. RIGHT: an early 20th-century photograph of a Dyak man.

1964
PAP wins only one seat in Malaysian general election. Communal riots ensue.

THE REPUBLIC OF SINGAPORE

1965
PAP wins Hong Lim constituency by-election. Singapore leaves Malaysian federation, becoming an independent nation. Joins the United Nations and the Commonwealth.

1967
Singapore, Malaysia, Thailand, Indonesia and the Philippines form the Association of Southeast Asian Nations (ASEAN).

1955
Rendel Commission granted by the British leads to elections and David Marshall becomes chief minister. A Legislative Assembly consisting of 32 members, 25 elected, is established. The Labour Front has a majority, but the People's Action Party (PAP) forms a powerful opposition.

1956
PAP Central Executive Committee election in which Communists decline to run. Chinese student riots; PAP leaders are arrested.

1958
A constitutional agreement for partial independence for Singapore is signed in London.

1959
PAP wins elections with 43 of 51 seats, with 53 percent of the popular vote. Lee Kuan Yew becomes

the country's first prime minister.

1962
A referendum is held on merger with Malaya: 71 percent vote in favour.

1963
Malaysia agreement signed in which Singapore, Sarawak and North Borneo (Sabah) are joined with the existing states of Malaya to form Malaysia. PAP wins Singapore general election.

1968
PAP sweeps first parliamentary general election, winning all 58 seats.

1971
British Far East Command ceases.

1972
PAP wins all seats in general election.

1981
In a by-election, J.B. Jeyaretnam of the Workers' Party wins the first seat to be held by a member of an opposition party.

1984
PAP loses two of 79 seats in the general election, its first loss of a seat since 1964.

1990
Lee Kuan Yew steps down as prime minister and is replaced by Goh Chok

Tong. The constitution is amended to provide for a president.

1991
PAP wins general election but loses four seats. Its share of votes falls from 61.8 to 59.7 percent, the lowest since it has been in power.

1996
Singapore is no longer regarded as a "developing nation" by the OECD.

1998
Singapore's economy is affected by the regional economic chaos in Southeast Asia.

1999
The economy makes a dramatic turnaround, growing 4–5 percent. Ong Teng Cheong steps down as

FAR LEFT TOP: Singaporean riot squad with the message "Disperse or we fire" in the 1960s. LEFT: Goh Chok Tong, prime minister 1990–2004. ABOVE: an aerial view of the 2009 Formula 1 Grand Prix. RIGHT: the Youth Olympic Games are awarded to Singapore.

president. S.R. Nathan from the minority Indian race is appointed president.

2000
Economic growth hits 10.1 percent.

2001
PAP wins 75.3 percent of votes in general election. A global downturn leads to a 4.7 percent unemployment rate, a 15-year high.

2002
Al-Qaeda-linked terrorist plot to bomb the US embassy uncovered. Some 15 suspects are arrested and jailed without trial.

2003
Outbreak of Severe Acute Respiratory Syndrome (SARS) in April, but quickly controlled. Northeast Line extension of the MRT opens.

2004
Prime Minister Goh Chok Tong steps down and Lee Hsien Loong takes office. The economy shows positive signs of recovery.

2006
PAP wins 66.6 percent of votes in general election, sweeping all but two seats.

2010
The world's first Formula 1 night race is held in September. Marina Barrage, Singapore's first reservoir in the city, opens. Resorts World Sentosa, Singapore's first integrated resort, opens in January; a second, Marina Bay Sands, opens in April. Singapore hosts the first Youth Olympic Games in August.

GROWTH OF A LION CITY

Singapore's role as a 21st-century hub for global growth is a throwback to its earliest days as a pivotal East–West trading post and rendezvous point for merchants and sailors

The story of how Singapore got its name reads rather like a fairy tale. The earliest (and most racy) of Malay histories, the 17th-century *Sejarah Melayu*, tells of the exploits of Sang Nila Utama, who assumed the title of Sri Tri Buana as ruler of Palembang, heart of the great Malay seafaring empire of Srivijaya. He was out searching for a place to establish a city one day when his ship was struck by a sudden and ferocious storm. The ruler reputedly saved the day by casting his crown into the waves. Ashore on an uncharted island, he was intrigued by the sight of a strange creature with a red body, black head and white breast. On enquiring of its name and told it was a lion, he decided to name the place Singapura, which means "Lion City" in Sanskrit.

Merchants and pirates

Singapore owes its reputation as a trading centre to the bustling activity in the region.

Traders from all over Asia stopped at Singapore, occupying a pivotal point on the tip of the Malay peninsula.

Even before the birth of Christ, Tamil seamen from southern India were plying heavy ships through the Straits of Melaka (Malacca). Later, the Greeks and then the Romans sought tortoise shell, spices and sandalwood from the Malay archipelago. By the 5th century, Chinese junks were sailing into peninsular waters, braving "huge turtles, sea-lizards and such-like monsters of the deep". The Arabs and Persians traded in the region too.

By the 14th century, Singapore was well established on this East–West trade route. Though its various rulers exacted duties from the passing ships, what most worried traders were the so-called "freelancers": pirates.

According to the 1350 Chinese text *Description of the Barbarians of the Isles*, the traders were unmolested as they sailed west. But on the way back, loaded with goods, "the junk people get out their armour and padded screens against

LEFT: contrasting faces of early Chinese businessmen.
RIGHT: 17th-century map of the Malay peninsula.

Towards the end of the 14th century, it came under attack, possibly by the Majapahits but more probably by the Thai state of Ayutthya or one of its Malay vassals.

Temasek came under the authority of the newly founded Melaka sultanate, and later devolved into an insignificant fishing settlement, becoming little more than an overgrown jungle. When Sir Thomas Stamford Raffles, the founder of modern Singapore, landed here on 29 January 1819, he found swamps, jungle and a lone village of some 100 Malay huts by the mouth of the Singapore River. Upriver lived 30 or so Orang Laut sea nomad families. It was, to put it mildly, a pretty bleak picture.

The island was controlled by the Temenggong, the Malay chief of the southern Malay peninsula, and the land was owned by Johor.

The Sultan of Johor had four wives but no clear heir, though he had two sons by two different commoners. When the sultan died, the younger of the two sons was placed on the throne, with the legitimacy of his rule recognised by both the British and the Dutch. The elder son, Hussein, who was away at the time, subsequently went into exile.

Raffles's shrewd move

Raffles knew the younger son would never permit the establishment of a British presence in Singapore and concocted his own plan. He invited the elder son Hussein to Singapore and proclaimed him heir to the throne of Johor. On 6 February 1819, Raffles signed a treaty with the Temenggong and the new sultan, giving the British East India Company permission to establish a trading post in Singapore. In return, the company would pay the Temenggong 5,000 Spanish dollars a year and the sultan 3,000 dollars. Raffles returned to Bencoolen, leaving Major William Farquhar in charge as the island's first Resident while retaining ultimate control as lieutenant-governor of Bencoolen.

Farquhar cleared the jungle, constructed buildings and dealt with the rat problem. The first settlers were traders and itinerants, mostly

arrow fire to protect themselves, for a certainty two or three hundred pirate junks will come out to attack them. Sometimes they have good luck and a favouring wind and they may not catch up with them; if not, then the crews are butchered and the merchandise made off with in short order." The scale of the pirate fleet seems inflated, but there is no doubt the threat was real.

Singapura, often called "Temasek" in the literature of that period, was most likely

> *On arrival in 1819, Raffles found "all along the beach... hundreds of human skulls, some of them old but some fresh with the hair still remaining, some with the teeth still sharp, and some without teeth."*

founded around 1390 by the Palembang ruler Parameswara. A scion of the former Srivijaya empire, he had fled Palembang after an abortive attempt to cast off allegiance to the great Javanese Majapahit empire (1292–1398). His Temasek settlement was short-lived, however.

LEFT: portrait of Sir Stamford Raffles. **RIGHT:** in the 19th century, most Chinese came to Singapore as indentured labourers.

Chinese, with others from the Middle East, Europe and Melaka. The population topped 5,000 by June 1819, from 1,000 in January.

When Raffles returned to Singapore in 1822, he drew up a detailed plan for its development. Among other things, he abolished gambling, going so far as to order that all keepers of gaming houses be flogged in public. Two years later, the British, having traded off other regions to the Dutch, took formal control of Singapore. Payments to Sultan Hussein and the Temenggong were increased in exchange for outright cessation of the island.

His health ailing, Raffles returned to England in 1823 and died three years later of a suspected brain tumour. The British put Singapore under the Indian colonial government, appointing a new Resident, John Crawfurd.

By 1824, the island was home to 11,000 people, mostly Malays, with a large number of Chinese and Bugis, and fewer Indians, Europeans, Armenians and Arabs. Under Crawfurd, Singapore began to make money for the British. He ran a tight ship and his strict adherence to the bottom line alienated many locals. He made

no friends among the Europeans either when he reopened the gaming houses.

As Resident, Crawfurd had his work cut out. In the early 1830s, much of the town area was still swampland. Floods and fires were major hazards, while the filth and bad drainage, and the resulting water pollution, caused cholera outbreaks. Violent crime was another problem; gangs of robbers raided the town almost every night. Added to these were poverty, malnutrition, overcrowding and excessive opium smoking, the last of which exacted the heaviest toll. Tigers were a menace, devouring as many as 300 citizens a year during the mid-19th century. The introduction of a government bounty led to the last tiger being shot in 1904.

By 1860, Singapore's trade had reached £10 million a year. Among the goods traded were Chinese tea and silk, ebony, ivory, antimony and sage from across the archipelago, and nutmeg, pepper and rattan from Borneo. From India and Britain came cloth, opium, whisky and haberdashery for the expatriates.

By this time a sense of permanence had been established; three banks had been set up and

Literary Greats

Singapore has been a source of inspiration for several international literary greats over the years

For more than 100 years, Singapore has been kind to the travelling scribe. Many stayed at the Raffles Hotel, a home away from home for the likes of Hermann Hesse and James Michener. But, above all, Singapore played host to the literary lions of the British

empire such as Conrad, Kipling and Maugham.

Joseph Conrad spent 16 years (1878–94) as a seaman in the Far East, with Singapore as his most frequent port of call. *Lord Jim* (1902) was inspired by a real-life incident in which a ship called the *Jeddah* was abandoned by her British crew when the vessel began taking on water after leaving Singapore. Conrad also drew material from his own life. He was first mate on the *Vidar*, a schooner circuiting between Singapore and Borneo. A few of his works can be traced to these trips, including his first novel, *Almayer's Folly* (1895), and *Victory* (1915).

Rudyard Kipling came to Singapore in 1889, when he was 24, and had just left his beloved India on a journey that would change his life for ever. Kipling's seven years in India were spent writing for English-language newspapers, and clever dispatches earned him a reputation as a rising star of British journalism.

Kipling was fond of strolling along the waterfront and seemed to have stumbled upon Raffles Hotel by chance, describing it as a place "where the food is as excellent as the rooms are bad. Let the traveller take note. Feed at Raffles and sleep at the Hotel de l'Europe." The latter was demolished in 1900.

When **Hermann Hesse** reached Singapore in 1911, he was already well known in Germany for works such as *Peter Camenzind* (1904) and *Gertrude* (1910). Hesse observed the English, and penned acerbic descriptions of tipsy Englishmen who "fought with each other half the night like pigs".

From his three visits to Singapore between 1921 and 1925, **Somerset Maugham** collected material for magazine articles that later went into his collection of short stories, *The Casuarina Tree*. In it, Maugham's descriptions of Singapore's inhabitants are perceptive: "The Malays, though natives of the soil, dwell uneasily in the towns, and are few. It is the Chinese, supple, alert, and industrious, who throng the streets; the dark-skinned Tamils walk on their silent, naked feet, as though they were but brief sojourners in a strange land... and the English in their topees and white ducks, speeding past in motor-cars or at leisure in their rickshaws, wear a nonchalant and careless air." ❑

LEFT: Somerset Maugham was a frequent visitor to Singapore in the 1920s.

> *Japanese prison camps were tropical hell-holes of rats, disease and malnutrition. Many of the prisoners sent to work camps in the jungles of Southeast Asia died, victims of disease and starvation.*

elaborate houses of worship built. Wealthy Europeans constructed Palladian-style houses. A writer described the charming city, with its bustling harbour, lush greenery and fine houses, as "the Queen of the Further East".

Immigrant entrepreneurs

By this time, the Chinese population had swelled to 61 percent of the total and showed no signs of slowing down. Most Chinese immigrants *(sinkeh)* came as indentured labourers and later struck out on their own. The number of Malays also increased, though less rapidly. Immigrants from South India came as well, some as merchants and labourers, others as con-

ABOVE: view of the waterfront in front of Fort Canning at the turn of the 19th century.

victs brought in by the British to build roads, buildings and other public works.

In these early days, Chinese men outnumbered the women 15 to 1, and the social lives of young bachelors revolved around secret societies. These societies used coercive tactics to run criminal rackets and secure territory. To control the situation, in 1877 the government installed a Chinese protectorate headed by W. A. Pickering, the first European who could read and speak Chinese.

In 1867, the Straits Settlements were made a Crown Colony under London's direct control, and a governor was appointed. In its early days, as sailing ships gave way to steam vessels, Singapore became a coal station for ships travelling to Europe through the Suez Canal, which opened in 1869. Singapore's trade expanded eightfold between 1873 and 1913 as a result, securing its permanent status as a major entrepôt on the leading East–West trade route, and a most vital commercial link in the chain of the British empire. By 1903, the little island had become the world's seventh-largest port in terms of shipping tonnage.

In 1911, the population stood at 312,000 and included 48 races speaking 54 languages,

THE EMERGENCY

The Japanese defeat and the restoration of British colonial rule to Malaya and Singapore did not go unchallenged, particularly by Communism. The Malayan Communist Party (MCP) had emerged from World War II with new-found strength, having built up its prestige as a patriotic resistance movement during the Occupation. It now sought to infiltrate the labour movement by inciting unrest to overthrow British imperialism and establishing a Communist state. This organised insurrection of the MCP from 1948 onwards was termed the "Emergency".

The MCP had its headquarters in Singapore, with branches in other Malayan towns. It operated through its General Labour Union cells to mobilise support among the workers and to gear the trade unions to its political ends. Attacks were launched in 1948 against European and local managers in tin mines and rubber estates to disrupt the economy and instil a climate of fear. In response, the British promulgated Emergency regulations in June 1948 that sanctioned arrest and detention without trial. They also initiated a campaign to win over the civilian population to erode the MCP's base among the populace, particularly the Chinese. The Communist insurgency began to lose steam by 1953, but it was only in 1960 that the Emergency officially ended.

according to census-takers. During this period, a large number of Europeans migrated here, marking perhaps the nadir of colonial snobbery. They distanced themselves from the "locals", eating Western food shipped in at great cost, and barring other races from their social clubs and prestigious civil service posts. Roland Braddell's *The Lights of Singapore* (1934) described life as "so very George the Fifth… if you are English, you get an impression of a kind of tropical cross between Manchester and Liverpool." With the

building of its airport a few years later, Singapore was headed towards modernisation. Then came World War II.

Britain, a firm Japanese ally during World War I, severed her treaty with Japan in 1921 at the suggestion of the US. As war tensions in the Pacific increased, Singapore was groomed as a regional base for British warships in the event of an outbreak of hostilities. In 1927, Japan invaded China, occupying Manchuria by 1931 and withdrawing from the League of Nations. Six years later, the Japanese formally declared war on China. Airfields and dry-dock facilities for the British fleet were completed in Singapore in 1938. The substantial-looking defences earned the island the moniker "the Gibraltar of the East".

Defence debacle

The only problem was that Singapore had all its defences pointing out to sea, while the Japanese, in a legendary manoeuvre, chose to invade it by land from the north, via Malaya. The Japanese 25th Army was led by Tomoyuki Yamashita, whose well-known discipline was said to be "rigorous as the autumn frost".

Japanese aircraft raided Singapore on 8 December 1941, the same day they devastated US ships and airfields in Pearl Harbor. When informed, Governor Shenton Thomas told Lieutenant-General A. E. Percival, "Well, I suppose you'll shove the little men off."

His nonchalance proved misplaced. The Japanese quickly established land and air supremacy, taking two British Royal Navy battleships. They pushed southwards through the Malayan jungle paths. Percival, realising his northern border was unprotected, grouped the last of his troops along the northeast coast. The Japanese, in collapsible boats and other makeshift vessels, cut around the northwest flank and invaded Singapore on 8 February 1942.

Reign of terror

After days of heavy shelling by the Japanese, Percival surrendered unconditionally. Prime Minister Winston Churchill called it "the largest capitulation in British history", while Yamashita, as he later wrote, attributed his success to "a bluff that worked". In fact, the Japanese troops were outnumbered more than three to one by the island's defenders.

The Japanese reign of terror began with the renaming of Singapore as Syonan – "Light of the South". The Chinese were singled out for brutal treatment, with many killed, imprisoned or tortured for the flimsiest of reasons. The Europeans were classified as military prisoners or civilian detainees, while the Malays and Indians were urged to transfer their allegiance to Japan or be killed. Syonan's economy deteriorated. Inflation skyrocketed, food was scarce and corpses were a common sight on the streets.

On 21 August 1945, the Japanese surrendered and the British returned in September. But Communist resistance to the Japanese had changed the political climate. The people had

Far Left: Tamil Workmen clear up debris in Singapore following a Japanese bombing raid in 1941.
Left: the formal British surrender to the Japanese, 1942.
Above: British policemen on the streets in 1946.

plans for their own destiny and the British would no longer write the rules.

"Neither the Japanese nor the British had the right to push and kick us around," recalled Singapore's former prime minister, now minister mentor, Lee Kuan Yew, in 1961. "We determined that we could govern ourselves and bring up our children in a country where we can be a self-respecting people."

The nationalistic itch among Singapore's population was not ignored by the British. One year after their return, the British ended their military rule of the Straits Settlements and set up separate Crown Colonies in Singapore and Malaya. The new governor instituted a measure of self-government on the island by allowing for the popular election of six members to a new 22-member Legislative Council. Elections were set for 1948.

Independence

Even before the war had ended, political activity had begun in Singapore. In 1945, the Malayan Democratic Union was formed with the goal of ending colonial rule, and merging Singapore with Malaya. *Merdeka* – Malay for independence – was the rallying cry. The first election in 1948 was a lacklustre affair, with a slim turnout and only 13,000 votes cast. The Chinese majority was sidelined in favour of the English-speaking minority, an unequal state of affairs that would later steamroll the Communist insurrection known as the Emergency *(see text box on page 40)*.

A British review recommended that all citizens be automatically registered to vote and that a Legislative Assembly with 32 members – 25 elected – be established with broadened

CONFRONTATION

The merger with Malaysia caused faultlines to appear not only on the domestic front but also on the international scene, with Indonesia. As leader of Southeast Asia's largest Muslim state, President Sukarno was opposed to the Malaysian Federation.

To destabilise it, he initiated a policy of coercive diplomacy from 1963–6 that amounted to an undeclared war against Malaysia. Although the confrontation was fought along the Indonesia–Malaysia border, it spilled over into Singapore, with Indonesian saboteurs infiltrating the island in 1964. Confrontation ended with Sukarno's downfall in 1966.

powers. The constitution was enacted in early 1955 and, later that year, Labour Front member David Marshall was elected Singapore's first chief minister. He led an all-party delegation to London the following year to negotiate complete independence from the Crown. He returned home empty-handed and resigned as he had failed to keep his *merdeka* promise.

Lim Yew Hock of the Singapore Labour Party took over as Chief Minister and made another bid in London in March 1957. The second delegation – which included a People's Action Party (PAP) member and a young Cambridge-educated lawyer named Lee Kuan Yew – accepted roughly the same terms Marshall had been offered: a fully elected Assembly of 51 members, no power over external affairs and representation on – but not control of – an internal security council.

Back home, the Legislative Assembly ratified the terms and, in 1959, the British parliament passed an act approving the new constitution. The general election was set for May. The PAP won a sweeping victory and Lee Kuan Yew became Singapore's first prime minister, a position he would hold until 1990.

The PAP takes charge

The new government immediately set about reviving the economy, which had been suffering from a steady decline in entrepôt trade, as Singapore's Asian neighbours increasingly took charge of their own trade. The PAP aimed for diversification: it beckoned multinationals with tax breaks, promises of protection against nationalisation of private enterprise and other attractive terms. A push on manufacturing also began.

The PAP's main concern was the abolition of colonialism. Exactly what form this would take caused a bitter split in the party. The PAP was divided into two wings – the relatively moderate, English-speaking social democrats (Lee Kuan Yew's wing) and the fiery, Chinese-educated Communists. The moderates were eager to join up with Malaya for independence – an approach approved by the electorate, which in a referendum in 1962 voted overwhelmingly for a merger.

Merger offered both raw materials and a wider market for Singapore's industrial products. An independent Singapore, Lee said at the time, with no raw materials and no appreciable

Left: David Marshall, Singapore's first chief minister, negotiating with Malaya's Tunku Abdul Rahman.
Above: Singapore sand-bagged guard post guarding against some 3,000 Communist-led bandits, 1950.
Right: the Singapore River in the 1950s with large commercial houses in the background.

internal market, was "a political, economic and geographic absurdity". The right-wing Malayan government would support the moderate Lee in his struggle with Singapore's leftist opposition Barisan Socialis. However, Malaya feared that absorbing Singapore's one million Chinese would adversely affect the balance of power in its Malay-dominant territory. But the greater evil of an "Asian Cuba" at its doorstep persuaded the anti-Communist Malayan prime minister Tunku Abdul Rahman to offer unification.

The merger took place on 16 September 1963. To balance the influx of Chinese from Singapore, the British colonial states of Sarawak and Northern Borneo (Sabah), with their largely indigenous Malay populations, also joined the Federation of Malaysia.

Within a week, the PAP held a general election, catching the opposition by surprise. Riding on the fresh success of the merger, the PAP won 37 seats against 13 for the Barisan Socialis. Almost immediately, the PAP arrested and detained 15 opposition leaders. This move decimated the Barisan Socialis, and was explained away by the PAP as necessary to wipe out the "Communist plot to create tension and unrest in the state".

The PAP entered the Malaysian political scene aggressively by insisting on an immediate common market, meeting head-on with Malaysian resistance. This was just one example of the tension-ridden differences between Singapore and its federation partners.

Divisive differences

But far worse was the racial tension. The PAP's foray into federal politics was viewed by Malaysia's Malays as a Chinese bid to challenge Malay supremacy. The discord culminated in two major race riots in Singapore between Malays and Chinese in July and September 1964, setting the stage for a split. On 9 August 1965, Singapore was expelled from the federation, and became independent. The next month, the island nation became a fully-fledged member of the United Nations.

For Singaporeans, independence was a matter of worry, not joy. How could this tiny state survive, surrounded as it were by giant unfriendly neighbours? Britain was to vacate its Singapore base – part of a general withdrawal of troops from east of Suez. For Singapore, this prompted economic concerns as much as security worries: the British bases accounted for some 20 percent of its GNP and employed a good chunk of the labour force. When the British left in 1971, Singapore introduced compulsory two-year national service for all 18-year-old males. Today, it has all the trappings of a modern-day fighting force, including an arsenal of sophisticated weaponry.

The newly independent country was also faced with high unemployment rates, inad-

POLITICIANS' BIG PAY PACKETS

Singapore may be a small country, but when it comes to paying its leaders, it's in the big league. Prime minister Lee Hsien Loong earns about US$2.7 million a year, while a cabinet minister in Singapore earns close to US$1.2 million. Singapore has the highest-paid leader in the world; the US president earns a mere US$400,000. Such high wages are due to Singapore's free-market philosophy of paying its ministers salaries competitive with top executives in the private sector. Only in this way does it expect the best brains to join the civil service. Needless to say, this is an area of much contention.

equate housing, no natural resources and little cash. It also lacked national cohesion, being essentially a disparate group of immigrants comprising the majority Chinese, and Malays, Indians and Eurasians. However, the fledgling state still had a few aces up its sleeve.

Its strategic location made it an established trading hub and it had inherited British rule of law. The other ace was the pragmatic – some would say ruthless – Lee Kuan Yew, who provided vision and the necessary drive. His government took to heart the basic economic premise that to attract foreign investment, a developing country had to offer political stability, cheap labour, a good location, and few or no restrictions on currency movement. As a result of his efforts, Singapore's industrial sector grew 23 percent a year from 1968 to 1972 – one of the highest rates the world has seen.

Nimble economic strategies

This growth was spurred by careful and far-sighted economic planning. Singapore has always adhered to an open market economy.

Each decade threw up its challenges, which the country overcame effectively. In the late 1960s and 70s, its capital and skill-intensive industries laid the groundwork for the entry of electronics giants such as Sony and Matsushita.

When the 1980s demanded knowledge-intensive industries, Singapore had in place by the decade's end a base of manufacturing capabilities. Companies undertook research and development, engineering design and software development. The upwards trajectory continued in the 1990s, with forays into Vietnam, India and China. Realising that it could not compete with other Asian countries in labour-intensive industries, Singapore aimed to be a world-class IT hub and Southeast Asia's banking and financial centre. The decade after the turn of the millennium, life sciences were identified as an engine of growth, while tourism received a boost with the opening of two "integrated resorts", mega-entertainment and leisure complexes complete with casinos, in 2010.

Along with economic growth, public housing was a top priority *(see page 198)*. Today, more than 87 percent of the population live in comfortable government-built Housing and

LEFT: Lee Kuan Yew making a speech in 1959. **ABOVE:** women make up nearly half of Singapore's work force.

Development Board (HDB) flats which they own, using funds from a compulsory retirement savings programme called the Central Provident Fund (CPF) to finance most of the mortgage.

The PAP at the helm

Over the decades, the PAP has proved itself a sturdy government able to deal decisively and competently with crises of different shapes and sizes: the 1970s oil crisis, the 1985 economic recession, the economic downturn of the late 1990s and the 2003 SARS epidemic.

If its increasingly sophisticated people chafe under a paternalistic style of government, such sentiments have hardly been reflected in the polls. The PAP, re-elected continuously since 1959, has only suffered a tiny hiccup in its history of political dominance – at the 1991 general election it lost four seats to the opposition, instead of the customary one or two.

Prime minister Goh Chok Tong, whose rule saw some political and social liberalisation in the last decade, retired in 2004, giving way to his deputy, Lee Hsien Loong, the eldest son of former prime minister Lee Kuan Yew (see opposite). There were concerns that the younger Lee may return to the more autocratic style of his father, but the critics have been proven wrong thus far.

In late 2004, he revealed the proposal to build two "integrated resorts", at Sentosa and Marina Bay. There were concerns that the casinos in these resorts would encourage gambling, so Lee suggested that safeguards should be implemented. As a result, Singaporeans and permanent residents pay an entrance fee of S$100 per visit or S$2,000 annually.

Both these integrated resorts were opened in 2010, just as Singapore came to the end of the global recession in 2009. The island recovered quickly from this, with close to 15 percent growth achieved in 2010 – the highest annual figure on record. ❑

PARLIAMENT AT WORK

Singapore has a system of parliamentary democracy, where members of parliament are voted in at regular general elections. The "life" of each parliament is five years from its first sitting after an election.

In the 1990s, nominated members of parliament (NMPs) were introduced – unelected members chosen by the parliamentary select committee. The aim is to allow citizens with no party affiliations to contribute to parliament. There's only been one legislative initiative from an NMP – in 1995, university lecturer Walter Woon introduced the Maintenance for Parents Bill, the first bill passed initiated by a non-PAP member.

ABOVE LEFT: Lee Hsien Loong. **ABOVE:** construction has now finished at Marina Bay Sands.

Lee Kuan Yew

The father of modern Singapore has had his share of criticism, but no one can deny that he's responsible for its roaring success

He stepped down in 1990 as Singapore's first prime minister, but Lee Kuan Yew remains a political force to be reckoned with. The Cambridge-educated, fourth-generation Singaporean is credited with shaping a tiny island comprising a disparate group of immigrants into a gleaming model of efficiency.

Lee's family origins reflect the migrant nature of the country: Chinese forefathers of hardy Hakka stock who moved to the area and married local Malays. Lee was born on 16 September 1923, when Singapore was still a British colonial outpost, to a father who worked for oil giant Shell before retiring to sell watches and jewellery. The eldest of five children, Lee topped candidates from the Straits Settlement and Malaya in the Senior Cambridge School Certificate examination in 1939 to win a scholarship.

A strong legacy

The story of how Lee Kuan Yew transformed Singapore is fascinating because no other leader in the modern world has had such a hand in influencing and directing his country's progress, right from independence to developed-nation status.

Lee helped found the People's Action Party (PAP) in 1954, shrewdly representing its moderate faction while the party itself courted the Chinese majority on an anti-colonial left-wing ticket. He was prime minister for 31 years until 1990, when he handed the reins over to Goh Chok Tong. While admired for his grasp of a wide range of issues and especially for his social and economic vision, Lee's uncompromising attitude and his critical, often intimidating, personal style was not always well received.

He has been described as autocratic, high-handed and authoritarian, with foreign critics describing Singapore's political system as intolerant. Still, it is undeniably a system that works, and the country's rise to affluence remains the greatest testament to Lee's personal beliefs.

Lee instilled good governance and bureaucratic efficiency, and dealt harshly with corruption while building modern ports, a top airport and other infrastructure to lure foreign investors. To compensate for the lack of local manpower, he implemented a policy of attracting foreign

workers, including top corporate managers and professionals.

Today, Lee is a well-respected statesman, an octogenarian whose views on Asia's emerging role in the world economy are sought by other world leaders. At home, in his advisory role as minister mentor, he continues to have a say in what goes on in Singapore's affairs. ❑

RIGHT: the much respected Lee Kuan Yew.

SOCIAL CAMPAIGNS

No other nation in the civilised world is as obsessed with spoon-feeding its people with social guidelines. These cover everything from courtesy to sanitation, marriage and childbirth

Singapore's earnest social campaigns, organised with much fanfare by its government, often draw mirth and scepticism from visitors who are used to more intrinsic behavioural values. While outsiders may find it strange for a country to spend millions of dollars on countless campaigns to tell people the seemingly obvious – be courteous; keep the country clean; flush public toilets – the majority of Singaporeans dutifully follow such exhortations on social behaviour.

Indeed, from the smiling immigration officer at a Changi Airport checkpoint to the helpful – and also smiling – taxi driver whisking visitors to their hotels in downtown Orchard Road, Singapore's social campaigns appear, on first impression, to have been successful. Non-Singaporeans may be puzzled by such an apparently socialist approach by a government that is a proponent of a free-market economy.

But it has a spin-off more in tune with capitalism – behind those smiles is a dollar sign. Take the ongoing Singapore Kindness Movement (formerly known as the Courtesy Campaign) for instance, which costs the government at least S$1 million annually. The fact is, it is simply good business to smile at tourists and visiting businessmen, to encourage them to return. Government-sponsored advertisements often feature a mix of Singaporeans flashing rows of perfect pearly whites.

And look at the message on why Singaporeans should smile. One advertisement says: "Just one thing to keep in mind when you next see our visitors. Simply smile and be gracious. Make our guests feel welcome. It will mean a better tomorrow for ourselves." So zealously was this campaign taken up that in 2006 the government sponsored a campaign to collect 4 million photos of smiling faces to welcome delegates for the IMF–World Bank forum in the city.

Socialist influences

Not all campaigns owe their origins to purely mercenary concerns, however, but have their roots in the socialist politics of the country. Singapore, with its majority Chinese population, was rife with Communist fervour in its early days. In the political struggle after World War II, democratic socialism emerged as the dominant ideology. Given this historical connection it is

> *After National Smoking Control Campaign, Anti-Drug Abuse Campaign and Anti-Drink Drive Campaign, Know the Line, which deals with gambling, is the latest campaign to help citizens control their vices.*

no wonder that social campaigns are an important part of the psyche of the Singapore government and its people. Over the years social campaigns have evolved from a Communist backdrop to take new meaning in modern Singapore.

Indeed, it seems there has been a campaign at every turn to match the needs of the day, from the perennial Courtesy Campaign to one which persuaded Singaporeans (not very successfully) to be punctual for wedding dinners.

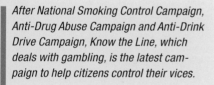

Preceding Pages: flag-waving at National Day, August 9. **Left:** a souvenir T-shirt pokes fun at Singapore's reputation for petty rules and regulations. **Top, Above and Above Right:** locals are encouraged to smile and be courteous.

One of the earliest campaigns was the Family Planning Campaign. Launched in 1966, just after Singapore was asked to leave Malaysia because of political differences, it was the government's knee-jerk response to a desperate situation: insufficient housing, unemployment and a declining trade economy. The solution: check the population growth.

To execute this, the Singapore Family Planning and Population Board was set up in 1966, to introduce population control and family planning. Many baby boomers will remember that they are the products of a nationwide campaign that exhorted their parents to "Stop at Two". It was an aggressive drive that emphasised the restriction of incentives in housing, education, tax and health-care benefits – if families had a third child or more. In true socialist fashion, women were called on to be sterilised after the second child. Medical assistance for sterilisation was made affordable and quick. However, the government was to realise the folly of this campaign two decades later.

The Keep Singapore Clean Campaign was another early campaign in post-independent Singapore. First launched by the former prime

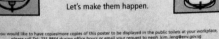

AIM WELL

Clean public toilets are possible.
Let's make them happen.

minister Lee Kuan Yew in October 1968, its aim was to educate all Singaporeans on the importance of maintaining a clean environment. Slogans such as "Keep Singapore Litter-Free" and "Clean and Green City" were generously articulated.

To ensure that the collective efforts were effective, fines were introduced by the government to punish those who spit and littered in public. Fines are such a commonplace feature of the country that Singapore is often infamously known as the world's "finest" city. Some snicker that the phrase "have a fine day" takes on new meaning in this island-state.

By the 1970s, unemployment was wiped out and adequate housing was provided, accompanied by spectacular economic growth. It testified that such campaigns were successful in achieving policy outcomes. The PAP, which enjoyed a monopoly over national politics and achieved political support from the majority, embarked on more social campaigns.

HOW TO TOILET TRAIN A NATION

You may be fined if you are caught not flushing a public toilet after use. To drive home this point, the local paper did a daily review of various "Toilets of Shame" in the 1990s, complete with pictures of urine- and excreta-splattered public loos. However, to date, the campaign has not successfully admonished people into peeing straight.

Thankfully, though, no one has ever actually been convicted of this "crime". It shows how difficult, if not ludicrous, it is to enforce such a rule – short of appointing toilet rangers to police every loo. But the situation is different in elevators. Ask any Singaporean who has lived in public housing in the 1970s and the 80s and they will tell you that people mistaking elevators for toilets used to be unpleasantly commonplace.

But Singapore's civil servants have found a solution. Using high-tech gadgets, elevators identified as being frequently abused are fitted with urine detectors and labelled with a sign which caricatures a young naked boy with pants at his ankles and cuffed at the wrists. The gadget, when it senses the offending fluid, jams the elevator midjourney until the doors are forcibly opened by officials. This has proved so effective that people now suspect that many urine detector signs in elevators are fakes, but no one wants to risk being caught with his (or her) pants down.

Campaign follies

By the 1980s, a decade of successful campaigning had resulted in fewer children. Singapore now suffered from a shortage of workers and the spectre of an ageing population had raised its ugly head: it has been estimated that by 2020 about one-fifth of Singaporeans will be aged 65 or above.

The government could now afford to be less heavy-handed. Rather than wave the stick of disincentives, it dangled carrots in the form of tax incentives. Never one to be cowed, the government launched a counter campaign, this time calling the people to "Have Three or More if You Can Afford It".

The Graduate Mothers' Priority Scheme was also introduced to offer incentives to female university grads who were mothers. They were encouraged to have more children and in return enjoyed hefty tax incentives. In contrast, the lowest-educated women were encouraged to stop at one or two children in return for a

FAR LEFT AND ABOVE LEFT: Singapore is known for its public information campaigns – in this case for public cleanliness. LEFT: the government has changed tack on family planning. ABOVE: marriage is encouraged.

cash grant of S$10,000 in their social security funds, which could be drawn upon to purchase public housing.

The move sparked a furore among Singaporeans and led to lengthy debates on the topic of "nature" versus "nurture". The PAP provoked considerable public criticism over its attempt at genetic engineering. The loss of two seats in parliament to the opposition in the 1984 general elections – for the first time since 1963 – and loss of nearly 13 percent of the votes cast from the election in 1980, showed the unpopularity of such a misguided policy. In 1985, the priority scheme for graduate mothers was terminated. Shortly after, the Singapore Family Planning and Population Board was closed.

To skirt around the issue, the government set up the Social Development Unit (SDU), conceived as a matchmaker for university-educated singles. Dubbed "Single, Desperate and Ugly" by its detractors, the SDU's mission is to bring singles together for the purpose of marriage. Its programmes include subsidised outings and get-to-know-you sessions. The scheme was later expanded, and separate units were set up for those with more basic qualifications. The government's unofficial policy of pairing off singles of similar educational backgrounds may raise hackles elsewhere in the world, but the success rate of the SDU and its sister organisations speaks volumes.

Then there was the Romancing Singapore Campaign, which started in 2002 to combat falling birth rates. The aim was to convey the message that "love is in the little things". Being more expressive with your partner at all times was encouraged and in 2005, it was taken over by the private sector and became a year-long festival.

Social campaigns today

In today's Singapore, more and more campaigns are merged with technology. The nature of campaigns is changing its shape from written form to electronic transmission through the the internet. Phrases such as "Cyber Courtesy" have emerged to help tone down the language in chat groups. In 1998, the Courtesy Campaign was further narrowed down to mobile phone users as technological changes brought about new areas of concern. Campaigns are also changing to a discreet, less direct format. The government is now more concerned with policy-making and launching social campaigns that are not directly related to racial, ethnic and religious issues.

Another change is that social campaigns today are supported by foreign investors. Most campaigns launched in the past few years secured large amounts of sponsorship from multinationals. Many have forgotten, it seems, the campaigns' original links to socialism.

What has been the effect of these campaigns

on the life of Singaporeans? On the socio-cultural plane, the Speak Mandarin Campaign has, for instance, reinforced racial differences in the community. Some think the millions of dollars contributed by taxpayers towards these campaigns promote the interests of the ruling party. For example, one journalist wrote in *The Straits Times* some years ago: "Here is what's really scary: what if a campaign like Smile Singapore actually works? I mean, what will that tell you about our people? Do you really want such a pliant population, even if the message it is absorbing seems to be a harmless one?" Others, meanwhile, think that social campaigns bring a positive benefit to society, and that is reason enough to continue them.

However, many people will agree that some of the campaigns have been successful. The Keep Singapore Green Campaign has kept the tiny island, for all its concrete, fairly green. As a result of another campaign, Tree Planting Day,

many more trees have sprung up, especially in the public housing estates. The PAP takes it so seriously that all its ministers are out in full force at this annual event to plant trees, assisted by numerous gardeners of course. The Great River Clean-Up Campaign to clean the once filthy Singapore River was also a great success. Coupled with river activities and the redevelopment of buildings along Boat and Clarke quays, the riverside is now a big draw for tourists and residents alike.

The government also realised that social campaigns needed to evolve to remain relevant to a more discerning society. In 2010, a well-produced and sleek $1.6 million social campaign ad to promote filial piety was broadcast on TV. It showed a patient middle-aged son caring for his bitter and angry aged mother, coupled with heartwarming flashbacks of how his mother cared from him when he was a child. The aim of this creative campaign was to inject some controversy and evoke a sense of passion among Singaporeans. This soft-sell campaign to promote family values created a buzz. It didn't only get the press and netizens talking, it also managed to move the public to tears. ❑

LEFT: students on an Social Development Unit course. **TOP:** Kindness Lion. **ABOVE:** separate entrances for Singapore residents and foreigners at the casino. **ABOVE RIGHT:** the Good English Campaign.

EVENTS AND FESTIVALS

Almost every month of the year, Singapore's streets, temples and ethnic enclaves come alive with a motley assortment of religious and cultural celebrations. A growing list of contemporary events now adds to the jam-packed calendar

With its multiracial character, it's no surprise that Singapore is a constant hive of activity, celebrating one cultural festival after another. The following festivals are among the most important in the calendar, and offer the most interest to the visitor.

January to March

Chinese New Year: The most widely celebrated festival among the Chinese, it falls on the first day of the lunar calendar, usually between mid-January and mid-February. Chinese custom decrees that the previous year's debts be paid, the home cleaned and new clothing purchased. It is also a time for reaffirming ties at the family reunion dinner that takes place on the eve. The 15-day festival, beginning with a two-day holiday, is commemorated by feasting and the giving of *hong bao*, red packets of "lucky money".

Catch the festive spirit in Chinatown, where the streets are all lit up and chock-a-block with people jostling for festive goods. Dragon and lion dancers throng the streets, making plenty of noise to keep the mythical monsters traditionally associated with Chinese New Year at bay. The celebrations end on a high note with the Chingay Parade – an exuberant procession which is held on the Sunday following the New Year. Lavish floats, stilt-walkers, martial arts troupes and mini-dramas illustrating classical Chinese myths are some of the parade's best-loved features.

Thaipusam: This Hindu festival is observed between January and February, in the Tamil month of Thai. Devotees honour Lord Muruga, god of bravery, power and virtue, by performing feats of mind over spirit. The festival begins at dawn at the Srinivasa Perumal Temple *(see page 168)* in Serangoon Road. Here, devotees who have entered a trance have their bodies pierced with metal hooks or spikes attached to a *kavadi*, a cage-like steel contraption which is carried on their shoulders. The procession makes its way to the Sri Thandayuthapani Temple *(see page 149)* at Tank Road, accompanied by chanting supporters.

April to June

Singapore International Film Festival: A varied diet of art-house films from various countries are showcased during this two-

Held island-wide from the end of May to early July, the Great Singapore Sale indulges those with a passion for shopping – with goods at shopping malls slashed down to bargain-basement prices.

week period, usually in April. Locally made films are also screened, and have been attracting an increasing following for their insightful vignettes of Singapore life. Fringe events include retrospectives, tributes, seminars and film-appreciation workshops.

World Gourmet Summit: A two-week-long gastronomic event with workshops and seminars on fine food and wines. Singapore's best chefs and restaurants are feted with awards, while guest chefs from around the world play host at selected restaurants with special menus.

Vesak Day: Usually celebrated in May, this

is the most important event in the Buddhist calendar, for it honours the birth, death and enlightenment of Buddha. Temple celebrations begin at dawn with a candlelight procession. As part of the celebrations, caged birds are released and free meals are distributed to the poor.

Singapore Arts Festival: This annual event in June showcases a bonanza of Asian and Western performing arts from dance and theatre to music. The festival also offers a Kidsfest and a fringe with free performances in public spaces.

Past performers have included the Washington Ballet and the London Philharmonic Orchestra, and also less commercial ventures, such as a Lithuanian adaptation of Shakespeare's *Othello*. The festival also features an eclectic fringe segment and workshops by visiting companies.

Dragon Boat Festival: Every June, colourful longboats with prows carved to represent dragons and birds crest the waves of Marina Bay, propelled by dozens of pairs of strong arms. The Dragon Boat Race is an international-class event that draws teams from Australia, Europe and the US, among others.

The festival honours a Chinese patriot, Qu Yuan, who drowned himself in 278 BC to

LEFT: Chinese New Year celebrations at the Marina.
ABOVE: the Chingay Parade marks the culmination of Singapore's Chinese New Year festivities with processions and costumes galore.

protest against the corruption of the imperial court. Fishermen tried to rescue him but failed. Small packages of rice were thrown into the water to distract fishes from his body, and villagers decorated their boats with dragon heads and tails with the same purpose in mind. Today, several varieties of these rice dumplings are available throughout the year.

July to September

Singapore Food Festival: The island celebrates another favourite pastime – eating – with a month-long food fiesta in July. Various food-tasting events and unique dining experiences that cover a gamut of cuisines are held.

National Day: For an entire month before 9 August, you'll hear children fervently practising songs of nationhood, and see performers and dancers with torches and flashcards rehearsing to perfect the National Day Parade. The pomp and pageantry, which celebrates the city-state's independence, culminates in a stunning fireworks display at night. The annual parade, traditionally held at either the Padang *(see page 103)* or the now demolished National Stadium will be held at the Marina Bay Floating Stadium until 2014 – when the new Sports Hub at Kallang is ready.

Festival of the Hungry Ghosts: Chinese believe the gates of hell are opened throughout the seventh lunar month, usually August/ September, to allow ghosts to wander the earth. To appease these wayward spirits, joss sticks and paper money are burned and feasts whipped up as offerings. Neighbourhood events such as *wayang* (Chinese opera) or *getai* (mini pop concerts) are held, climaxing in a lively auction.

Monkey God's Birthday: The Monkey God is a character from the Chinese classic *Journey to the West*, who is celebrated for protecting his master, a monk of the Tang dynasty, dispatched to India to collect the Buddhist *sutras* (holy books). During this festival in September, acrobats perform at various temples.

October to December

Mid-Autumn Festival: This traditional harvest festival takes place on the 15th day of the eighth lunar month, usually in October. There are various legends behind this festival, the most popular one about Chang-E, a fairy who flew to the moon. Mooncakes – pastries filled with lotus paste and egg yolks – are eaten on this day, and children carry lanterns around the neighbourhood. Don't miss the impressive display of lanterns at the Chinese Garden *(see page 200)* in Jurong.

Navarathri: Sanskrit for "nine nights", Navarathri pays homage to the three consorts (Durga, Lakshmi and Saraswati) of the Hindu gods, with nine days of traditional Indian music and dancing at all Hindu temples. The festival

concludes with a procession. This October event provides a rare opportunity to experience Indian arts; elaborate performances are held at the Sri Thandayuthapani Temple *(see page 149)* and other Hindu temples.

Thimithi Festival: This breathtaking fire-walking ceremony occurs in October at the Sri Mariamman Temple *(see page 125)* on South Bridge Road. Male devotees sprint barefoot across glowing coals, without any apparent injury to their feet, in honour of Draupathi, a legendary heroine deified by South Indian Tamils. On the eve of the festival a magnificent silver chariot honouring Draupathi makes its way from this temple to the Srinavasa Temple in Little India.

Deepavali: Also known as the Festival of Lights, to symbolise the conquest of good over evil, this is the most important festival in the Hindu calendar. Usually occurring in October or November, it is celebrated by the traditional lighting of oil lamps at homes and in Little India, which is turned into a fairyland of twinkling lights. Prayers are recited in temples and statues of deities carried around the grounds.

Christmas: Almost everyone, regardless of religious affliation, gets into the spirit of exchanging gifts come Christmas time. Orchard Road is transformed into a riot of lights and glitzy displays, while shopping malls and hotels try to outdo each other with the most imaginative decorations and vie for the "best decorated award". Nevertheless, as with all things Singaporean, Christmas here is celebrated with a difference – just tuck into a tandoori turkey and you'll see!

Variable dates

Hari Raya Puasa: This Muslim celebration falls on the first day of the 10th Muslim month; the date varies from year to year. During Ramadan, the month preceding Hari Raya Puasa, all able Muslims observe a strict fast from sunrise to sunset – so that they are better able to commiserate with the less fortunate. On Hari Raya Puasa, celebrants ask for forgiveness from family members, make new resolutions and feast on traditional food.

The other Muslim festival celebrated with a holiday is **Hari Raya Haji**, which marks the sacrifices made by Muslims who undertake the pilgrimage to Mecca. ❑

CONTEMPORARY EVENTS

A boom in world-class venues plus a growing population of fun-seeking city-dwellers has led to a significant increase in events, from the Singapore Fashion Festival and the New Year Countdown Party to the Huayi Chinese Festival of Arts and the Mosaic Music Festival. A more recent addition is the Singapore Biennale, an exhibition of international contemporary art.

For the most current list of events and celebrations, check the Singapore Tourism Board website at www. yoursingapore.com or go to any of its Visitor Centres. *The Straits Times* and free tourist magazines like *I-S, Where* and *Changi Express* also provide details.

LEFT: helicopter fly-by at the National Day Parade.
ABOVE: Deepavali. **ABOVE RIGHT:** Hari Raya Haji.

A POTPOURRI OF FESTIVALS

Where else can you see snow in a tropical island, watch bodies being pierced and skewered without bleeding, and burn money for the dead?

Singapore is a fascinating melting pot of Chinese, Malays, Indians, Eurasians and expatriates from around the region and the West. Add to this a diversity of religions and you have a virtual kaleidoscope of rituals and ceremonies – some seemingly strange to the foreign eye. The Chinese make up the majority, and their distinctive cultural identity is manifested in many customary and religious practices, both Buddhist and Taoist, and often a combination of both. Despite the city's outward modernity, Chinese temples are bustling and noisy places thronged with devotees going about their rituals. Most Hindu temples and Muslim mosques also welcome visitors, but make sure that you're modestly attired (no shorts or revealing tops) and remember to remove your footwear before entering. There is always something going on at these places – all of which provide ample fodder for avid photographers.

ABOVE: mooncakes, rich pastries filled with lotus seed or red bean paste and egg yolks, are sold to mark the Chinese Mid-Autumn Festival in late September or early October.

LEFT: *wayang* or Chinese opera is a colourful stage entertainment that combines mime, dance, songs and dialogue, and is often performed during the Festival of the Hungry Ghosts. Shrill voices punctuated by loud gongs, clashing cymbals and droning stringed instruments may seem quite alien, but the plot is usually a familiar story of heroes fighting against evil and lovers escaping from disapproving parents.

ABOVE: in an intense and dramatic demonstration of belief and devotion, the body of a Hindu devotee is pierced with spikes and skewers as he carries a heavy steel *kavadi* decorated with peacock feathers and flowers during a Thaipusam festival procession. This almost inhuman feat requires devotees to undergo weeks of rigorous spiritual preparation before they can take part in this ritualistic journey. During their tranced state, no blood is shed even with steel rods pierced into their tongues, cheeks and other parts of the body – definitely not a sight for the squeamish. The procession also sees some devotees walking on a bed of nails.

FESTIVAL LIGHT-UPS AND DECORATIONS

The Christmas light-up on Orchard Road is a yearly tradition; the street is set ablaze with thousands of fairy lights, and shopping malls deck their facades with decorations in the spirit of the season. From snowmen to log houses and larger-than-life Santa Claus figures, almost every Yuletide cliche is played out – never mind that it's alien to local culture.

Another colourful festival to look out for is the Chinese Lunar New Year. In the days leading up to it, the streets of Chinatown are decorated with lights and lined with bazaar stalls selling festive food like waxed duck and barbecued meats. The excitement culminates on the eve when revellers congregate to ring in the Lunar New Year and watch a dramatic fireworks display.

Likewise, Deepavali sees a riot of neon lights on the streets in Little India at Serangoon Road, while Geylang Serai is all abuzz during the Muslim festival of Hari Raya Puasa.

ABOVE: Chinese New Year is celebrated in style in Singapore. The Chingay parade is held on the Sunday following New Year's Day.

LEFT: apart from the street decorations and festival light-up at Geylang Serai, another hub of activity during the Muslim Hari Raya Puasa is Kampong Glam.

SINGAPORE AFTER DARK

The city rocks after dark. Come dusk, pubs shift gears,
clubs rev up their music, and theatre and dance come alive
on stage. There's something for just about everyone,
whether they prefer a night at the opera or a pub crawl

Once sidelined as a sterile city with no soul, Singapore has undergone a remarkable transformation into a lively arts and entertainment hub. Whether it's a night of pub-crawling or one of non-stop clubbing (bar-top dancing was famously legalised in 2003), the options are plentiful. There are chill-out alfresco bars set in lush gardens or on rooftops, chic lounges for the design-conscious, pubs with world-class bands, and dance clubs that rank among some of the best in the world.

Of late, the Lion City has been taking itself less seriously. Not only is Singapore the first city in the world to host a Formula 1 night race, some clubs operate 24/7, a reverse bungee-jump outfit sends people hurtling into the night sky, busking is no longer illegal, gay bars make no bones about their inclinations, and gambling in luxury casinos is the talk of the town – after eat-

> Whether your idea of fun is being moved to tears at the opera, having a chuckle at a comedy act, tossing back a whisky at a dimly lit karaoke lounge, or shooting pool at 3am, you will find it in Singapore.

ing and shopping, that is. Sticky issues still exist – sugar-free "therapeutic" chewing gum is only available after giving your name and ID card number to the pharmacist – but Asia's little red dot is having a fine time playing hard and still working as hard. And if you reach down deep enough, you'll hit the underbelly of Singapore society – as vibrant and decadent as the best of them.

The art of entertainment

There is an incredible number of arts and entertainment events throughout the year for a tiny city like Singapore. Arts venues such as the stunning Esplanade – Theatres on the Bay offers a year-round calendar of events, both free and ticketed. The Arts House, an arts venue overlooking the Singapore River that was transformed from the historic Old

LEFT: barman at a modish downtown nightclub.
RIGHT: dancing at the Pump Room.

Parliament House, serves up a refreshing line-up of cultural, visual and performing arts events. In 2006, Singapore staged its first biennial international visual arts event, the Singapore Biennale. The Singapore Arts Festival takes place each June *(see page 57)*.

The National Arts Council, the government body that looks after Singapore's cultural soul, organises year-round free concerts at lush Singapore parks. Other annual fixtures are the Mosaic Music Festival, the International Comedy Festival and the Singapore Dance Theatre's Ballet Under the Stars series.

The theatre scene

New Broadway-destined shows with an Asian focus occasionally premiere in Singapore, while long-running shows like *Les Misérables, Oliver!* and *Phantom of the Opera* have made appearances here. The latest production to be unveiled (March 2011) is the Southeast Asian premiere of *The Lion King*, at The Sands Theatre at Marina Bay Sands.

All these exist alongside a very healthy Singapore theatre scene, which features both locally written and produced works and inter-

national collaborations. Wild Rice, a theatre company that creates "glocal" works inspired by Singapore society and universal issues, has showcased its productions in cities such as Wellington, (*Animal Farm*, 2004), Moscow (*Generation/s*, 2008) and Hong Kong (*Animal Farm*, 2010).

The Singapore Repertory Theatre is most associated with Broadway-scale productions which bring together the world's most talented Asian stars – like David Henry Hwang, Lea Salonga, Pat Morita, Tsai Chin and Shabana Azmi – along with award-winning directors, playwrights and lighting, set and costume designers. It has also presented productions starring international actors such as Ian McKellen and Ethan Hawke. Its recent productions include *A Midsummer Night's Dream*, *The Pillowman* and *Much Ado About Nothing*.

Dance and music

Classical music in Singapore revolves around the Singapore Symphony Orchestra, which traces its history back to 1979. The critically acclaimed orchestra gives more than 50 concerts a year at Esplanade – Theatres on the Bay.

Its repertoire tends to be mainstream; most concerts comprise the standard overture, concerto and symphony, but it also performs more accessible classical and contemporary music. Big names that have performed with the SSO include percussionist Evelyn Glennie and tenor José Carreras.

Dance in Singapore is dynamic, with a corps of dancers and choreographers moving between projects and ensembles. The most important is the Singapore Dance Theatre, with a repertoire ranging from *The Nutcracker* and *Sleeping Beauty* to contemporary dance. Choreographer Jamaludin Jalil's *Juxtamotion*, and Paul Ocampo's *Who Cares?* set to the music of the pop group Queen have all entered into its repertoire, and some have been included in overseas tours.

Film fare

Recent years have seen the local film industry grow at an unprecedented rate, with a glut of

LEFT: a costume drama performed at the Singapore Art Festival. TOP: the Singapore Symphony Orchestra at Victoria Concert Hall. ABOVE: Night Festival at SMU Campus Green. ABOVE RIGHT: performance at the Odyssey Dance Theatre.

> To get revellers back home safely, bus operators SBS Transit and SMRT have late-night services that operate during festive seasons, weekends and holidays from 11.30pm to 4.25am.

high-grossing films tackling social issues with both humour and style. Local directors such as Jack Neo, Eric Khoo, Kelvin Tong, Tan Pin Pin and Royston Tan are increasingly enjoying the limelight at home and overseas with their award-winning movies and short films. Singapore's young film industry has far outstripped its sister, the television industry, in terms of quality and depth.

For the visitor, it's no longer a matter of luck or timing when it comes to catching a well-produced local film. The Sinema Old School in Mount Sophia is an independent cinema house that screens only Singapore-made films – an excellent way of gaining insight into local culture. Another thing you can count on are the year-round foreign film festivals. One highlight is the Singapore International Film Festival

held in April – going strong for over 20 years – which showcases some of the world's (and Singapore's) best. Film buffs can also catch art-house flicks at The PictureHouse at the Cathay Building, Cinema Europa at VivoCity and The Arts House.

The moviegoer here is spoilt for choice. Virtually every shopping mall in Singapore boasts a multi-theatre cineplex, albeit screening mainly Hollywood pulp fare, up to six times a day. Mid-night shows in the past were confined only to weekends, but today movie-lovers can watch all-night movie marathons. At Cathay Cinelei-sure on Orchard Road, for instance, movies on Fridays, Saturdays and the eves of holidays run overnight until the crack of dawn. Golden Village Cineplex in Great World City on Kim Seng Road offers – for a price – plush sofa-style seats for two, with the option to enjoy a meal as you watch the movie.

COURTING THE PINK DOLLAR

Singapore, like other large international cities, has wised up to the increasingly large and cash-rich international pink dollar market. While not openly offering welcome banners, efforts are well under way to put out the word – through the right channels – that the gay and lesbian community can comfortably enjoy a vacation in Singapore, without fear for personal safety or persecution.

In fact, Singapore's former prime minister Goh Chok Tong may have inadvertently sparked this change in official mindset when he remarked in 2003 that the civil service did not discriminate against the hiring of gay people. Taking the cue, the local and international press ran several articles on Singapore's gay community. These days, gay-themed plays have become commonplace, along with a rash of gay-friendly bars and saunas, especially in the Chinatown area. Gay-cruising spots, too, have emerged from the shadows. Local gay rights advocacy group People Like Us (www.plu.sg) seeks to champion the cause of the community but has so far failed in lifting regulations in Singapore which outlaw homosexual sex. And it looks like it has a long way to go in still conservative Singapore. Community-specific platforms on the internet (like www.fridae.com) advise gay and lesbian travellers on what's out there for them.

Above: Boat Quay is a major nightlife hub.

Favourite nightlife haunts

Singapore offers plenty of nightlife choices. There is a bar or club to suit every taste and quirk. If you don't have much time and want a definitive after-dark experience, a multi-venue destination could be the answer.

St James Power Station at HarbourFront opposite Sentosa Island was formerly a coal-fired power station; it's now been given a new lease of life as a multi-venue hotspot – with a total of nine party outlets. There's The Boiler Room with an energetic cover band belting out Top 40 pop, R&B and rock, the world-music club Movida (where an enthusiastic crowd dances to sexy Latin tunes), and Powerhouse with its hip pop-house beats.

Better known in international clubbing circles is Zouk, at Jiak Kim Street, whose diehard fans continue to worship it as the ultimate in cool. Zouk plays a diet of edgy underground and house music, and has hosted in the past DJ luminaries like Paul Oakenfold, John Digweed and Sasha. The annual ZoukOut, which began in 2000, is now touted as Asia's largest outdoor

dance-music festival. This beach dance party held in December at Sentosa's Siloso Beach lures in throngs of clubbing fans to party from 8pm to 8am.

The Butter Factory, a hip hop and R&B dance club at One Fullerton, is another spot where beautiful people gather. Boat Quay might be considered just for tourists, but a fair amount of locals can be seen stumbling out of the bars here too. Favourites include Harry's (where they have a cocktail, Bank Breaker, named after Nick Leeson, who brought down Barings in 1995 and used to hang out in this bar) and The Penny Black, where you'll get a feel of Victorian England. Many bankers from the CBD area throng these bars after work.

A makeover has transformed the once sedate Clarke Quay into the city's hottest nightlife haunt with a rash of hip restaurants, bars and dance clubs. Home-grown favourites at Clarke Quay are Attica/Attica Too, where DJs spin everything from hip-hop to electronic dance, and The Pump Room, where hot local band Jive Talkin' performs nightly (except Mondays).

Sentosa has warmed up as an after-dark destination with the entry of several hip beachside

bars, including the Ibizan import Café del Mar, complete with ambient music, cabanas and outdoor daybeds. At the casual bar set-up called Coastes next door, one can sip cocktails while lazing in a hammock. Or you might prefer the classy surrounds of il Lido Lounge Bar at the Sentosa Golf Club, where the beautiful sunsets, designer decor and DJs playing soul and chill-out music make for a posh night out.

The opening of the integrated resorts in 2010 has also added some new nightlife options, of which the most exciting is Ku De Ta, perched on the magnificent Sands SkyPark.

Lounges and jazz bars

For those seeking a quiet drink, there are a large number of chic bars and lounges, many with alfresco seating. Located by the Singapore River is Bar Opiume at Empress Place (next to Asian Civilisations Museum), a sophisticated chill-out place.

Also high on the "be seen" scale are drink hotspots like New Asia Bar and City Space at the Equinox Complex at Swissotel The Stamford, Ink Club Bar at Fairmont Singapore, and Post Bar at the Fullerton Singapore hotel (*see page 119*).

If jazz is your thing, there are a handful of places worth checking out. For international jazz acts, head to Harry's Bar at either of its branches in Boat Quay or The Esplanade, and Blu at Shangri-La Hotel. Local jazz acts can be found bringing the house down at Blu Jazz Café near Arab Street and Esplanade Mall's Southbridge Jazz @7atenine.

One of the top tourist bars is The Long Bar at Raffles Hotel, where guests can down glasses of the iconic Singapore Sling while enjoying live music by the resident band.

Theme pubs

Theme pubs are popular; among the long-standing favourites are Hooters at Clarke Quay with its well-endowed waitresses (enough said) and Ice Cold Beer on Emerald Hill for 9-inch hot-dogs and 30 varieties of ice-cold beer. Paulaner Brauhaus at Millenia Walk is a German micro-brewery specialising in freshly brewed light and dark lagers, while Que Pasa at Emerald Hill is an old shophouse converted into a Spanish-inspired bar serving tapas, sangria and cigars. Irish pubs are found all over Singapore – even along the beach in East Coast (Scruffy Murphy's) – and Muddy Murphy's at the Orchard Hotel was

reportedly built in Dublin, taken apart, shipped to Singapore and painstakingly reconstructed.

Karaoke

Karaoke lounges are everywhere, with membership clubs offering private rooms for rowdy sessions without punishing other patrons. K-Box Karaoke Lounge has about a dozen outlets in Singapore, and is open until 3am – when no one cares any longer who's singing what. Some outlets even have extended hours, on some nights.

Tanjong Pagar, once home to a rash of pubs, has seen its fortunes dwindle, and the district is now home to a more lucrative slice of the entertainment pie. Behind gaudy, neon-lit facades, drunken off-key renditions of Chinese and English classics are rendered, with hostesses who ply their groping male customers with drinks – and whatever else takes their customers' fancy.

> Rooftop bars offer breathtaking views of the city. Try 1-Altitude at UOB Building, Orgo at The Esplanade, Breeze on top of the boutique Scarlet Hotel, or Lantern at the Fullerton Bay Hotel.

Red-tinted pursuits

Yet another underworld is Claymore Rise near Orchard Towers in Orchard Road, packed with "working girls" and their agents. If you are female and alone, don't choose this as a meeting place – unless getting unwanted overtures or the sleazy eye from agents doesn't faze you. Inside Orchard Towers are well-known pick-up joints like Ipanema and Peyton Place.

All-you-can-drink alcohol buffets, drag nights, sex-for-sale joints disguised as health clubs and gyms, it's all here in Singapore, if you know where to look and who to ask.

• *Individual nightlife spots are listed in the Travel Tips section (pages 247–9).* ❑

LEFT: revellers at the Pump House. **TOP:** DJ at work. **ABOVE:** Harry's Bar at Boat Quay. **RIGHT:** band at the Substation.

CUISINE

Singapore's extraordinary cultural diversity has given the
island-state an explosion of flavours – Chinese, Malay,
Indian – and a delicious hybrid Peranakan cuisine that is
entirely its own. Add to this the world's major cuisines,
and you have a city that never stops eating

There are few places in the world where life revolves around food like it does in Singapore. Singaporeans talk about food all the time, just like the English talk of the weather. People from all walks of life display remarkable critical abilities in matters culinary. They can debate on where to get the freshest seafood, the hottest chilli sauce, the best chicken rice or *satay* for hours on end – preferably over a meal. Whether served on polystyrene in a rough-and-ready food centre or on bone china in a chichi restaurant, food is a major focus in Singapore.

The racial mix of Chinese, Malays and Indians, as well as an expatriate population from the world over, has led to a range of cuisines which is nothing less than incredible. These immigrants brought their favourite dishes, ingredients and techniques, resulting in a variety of food which has merged then re-emerged as unique, and is available today in venues ranging from hawker stalls to world-class restaurants.

There are few cuisines which aren't represented in Singapore, so much so that the choice is wonderfully daunting. For most Singaporeans, however, nothing beats hawker-style Indian, Chinese, Malay and Peranakan specialities – and home-grown favourite dishes like fish-head curry and chilli crab.

> Chilli crab is Singapore's unofficial national dish and a must-try. Just as delicious is the drier, but no less spicy, black pepper crab. Whichever you choose, be prepared to use your fingers and get messy.

Peranakan

The combination which really has its own identity and provides Singapore with its most indigenous cuisine is Peranakan or Nonya food. Peranakans *(see page 22)* are descendants of early migrants from China who settled in Penang, Melaka and Singapore, and married local Malay women. The product of this union is the unique Peranakan culture and a cuisine which

LEFT: *dim sum* at Chinatown's Yum Cha Restaurant.
RIGHT: *nasi briyani,* a fragrant rice dish.

deftly blends Chinese ingredients with Malay spices and herbs – resulting in food that is both imaginative and tasty.

Central to Peranakan cuisine is the *rempah*: a mixture of spices such as chillies, shallots, lemongrass, candlenuts, turmeric and *belacan*,

> Laksa – *Peranakan spicy noodle soup –* comes in many versions, including rich, coconut-laden nonya laksa. *The most popular* laksa *in Singapore is found at Katong on the East Coast.*

or prawn paste, ground by hand in a stone pestle and mortar (*batu tumbuk*). It is this nose-tickling mixture which imparts a distinctive flavour and aroma to Peranakan cuisine.

Although best eaten in a Peranakan home, the food can be enjoyed at a small number of restaurants. Look out for dishes such as *otak otak*, a blend of fish, coconut milk, chilli paste, galangal and herbs wrapped in banana leaf, or *ayam buah keluak*, which combines chicken with Indonesian black nuts to produce a rich gravy. Although fused with Malay influences, Peranakan cuisine includes many pork dishes

such as *babi pongteh*, made of cuts of tender pork belly with salted bean paste. Be sure to leave room for desserts – colourful cakes and sticky sweet delicacies, many perfumed with coconut milk and fragrant pandan leaves.

Chinese cuisine

The Chinese have a way with food. Whether it's fresh fish and pork, preserved meats and dried seafood, or exotic abalone and bird's nest, Chinese cooks will whip up the tastiest of dishes. In recent years, Chinese food has also taken a turn for the healthy; increasingly cooks make do without lard and fatty cuts of meat, preferring instead slivers of lean meat or fresh seafood, accompanied by a range of fresh vegetables quickly stir-fried to preserve their flavours.

While there are uniquely Singapore-inspired Chinese dishes like chilli or pepper crabs, the large Chinese population here generally ensures the authenticity of the cuisine. The meal is always eaten in traditional style – by helping oneself with chopsticks (or more likely these days, spoon and fork) from a selection of dishes shared by all the diners.

The adaptation to regional and climatic demands, as well as the absorption of foreign influence, has led to a fascinating variety of tastes from all over China. In Singapore you

don't just say you'll eat Chinese; you say you'll eat Sichuan (for Szechuan), Cantonese, Teochew, or any of a dozen distinct types of food from China's various regions. You can sample anything from light Cantonese dishes to crispy Peking duck (from Beijing), and piquant hot and sour soup (Sichuan).

An ancient Chinese proverb advises living in Suzhou (noted for its refined manners and beautiful women), dying in Liuzhou (where teakwood coffins are made), but eating in Guangzhou (Canton). As more Cantonese than any other Chinese from other regions settled in the West, their cuisine is perhaps the best known of all, with its fresh ingredients and light sauces. Although the Cantonese form only a fraction of the Chinese population in Singapore, they are still the most prolific restaurateurs here. The oldest Cantonese restaurant in Singapore, Spring Court, was established in 1929 by an immigrant from China. Today the stalwart is still being managed by the same family.

LEFT: a typical Chinese restaurant in Geylang, with outdoor seating. TOP: food courts are a feature of Singapore. ABOVE: street vendor. ABOVE RIGHT: tofu dishes feature in Singaporean-Chinese cuisine .

Cantonese dishes are simply flavoured, and cooked using a variety of methods: steaming, stir-frying, roasting, poaching and deep-frying. A perennial Cantonese favourite is *dim sum* (meaning "to touch the heart"), small steamed or fried buns, pastries and dumplings served in bamboo baskets. These little delicacies are usually stuffed with a variety of meat, prawns, minced vegetables and herbs, and are available at most restaurants during lunchtime.

Less common but equally good is Hakka food, simple and hearty fare that often features beancurd as one of the main ingredients. The guest people, as the Hakkas were known when they came from the western border of Canton, use their ingenuity to make the most of every scrap of food. Home-made wine is used to make heady soups such as beefball soup, while *yong tau foo*, beancurd stuffed with minced fish and vegetables and served with a dark sweet sauce, is another speciality.

Seafood with well-flavoured sauces is typical of Hokkien cuisine. But perhaps most popular of all is *Hokkien mee*, thick egg noodles sauteed with pork, squid, prawns and vegetables in a rich sauce, usually served with half a fresh lime and a dollop of chilli paste. Also worth trying

are *poh piah*, paper-thin crepes filled with shredded turnip, prawns, sausage and eggs seasoned with garlic, chilli paste and sweet bean sauce.

Then there is Hainanese food: the most famous dish of all is Hainanese chicken rice, a combination of boiled or roasted chicken, splashed with a touch of sesame oil and soy sauce, and served with rice cooked in chicken stock and a side dish of spicy chilli-garlic sauce. Early Hainanese immigrants who first came to Singapore worked as cooks and waiters for rich families. They eventually created a range of unique dishes such as the chicken rice that we know so well today alongside pork chop and other Western-style dishes,

Vegetarians need not despair: tofu (soya beancurd), widely used in Chinese cuisine, makes a protein-packed meal for non-meat-eaters, and there are endless ways of preparing and flavouring it. Chinese vegetarian restaurants also use wheat gluten to create dishes that resemble meat and poultry.

Seafood

Surrounded by tropical waters, Singapore is assured of a plentiful supply of fresh fish and seafood. Succulent prawns, crayfish, lobster, crab, pomfret, *ikan merah* (red snapper) and *tenggiri* (mackerel) are featured in many local dishes. Next to Peranakan food, seafood-based cuisine is perhaps the closest there is to a home-grown culinary art. Asian spices combined with Chinese cooking methods make for concoctions like chilli or pepper crab, steamed prawns and crispy fried *sotong* (baby squid).

Singaporeans adore seafood and will happily make the pilgrimage to the East Coast to find the best seafood restaurants (although there are smaller numbers scattered in other parts of Singapore as well).

DINING ENCLAVES

Throughout the city, the number of areas with a concentration of restaurants make it fun – or frustrating – when making a choice. Among these are ION Orchard, 313@ Somerset and Ngee Ann City along Orchard Road (all malls packed with eating outlets); Clarke Quay, Robertson Quay and Riverside Point with rows of restaurants (all three are strung along the Singapore River); Tanjong Pagar Road and Club Street (restaurants in old shophouses); One Fullerton and Marina Bay Sands; Tanglin Village at Dempsey (a cluster of restaurants in an old military barracks); popular Holland Village (casual eateries) and East Coast Parkway (great seafood restaurants).

For chilli crab, sometimes said to be Singapore's national dish, crabs are stir-fried in their shells with a thick sauce of garlic, sugar, soy sauce, tomato sauce, eggs and, of course, lots of chilli. The result is a pile of bright-red crustaceans to be tucked into, an utterly delicious experience made even better when crusty French bread or deep-fried Chinese buns are used to mop up the sauce. Black pepper crabs, coated in a tongue-tingling sauce, are, some say, even better.

Malay cuisine

Malay food in Singapore is an amalgam of traditional dishes from peninsular Malaysia, with strong influences from the Indonesian islands of Sumatra and Java. Rice is the staple that counterbalances the spiciness of the food. Coconut is also important, with the flesh grated and squeezed for the rich milk used in countless gravies, as well as cakes, desserts and drinks. Malay dishes are flavoured with a startling array of spices and herbs: lemongrass, shallots, galangal, tamarind, turmeric, cumin, ginger and garlic. Another vital ingredient is *belacan*, a pungent dried shrimp paste often combined with pounded fresh chillies to make *sambal belacan*.

Nasi lemak is a popular dish traditionally wrapped in a banana leaf and eaten at all times of the day. *Nasi padang*, originally from the Padang area of West Sumatra, combines a variety of spicy meat, chicken and vegetable dishes served with rice and placed in the centre of the table. A typical meal would include beef *rendang*, a thick and spicy curry made from coconut milk, spices and herbs, served with a fragrant rice dish, *nasi minyak*, to which cardamom and cinnamon have been added, a vegetable curry called *sayur lodeh* (mixed vegetables in coconut) and *sambal goreng* (an aromatic dish of tofu), *tempeh*, a preserved soya bean cake, and long beans.

One of Singapore's all-time Malay favourites is *satay*. These are small bamboo skewers of marinated beef, mutton or chicken which are grilled over coals and served with sliced onion, cucumber, *ketupat* (compressed rice cakes) and peanut sauce. Not to be outdone, the Chinese have come up with their own version, made with either pork (which is taboo for Malays) or chicken, and served with a sweeter version of the traditional peanut sauce.

Indian cuisine

Indian food, characterised by its complex use of spices to make its staple curries, is not always spicy. Northern Indian cuisine is more aromatic than spicy, its rich flavour resulting from a complex use of spices tempered by yoghurt. Food

LEFT: curry, rice and vegatable dishes at a food festival. **ABOVE:** *nasi lemak* is considered the national dish of Malaysia. **RIGHT:** *laksa*, a spicy noodle soup, comes in many different varieties.

SPICY FISH-HEAD CURRY

Another leading contender for the national dish is fish-head curry, which comes in spicy Indian, Malay and Peranakan variations. Despite the somewhat unappealing sight of a giant fish head floating in a thick sea of gravy, the succulent flesh and the accompanying hot and sour gravy flavoured with curry powder and tamarind juice is a delicious and satisfying taste sensation. The dish is accompanied by vegetables like brinjal and okra.

Fans of the dish wax lyrical about the eyeballs and the cheeks of the fish head; true blue aficionados even resort to tossing a coin to see who gets to eat the choice parts. Most people, thankfully, are happy just slurping the gravy.

cooked in a *tandoor* or clay oven is one of the highlights of northern Indian cuisine. It is used for baking leavened *roti* (bread) or naan, and to produce delicious marinated fish or chicken dishes, using either whole (tandoori) or small pieces (tikka) of meat. The bread is perfect for sopping up the yoghurt-based gravies, an influence of the nomadic tribes and their hill-grazing cattle.

In the south of India, fiery curries are a speciality and coconut milk is often used in the gravy instead of yoghurt. Southern food is also distinctive for its use of mustard seeds and fragrant mint, curry and coriander leaves. *Korma* dishes are generally mild, although anything prefixed by the word *masala* is likely to be hot and will be reddish in colour. The so-called "banana leaf" restaurants of Serangoon Road are well known for their spicy fare served on banana leaves. Ice-cold beer or lime juice is the perfect accompaniment to douse the fire.

Indian Muslim food is very popular in Singapore. One speciality is *roti prata*, fluffy griddle-fried bread served with curry sauce. These days besides plain *prata*, you can have it with egg, cheese and even chocolate. Another favourite is *murtabak*, the same fluffy bread stuffed with heaps of onions and minced mutton or chicken. The oldest Indian Muslim restaurant, Singapore Zam Zam, has been serving *murtabak* to its fans since 1908. Another popular dish is *nasi briyani*, a fragrant rice dish redolent of saffron and cooked with seasoned mutton or chicken.

There are also a variety of vegetarian dishes, savoury snacks, lentils and breads, as well as cloyingly sweet milk-based desserts. Vegetarian meals are often served on a banana leaf, or on a *thali*, a large tray holding a mound of rice, on which smaller bowls or *katori* are placed, filled with the accompanying dishes.

Eurasian food

Eurasian cuisine – which hails from Singapore's minority community of Portuguese, Dutch, Malay, Javanese and Indian ancestry – is typically multicultural. Malay herbs spice up pork, further enhanced by Indian mustard seeds and chillies. Typical is devil curry, a fire-and-brimstone name for a spicy dish of chicken pepped up with vinegar, mustard and chillies. Similarly, English dishes such as stews and roasts are transformed with the addition of soy sauce, green chillies or sour tamarind juice. The Eurasian family's Christmas table is always laden with these dishes, including a traditional item called *feng* – a type of curry made of pork and offal.

International cuisines

If local fare doesn't grab you, take your pick from any number of French, Italian, Spanish and Mediterranean, or Thai, Japanese and Korean restaurants. Many foreign chefs have made Singapore their home, and set up ven-erable restaurant groups around the island. Whether it's a plate of hearty risotto, pan-fried foie gras or tapas you fancy, or perhaps the most pristine sushi and sashimi, it's easy to find a satisfying meal here.

Latest trends

The trend in Singapore's high-end restaurants these days is for highly innovative modern European cuisine using the freshest seasonal ingredients and fine techniques such as "sous-vide" (cooking under vacuum). Although there is no Michelin Guide in Singapore, the city has attracted many Michelin-starred chefs. Boosting Singapore's reputation as an energetic gastronomic city are top-notch restaurants by celebrity chefs from Tokyo, Paris and New York. High-profile names such as Joel Robuchon, Santi Santamaria, Tetsuya, Daniel Boulud and Guy Savoy have all set up their outposts in Singapore thanks to the opening of the two "integrated resorts", Marina Bay Sands and Resorts World Sentosa, in 2010. The island has embraced these culinary heavyweights with open arms and is expecting more to come.

• *Individual restaurant recommendations are listed at the end of each chapter in the Places section.* ❑

LEFT: Indian cuisine. TOP: Japanese chef Tetsuya.
ABOVE: Lebanese restaurant in Holland Village.
ABOVE RIGHT: Daniel Boulud burger – a premium quality interpretation of the fast-food staple.

SINGAPORE-STYLE HAWKER FOOD

A visit to the city-state is incomplete without a meal at one of its food centres, where an astonishing variety of dishes are cooked on the spot

The hawker centre offers multi-ethnic Singapore cooking at its best. Whether it's a simple dish of noodles for S$3 or a S$20 three-course meal of barbecued fish, chilli prawns and fried vegetables with rice, the cost is a fraction of what you would pay for a similar meal in a restaurant. Prices apart, the experience is unique, and a pleasant reminder of your stay in this food-crazy city. When celebrity chef Anthony Bourdain visited Singapore, he proclaimed, "I love the hawker centres. The whole style of casual eating here is sensational."

For the uninitiated, here's how you order a meal at a hawker centre. If there's a group of you, have one person sit at a table to *chope* (meaning reserve in local parlance) seats for the rest of the party. Don't be surprised if you see seats with bags or packets of tissue paper on them; it's a sign that they have been taken. The others, having noted the table number, should order their food and tell the stall owner the table number they are seated at, unless of course it's a self-service operation. If you're on your own, you can share a table with strangers. As you savour your meal, you will realise why true-blue local gourmets will head for their favourite food stall at every opportunity.

ABOVE: plate-sized and bright-red crabs smothered in a piquant chilli and tomato sauce is a typical Singapore dish that you'll find at hawker stalls that specialise in seafood. The dish isn't as robustly spicy as it looks, but if you're not feeling particularly adventurous, order black pepper crabs instead, which are just as delicious.

CHANGING TIMES FOR THE HAWKERS

In the old days, there was no such thing as a hawker centre. Instead, the roving hawker was a familiar fixture in the neighbourhood. The sound of an ice-cream bell, or the clacking of a bamboo stick against a wooden block, or the chant of the *mua chee* man selling sticky nougat-like candy, would send children – and their parents – scrambling from their homes into the streets to buy their favourite snack. The fare on offer was amazing, from bread and bowls of steaming noodle soups to peanuts and *poh piah* (spring rolls).

Then came the roadside hawkers, who set up their makeshift stalls on the streets after dark, when parking lots were emptied of cars and replaced by wooden tables and stools, and push-carts which doubled as mobile kitchens. By 1987, with urbanisation and an obsession with cleanliness, the last of the roadside hawkers were cleared. The only places where you can find roadside hawkers today are Chinatown's Smith Street and Glutton's Bay at The Esplanade. These sanitised recreations of yesteryear do their best to resemble the city's once bustling and colourful street life.

ABOVE: satay vendor at Lau Pa Sat Festival Market in the Central Business District.

LEFT: a food centre at Geylang sells a large range of dishes. Most establishments include photographs of each dish for ease of identification.

BELOW: *cha kuay teow* is made from wok-fried flat rice noodles (*kway teow*) and yellow noodles *(mee)* with garlic and bean sprouts and various other ingredients including fish cakes or fresh shrimps.

RIGHT: *mee rebus*, literally "boiled noodles". Wheat noodles are dunked in a spicy-sweet brown gravy and topped with chopped tofu, spring onions, green chillies, a hard-boiled egg and dark soya sauce.

SHOPPING

It's not for nothing that Singapore is renowned the world over as a shopping haven. The range is stupendous, with malls so huge one could lose oneself for days within their labyrinthine corridors. If retail therapy is your idea of heaven, you'll find bliss in Singapore

The notion seems implausible, even laughable – that shopping, along with eating, are serious pastimes for many Singaporeans. People in Singapore shop all the time – during lunchtime, after work and at weekends. Call it retail therapy or a necessary evil, the buying culture is so firmly embedded that Singaporeans are easily spotted – by like-minded Singaporeans when they shop outside the country.

The result? Every neighbourhood on the island has at least one mall, never mind that they all offer similar things. The guiding principle appears to be, if there's an empty plot of land, let's build a shopping centre. If a historical

building is falling apart, let's give it a lick of paint, and put in some shops and restaurants (as opposed to, say, a museum).

Is there such a thing as too much of a good thing? Not if you look at shopping mecca Orchard Road *(see page 147)*. It is *the* place for all things hot, trendy and newly minted. With over 30 malls stretching along a tree-fringed road, it's truly a testimony of the country's number one passion.

Service levels have improved over the years, especially at department stores. The staff are very helpful, and most salespeople will oblige and make an effort to follow up requests.

Astounding diversity

The joy of shopping in Singapore lies in its diversity. From swanky air-conditioned malls to steamy bazaars, sleepy ethnic neighbourhoods to buzzing department stores, it's up to you to decide how to vary your shopping experiences. Singapore is also a city of duty-free luxury goods, of cutting-edge technology and high fashion, as well as a centre for traditional Asian exotica such as tea, silk, porcelain, traditional medicine and spices.

Despite keen competition from up-and-coming shopping destinations in the region, shopping in Singapore is a pleasure. It's easy to buy because English is the lingua franca. With the efficient transportation network, zipping around with your shopping bags in tow is a breeze. Some malls are so well connected by pathways and underground tunnels, you can easily walk from one to another without getting wet on a rainy day, or seeing the light of day.

An even greater delight is how hassle-free it is. Touting is virtually absent along the main shopping districts – and most stores accept major credit cards. ATMs are plentiful, and stores are open from about 10am–9pm daily. It's highly likely you could shop 'til you drop.

The best times to shop

The Great Singapore Sale, from late May to early July, has become a much anticipated annual shopping bonanza for both locals and visitors. The generous discounts – sometimes up to 70 percent – see even the most tight-fisted parting with some cash. If there's one time to max out on your credit card, it would be during this retail blowout.

Fashionistas should consider another important event on the local fashion calendar. The star-studded Singapore Fashion Festival, an annual event in April, aims to position the city as the region's fashion capital. Young and talented Asian designers share the limelight with international fashion powerhouses and cutting-edge couture designers from the world's most renowned fashion capitals. Expect chichi

fashion runway shows, fashion-related exhibitions and glamorous parties.

The mall, the merrier

Tip for shopping in Singapore: temptations are everywhere – everything and anything money can buy and you can possibly want – lustrous pearls, age-old *huanghuali* (golden rosewood) desks, vintage handbags and the latest digicams – are found along the prime shopping districts of Orchard Road and Marina Bay.

TOYS FOR BOYS

It's no secret that Singapore is one of the world's best places to shop for gadgets and all things electronic. You name it, PDAs, computer hardware and software, the latest cameras and MP3 players, you'll find them at specialty malls such as Funan DigitaLife Mall and Sim Lim Square. Electronic stores like Harvey Norman and Best Denki have outlets all over town and merchandise is very competitively priced. Be sure to ask for an international guarantee, though.

LEFT: VivoCity. **ABOVE:** shoppers at Bugis Junction.

On the surface, Orchard Road looks like a relentless stretch of gleaming five-star hotels and shiny malls. For shopaholics in the know, however, every shopping centre is a shrine replete with inimitable finds. Tangs, at the corner of Scotts Road and Orchard Road, for example, has an illustrious history dating back to the 1930s. Despite a traditional architecture that's modelled after the Imperial Palace in Beijing's Forbidden City, its Beauty Hall is *the* place for cult cosmetic and skincare labels; the Home department in the basement is crammed full of extraordinary gadgets for modern homes.

Just down the street, the brand new ION Orchard and formidable Ngee Ann City are places with a good balance of luxury brands, high-end retailers and mid-priced stores. These two malls have a mind-boggling number of eateries too, perfect for a pit-stop in between shopping. Further down is the new 313@Somerset mall, which is conveniently built just above Somerset MRT station.

Over at the simply colossal 93,000-sq-metre

BUY BUY SINGAPORE

Singapore's multicultural heritage has given birth to uniquely local gifts. Here are a few worth carting home.
• **RISIS**, known for its orchid accessories plated in 24ct gold, also has other nature-inspired jewellery (01-084 Suntec City Mall, tel: 6338-8250; www.risis.com.sg).
• Purple gold jewellery by **Lee Hwa** is a unique amalgam of yellow gold and aluminium (01-37/40 Wisma Atria, tel: 6736-0266; www.leehwa.com.sg).
• The ground floor of **MICA Building** is the best one-stop shop for works by local and Asian artists. There are several galleries here, but of note is Art-2 (01-03 MICA Building, 140 Hill Street, tel: 6338-8713; www.art2.com.sg).

• **Boon's Pottery** has vases, teapots and crockery – all crafted by local potters (01-30 Tanglin Mall, tel: 6836-3978; www.boonspottery.com).
• **Museum Shop** at Asian Civilisations Museum, Empress Place, stocks repros of treasures and trinkets (1 Empress Place Road, tel: 6336-9050; www.museumshop.com.sg).
• Fresh, handmade pralines, including durian and mango varieties, are found at **SINS Choc Shoppe** (Level 1 Atrium Centrepoint, tel: 6734-3469; www.sinschocs.com).
• Take home ready-to-cook versions of spicy *laksa* or *satay* by **Prima Taste** (www.primataste.com.sg), available at Cold Storage or NTUC supermarkets.

(1 million-sq-ft) Suntec City Mall, just a five-minute drive away in the Marina Bay area, you will go wild over the choice of merchandise in the 300 or so shops. The mall was once the largest of all malls in Singapore, only to be supplanted by 102,000-sq-metre (1.1 million-sq-ft) VivoCity, located further afield in the Har-bourFront area near Sentosa. It has a cineplex, a hypermart and hundreds of shops and restaurants, some of which overlook Sentosa Island.

What's also worth your time are the shopping carts parked at the ground floor of Raffles City Shopping Centre and Parco Bugis Junction. Young entrepreneurs often peddle one-of-a-kind wares sourced from all over the world.

There are also shopping malls with attitude for the younger crowd, such as The Heeren on Orchard Road and Level One at Far East Plaza at Scotts Road. The manufactured grittiness comes complete with thumping techno pop. Their edginess may seem a bit manufactured – this is after all squeaky-clean Singapore – but many young, bold and very talented Singapo-

rean designers have their fashion boutiques there. Definitely worth a peruse if you're planning to bring home more than Chanel and Prada.

Uniquely Singapore

Local fashion designers, being at a cultural crossroads, are inspired by Eastern and Western influences. Whether it's a modern cut on a cheongsam or a subtle addition of beads to an elegant evening dress, their designs show off cosmopolitan Singapore.

ORCHARD ROAD

This is by far the most famous shopping precinct, an endless stretch of smart boutiques, malls and department stores. New glitzy malls have been launched since 2009, including Orchard Central, 313 Somerset, Mandarin Gallery and ION Orchard, while the older malls, like Paragon, The Heeren and Centrepoint, are constantly reinventing themselves to keep up with the new kids on the block. The shopping on Orchard Road tends to be more upmarket, so don't expect bargains. Christmas in the Tropics is a highlight every year, when the entire stretch from Tanglin to Dhoby Ghaut and beyond sparkles with lights and at times over-the-top decorations.

FAR LEFT: shoppers at ION on Orchard Road.
TOP LEFT: sales at Ngee Ann City Square. **LEFT:** shopping at the Resorts World Sentosa. **ABOVE:** antiques for sale at Asia Ancient.

The best places to seek out home-grown, edgy fashions are at The Heeren (Fourskin and Punkstar), Far East Plaza (WoodWood), Haji Lane off Arab Street (Know It Nothing and White Room) and Stamford House (Hansel). Plenty of designed-in-Singapore, ready-to-wear clothes can be found at independent boutiques

The Chinatown Night Market has more than 200 street stalls hawking all manner of goods, from contemporary jewellery to more traditional Chinese goods like calligraphy, lanterns and masks.

such as M)Phosis (Ngee Ann City) and GG<5 (ION Orchard).

For a slice of everyday Singapore life, hop onto the train and head to the heartlands. There is always a mall to lose yourself in – if you haven't had enough in the city. Tampines Mall (Tampines MRT) and Junction 8 (Bishan MRT) will give you a good idea of what people in the suburbs buy. Fendi and Gucci may not be represented there, but prices tend to be lower and bargaining is acceptable at some shops. If you're

lucky, you may chance upon a *pasar malam*, a makeshift nightmarket selling all manner of food and goods at empty spaces near MRT stations. Those looking for Asian arts can head over to Holland Village, just outside the centre of town. Holland Shopping Centre is home to **Lim's Arts & Living** at 02-01 (tel: 6467-1300), a real oriental treasure trove spread over three floors. Across the road at **Chip Bee Gardens** are a collection of galleries selling Asian art.

If it's colour and atmosphere you're after, the city's ethnic pockets – Chinatown, Little India and Kampung Glam – are flush with quirky finds. Hit Chinatown for Chinese silk, exotic herbal cures and antique furniture; Kampung Glam for handmade perfume bottles, basket ware and fabrics; and Little India for henna tattoos, incense and Bollywood VCDs.

Oddly, though Singaporeans fervently embrace the concept of market shopping outside Singapore, the culture has not caught on here. Unlike Bangkok's Chatuchak or Sydney's Paddington, such markets in Singapore are dismal and sometimes contrived affairs. If, however, you are looking for a little adventure, flea markets make interesting detours.

Sungei Road's Thieves' Market is the oldest. Broken radios, chipped crockery and used

clothing spread haphazardly on the floor are hardly the sort of things you would want to buy, but the market is an insight into the city's underbelly. The market at Tanglin Mall, held on the first and third Saturday of the month, is especially good for second-hand clothing. The Market of Artists and Designers (MAAD) is a unique showcase for emerging local designers' handmade, one-of-a-kind accessories, paintings and artwork. It's held at Red Dot Museum (28 Maxwell Road; www.maad.sg) the first weekend of every month. The weekend afternoon bazaar outside Chinatown Complex hawks a stash of treasures – like antique bronze ware, Chairman Mao memorabilia and handmade beaded handbags – mementos from a fast-disappearing side of Singapore. Clarke Quay's Mille Fleur night bazaar, which takes place roughly every three months on a Friday and Saturday night from 6pm to midnight, features about 30 vendors selling handmade jewellery, accessories and clothing for men and women.

Besides flea markets, souvenirs and knick-knacks can be found at Chinatown Night Market (Trengganu, Pagoda and Sago streets) in the evening. In the day, Chinatown Complex on Smith Street is a hive of activity, particularly the "wet market" in the basement, where all kinds of fresh ingredients are sold. Another place to find the freshest produce is at the popular Little India's Tekka Market. In the same district too is Campbell Lane, where you can find vegetables, spices, jasmine garlands and fragrant incense.

• See also Orchard Road (pages 147–54) for more information on shopping.   ❑

ARAB STREET

In Arab Street, off Beach Road, and its adjoining streets, a strong Muslim atmosphere lingers from the early years of Singapore when Malays, Bugis and Javanese settled here. You will see men making their way to the Sultan Mosque at prayer time, or smoking apple-scented sheesha pipes in doorways. Prayer mats, holy beads and lace skullcaps for those who have made the pilgrimage to Mecca are all sold in the old shophouses that line the streets. This area is also the place for cheap batik and textiles, including everything a tailor needs: lace, sequins, beads, buttons and bows. Other good buys are baskets, leather bags, purses and shoes.

LEFT: clothes at Bugis Junction. TOP: bangles in Little India. ABOVE: silk in Chinatown.
ABOVE RIGHT: saris in Kampung Glam.

PLACES

A detailed guide to Singapore and its surroundings, with the principal sites numbered and clearly cross-referenced to maps

Singaporeans used to joke that if they left the city-state for more than three months, they wouldn't be able to recognise many familiar places on their return, so relentless was the pace of urbanisation. Although true to a certain extent, this has changed thanks to conservation efforts. If a building is of architectural or historical significance, the tendency is to restore it rather than replace it with a new-fangled one.

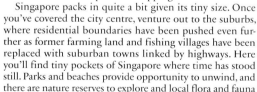

The results are apparent everywhere – in Chinatown, the Civic District, Kampung Glam, Little India and the old residential neighbourhoods. The gentrification of these places, apart from giving the city added charm, has also helped develop among Singaporeans a sense of their own history and a link with the past of their forefathers. This is appropriate, for Singapore remains largely carved up according to Stamford Raffles's plans for the layout which he implemented in June 1819.

The colonial hub of the city, today's Civic District, is still the heart of administration, as it was in Raffles's time. The clamour of Chinatown and the hum of business in the Central Business District around Raffles Place have not diminished. The Muslim area of Kampung Glam, and the predominantly Hindu Little India, retain their ethnic feel. Chic Orchard Road is one of Asia's premier shopping areas.

Singapore packs in quite a bit given its tiny size. Once you've covered the city centre, venture out to the suburbs, where residential boundaries have been pushed even further as former farming land and fishing villages have been replaced with suburban towns linked by highways. Here you'll find tiny pockets of Singapore where time has stood still. Parks and beaches provide opportunity to unwind, and there are nature reserves to explore and local flora and fauna to discover. In the south of Singapore (besides Sentosa), there are a number of small islands such as Kusu, Lazarus and Hantu, with tranquil beaches and clear waters. The average visitor, say the statistics, spends four days in Singapore. This book is filled with ideas on how to extend your stay to a week or more – and still be sufficiently enthralled at the end of it. ❑

PRECEDING PAGES: night-time view from the top of Raffles Place; Lian Shan Shuang Lin Temple; crowd enjoying the light display at the Night Festival, National Museum.
LEFT: Chinatown rooftops. **ABOVE LEFT:** National Arts Gallery. **ABOVE RIGHT:** Little India.

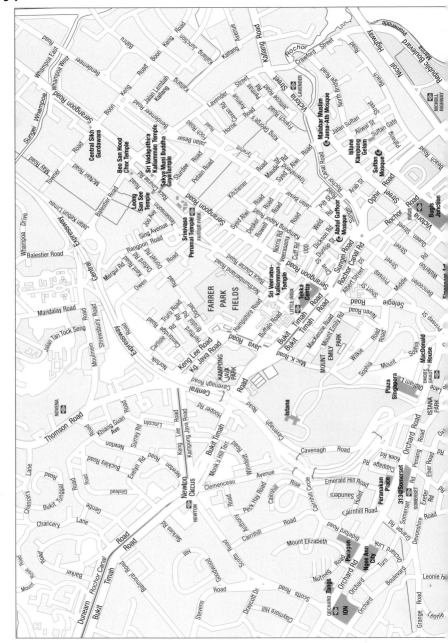

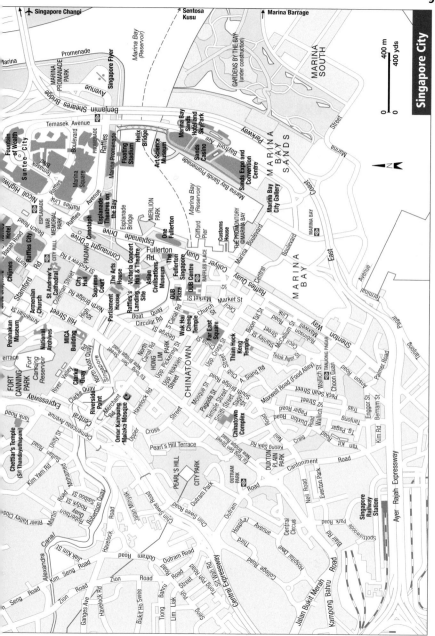

THE CIVIC DISTRICT

From the site where Raffles first landed in 1819, you can explore the heart of Singapore, speckled with stately colonial buildings and majestic churches, and a mix of lively quays, theatres and museums

Nearly two centuries after Stamford Raffles first set foot in Singapore, the island is still governed from the colonial nucleus he established on the east bank of the Singapore River. A walk in this **Civic District** – the heart of colonial Singapore – is essentially a stroll down memory lane, featuring sights and monuments that reflect the city-state's rich historical past.

Raffles's Landing Site

It's appropriate to start this walk from where it all began – at **Raffles's Landing Site ❶** on the left bank of the **Singapore River**, the commercial lifeline of Singapore for more than a century. It was here, on the very spot where a replica white marble statue of Sir Thomas Stamford Raffles stands, that the founder of modern Singapore stepped ashore on 28 January 1819. The view of the skyline on the opposite side of the river from the landing site is stunning: an arc of beautifully restored shophouses above the steps of **Boat Quay** set against the dramatic backdrop of soaring towers in **Raffles Place** *(see page 136)* – a wonderful contrast of the old and the new.

LEFT: City Hall. **RIGHT:** Raffles's Landing Site, where the founder of modern Singapore stepped ashore in January 1819.

The Arts House

Just behind is **The Arts House ❷**, a performing arts centre that took over the premises of the Old Parliament House, Singapore's oldest state building (box office tel: 6332-6919; www.theartshouse.com.sg). Refurbished but still retaining its original spaces, it features a 200-seat chamber for music and drama performances – previously used by members of parliament for debate – a visual arts gallery and a 75-seat art-house cinema.

ABOVE: the Asian
Civilisations Museum.

Built in 1827 as the home of a British merchant, the building was the work of George Coleman, the architect responsible for shaping much of colonial Singapore. It was turned into a courthouse and later became the parliament house for the incumbent government. Keep an eye out for the bronze elephant statue in the courtyard, a gift from Thailand's King Chulalongkorn in 1871.

The new **Parliament House**, just next door, was completed in 1999 – five times larger but still retaining the colonial architectural style. Porcelain dating back to the Ming and Yuan dynasties was found on the site during construction and is now displayed in the new complex. Parliament proceedings are open to the public; guided tours by appointment only.

Asian Civilisations Museum

Address: 1 Empress Place,
www.acm.org.sg
Tel: 6332-2982
Opening Hrs: Mon 1–7pm, Tue–Sun 9am–7pm, Fri 9am–9pm
Entrance Fee: charge
Transport: Raffles Place MRT

Adjacent to The Arts House is the **Asian Civilisations Museum ❸**.

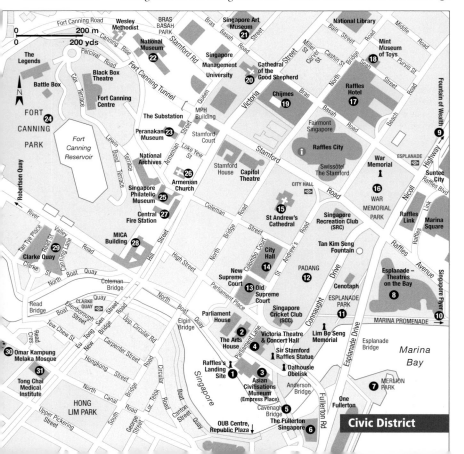

Civic District

Housed in the neoclassical **Empress Place Building**, this is one of the oldest structures in Singapore. Built by Indian convicts between 1864–7 and designed by J.F.A. McNair, it was first unveiled as a courthouse for the colonial government and later housed Singapore's legislative assembly. By the early 1980s, the building had seen better days, and there was talk of demolition. Fortunately, the Singapore Tourism Board came to the rescue and spent millions renovating it. It engaged the services of a French Gothic and neoclasssical conservationist, Didier Repellin, who helped restore the building to its original splendour. In 1989, it reopened as a museum showcasing Chinese artefacts, but it closed after a few years.

More restoration work followed, and in March 2003 it became home to the Asian Civilisations Museum. At 14,000 sq metres (151,000 sq ft), this outstanding museum *(see also pages 120–1)* provides generous space to display its sizeable collections on the civilisations of East, Southeast, South and West Asia.

With 11 galleries spread over three levels, each of the four regions has its own thematic storyline and permanent displays integrated with interactive kiosks and discovery corners, along with a centre specially dedicated to younger visitors.

Victoria Theatre and Concert Hall

Facing the side of the Asian Civilisations Museum are two distinctive and venerable structures well known to local drama fans and concert-lovers: the **Victoria Theatre and Concert Hall** ❹ (originally known as Victoria Memorial Hall). Both were built in the 1880s to commemorate Queen Victoria's Diamond Jubilee. The Victoria Theatre was originally built as Singapore's town hall in 1862 before being converted into a theatre in 1905. It features a distinctive clock tower with a Westminster chime that has never stopped pealing on the hour since its installation in 1906.

The concert hall stages opera, ballet and classical music, while the

ABOVE: the new Parliament House.

The bronze statue of Stamford Raffles outside the Victoria Theatre and Concert Hall was crafted by Thomas Woolner and first unveiled in 1887, before being moved to its present site in 1919.

ABOVE: the Fullerton hotel once housed the city's General Post Office.
ABOVE RIGHT: the Merlion. **BELOW:** locals refer to the Esplanade – Theatres on the Bay as the Durian. The spiky facades of the twin domes of the theatre and concert hall resemble the thorny exterior of the tropical fruit.

theatre is a principal performance venue for dance and plays.

Just opposite is the **Dalhousie Obelisk**, a memorial dedicated to Marquis Dalhousie, India's governor-general from 1848–56, who visited Singapore in 1850.

Cavenagh/Anderson bridges

A walk from the Asian Civilisations Museum, along the riverside, leads to **Cavenagh Bridge ❺** and **Anderson Bridge**. The latter was built in 1910 when the Cavenagh, constructed in Scotland and assembled here by Indian convict labour in 1868, could not cope with increasing traffic. During the Japanese Occupation, Anderson Bridge served a macabre purpose: severed heads of criminals were hung from it.

Cross Cavenagh Bridge, and on the left are whimsical bronze statues of five boys leaping into the river. Tucked away on the right of the bridge are tiny bronze sculptures of *Kucinta* cats, indigenous to this part of the world (*see text box opposite*).

The Fullerton Singapore

The grand Palladian-style building across Cavenagh Bridge is Singapore's former General Post Office, restored to its current reincarnation as a five-star hotel, **The Fullerton Singapore ❻**. Originally built in 1928 and named after Sir Robert Fullerton, the first governor of the Straits Settlements, the building, distinguished by tall Doric columns, is a wonderful example of the neoclassical style that once dominated the district. Artfully renovated for an astounding S$400 million and reopened in 2001, the hotel is deceptively contemporary within its stately walls – best described as modern Art Deco. The historical landmark offers 400 broadband-ready rooms, excellent restaurants and the stylish **Post Bar**, which attracts a well-heeled crowd. Enter by the massive revolving main door and see the central atrium, created by punching out several floors and the old ceiling.

For a study in architectural contrast, take the underpass beneath The Fullerton to the glass-and-steel **One**

Riverside Sculptures

Start your art trail from Colombian sculptor Fernando Botero's lovably fat *Bird* outside UOB Plaza. Walking along the Singapore River towards The Fullerton hotel, local sculptor Aw Tee Hong's *The River Merchant* depicts Alexander Johnston, one of Singapore's early merchants. Just before Cavenagh Bridge, the lifelike bronze *Kucinta* cats on the left often attract real stray cats. Outside The Fullerton, the scene of five playful, naked boys leaping into the river is the work of Chong Fah Cheong. Across the bridge two sets of sculptures tell the story of Singapore's development from port to financial centre: *The Great Emporium* and *From Chettiars To Financiers*.

Fullerton, a dining hub by the waterfront. Swanky restaurants with floor-to-ceiling windows offer stunning views of **Marina Bay**. Just a stone's throw away is the newly refurbished Clifford Pier: this historic landmark was the first port of call for early immigrants. Thankfully the original architecture of the pier, with its high ceilings, has been maintained. Just a few steps away is the chic new Fullerton Bay Hotel with its rooftop bar, Lantern, affording gorgeous views of Marina Bay Sands.

Next to the hotel is the well-preserved Customs House, which now houses restaurants and bars. This entire area, including the Fullerton hotel, has been re-branded The Fullerton Heritage (http://thefullerton heritage.com) and is set to become one of the trendiest areas in town.

Merlion Park

At the northern end of One Fullerton is the **Merlion Park** ➐ anchored by the Merlion statue, the rather kitschy half-fish, half-lion creature that has been adopted as the city's tourism mascot. Visitors, however, seem to fall for it, judging by the crowds here at any time of the day.

The Merlion was inspired by the creature that Prince Sang Nila Utama *(see page 35)* saw when he arrived in Temasek in the 13th century. Believing it to be a *singa* (lion), he renamed Temasek *Singapura* (Lion City).

The Esplanade Theatres

Looming across the waters of Marina Bay is the prickly hedgehog-like outline of **Esplanade – Theatres on the Bay** ➑, a S$600-million performing arts centre with the equally grandiose aim of establishing itself as a cultural landmark and Asia's performing arts hub (tel: 6828-8377; www.esplanade. com). The massive complex, which seems a little hemmed in by its waterfront location, opened with much fanfare in October 2002. The 6-hectare (15-acre) complex houses a 1,600-seat concert hall that has one of the world's finest pipe organs, a 2,000-seat theatre, smaller recital and theatre studios, an outdoor amphitheatre, and sculpted gardens by the waterfront. The design of

TIP

Take a "bumboat" ride along the Singapore River. Departures are from the jetties at Raffles's Landing Site and Merlion Park. Tickets cost S$15 for the Singapore River Experience (Boat Quay, Clarke Quay and Marina Bay) and $20 for New River Experience, which includes Robertson Quay (daily 9.15am–10.30pm). Contact Singapore River Cruises, tel: 6336-6119, or check www.rivercruise. com.sg.

BELOW: bronze sculptures, titled *First Generation*, outside the Fullerton hotel.

this landmark icon – which people either love or hate – with its distinctive facade of sharp-edged metal sunshades, has been mired in controversy since the model was first unveiled in 1992. Michael Wilford, the British architect who designed the edifice, quit the project in 1995 over unexplained differences, leaving home-grown company DP Architects to complete the job.

Design controversies aside, the Esplanade has so far played host to top names like José Carerras, Dee Dee Bridgewater and the Lincoln Center Jazz Orchestra. The concert hall is especially lauded for the acoustics, designed by celebrated American sound scientist Russell Johnson. Avant-garde installation art is a regular feature at the concourse level. Its attempt to bring arts to the masses sees free performances on Friday and weekend evenings at the Outdoor Theatre by Marina Bay.

The adjoining **Esplanade Mall** houses an interesting array of shops and restaurants such as My Humble House. Walk along the Marina Bay Promenade just outside; this is one of the best spots to view the CBD skyline.

Suntec City

Rising behind the Esplanade Theatres is the outline of Marina Square and Suntec City – all built on reclaimed land. This area is virtually a self-contained city. **Marina Square** is a huge American-style mall linked to the trio of John Portman-designed hotels, the **Marina Mandarin**, **Mandarin Oriental** and the **Pan Pacific**, and the **Ritz-Carlton Millenia** designed by Kevin Roche.

Across Raffles Boulevard is a massive convention and shopping development called **Suntec City**, noted for its gigantic water-spewing **Fountain of Wealth ❾**, the world's largest of its kind. The purportedly auspicious bronze structure was inspired by the Hindu *mandala* but in fact looks more like an alien mothership about to take off. Interestingly, Suntec City's design was closely governed by the principles of Chinese geomancy or *feng shui (see pages 144–5)*.

Shopping options abound here – both at the massive **Suntec City**

ABOVE: the Cenotaph memorial at the Esplanade Park honours "Our Glorious Dead" – the soldiers who died in the two World Wars. **BELOW:** Suntec City Mall dining. **BELOW RIGHT:** the Fountain of Wealth.

Mall, Singapore's largest, as well as nearby **Millenia Walk**, where there are many stores to empty the most padded of wallets. Oscar's Café at the adjacent **Conrad Centennial** hotel or the myriad pubs and restaurants in this area are perfect for flopping out.

Singapore Flyer

Address: 30 Raffles Avenue, #01-07; www.singaporeflyer.com
Tel: 6734-8829
Opening Hrs: daily 8.30am–10.30pm (ticket sales 8am–10pm)
Entrance Fee: charge
Transport: Promenade MRT

Another of Singapore's attempts at superlatives, the **Singapore Flyer** ❿ opened in 2008 along the Marina Bay waterfront. At 165 metres (541ft), it is the world's highest observation wheel and offers stunning views of the city. On a good day, even parts of Malaysia and Indonesia's Riau Islands can be seen. The ride takes 30 minutes to complete. To lure in more visitors, this attraction also offers a dining experience dubbed "Full Butler Sky Dining", complete with in-house butler, fine wines and gourmet food prepared by various guest chefs. A revamp has been planned for the Flyer, and S$10million will be invested in a food hub, offering waterfront dining and a 1960s-themed food street.

Within walking distance of the observation wheel is a large area where all the Singapore Formula 1 night race action takes place in September each year. The grandstand, entertainment stage, pits and performance area are all located here.

Esplanade Park

Flanking Esplanade Theatres and the Esplanade Bridge is **Esplanade Park** ⓫ and the tree-lined **Queen Elizabeth Walk**, formerly a seafront promenade where colonial-day Europeans spent their leisure time strolling or playing cricket.

At the park's southern end is the **Lim Bo Seng Memorial**, with its four bronze lions. It is dedicated to a local hero and martyr, Lim Bo Seng (1909–44), a member of an underground resistance movement against the Japanese during World War II. Further along is the **Cenotaph**, built to remember the soldiers who died fighting in the World Wars.

At the park's northern end is **Tan Kim Seng Fountain**, built in gratitude for a donation "towards the cost of the Singapore Water Works" given in 1857 by the trader and public benefactor Tan Kim Seng (1805–64). His £13,000 donation to the waterworks was a princely sum in those days.

The Padang

Adjacent to the Esplanade Park across Connaught Drive is an expanse of green called the **Padang** ⓬ ("field" in Malay), the occasional venue of Singapore's National Day celebrations on 9 August. Known as the Esplanade in colonial times, this is where the British took a turn in the cool of the evening in their

ABOVE: the Singapore Flyer.

TIP

The DUCKtour is a great way to see Singapore. The amphibious craft drives past key landmarks in the Civic District before splashing into Kallang River for a scenic ride around Singapore River. Tel: 6333-3825, or check www.ducktours.com.sg.

horse-drawn carriages, exchanging the latest gossip at the so-called Scandal Point. After the Japanese captured Singapore in 1942, European civilians were rounded up on the Padang and marched to Changi Prison. The Padang is flanked by two of the city's oldest leisure clubs – the **Singapore Recreation Club** (1883), now rebuilt on its original site, and the **Singapore Cricket Club** (1852), also the venue for cricket and rugby matches.

Old Supreme Court/ City Hall

Adjacent to the Cricket Club, across St Andrews Road, is the **Old Supreme Court ⓭**. Dating back to 1927, this regal-looking structure has stout Corinthian columns and a green dome. Behind is the **New Supreme Court**, a Norman Foster-designed glass-and-steel structure capped by a dramatic circular disc. There is an observation deck on the eighth floor and a gallery on the ground level (tel: 6226-0644; both daily 8.30am–6pm) that traces Singapore's legal history.

Next to the Supreme Court and facing the Padang is **City Hall ⓮**,

once Singapore's most important government building. Completed in 1929, with a facade of Greek columns and a grand staircase, it was on these steps that Lord Louis Mountbatten accepted the surrender of Singapore by the Japanese General Itagaki in September 1945. Singapore's former prime minister Lee Kuan Yew declared the island's independence from Britain on the same spot 14 years later. Both the Old Supreme Court and the City Hall are now being converted into Singapore's National Art Gallery, which will open in 2014.

St Andrew's Cathedral

Across Coleman Street amid an expanse of greenery rises the spire of **St Andrew's Cathedral ⓯** (tel: 6337-6104; www.livingstreams.org.sg/sac; daily 7am–7.30pm). The church, a gazetted monument, owes its smooth white surface to the plaster used by the Indian convict labourers. Called Madras *chunam*, it was made of egg white, eggshell, lime, sugar, coconut husk and water, and gave the building a smooth, polished finish.

ABOVE: enjoy a Singapore Sling at the Long Bar. **BELOW:** National Day Parade at the Padang, with City Hall in background. **BELOW RIGHT:** St Andrew's Cathedral.

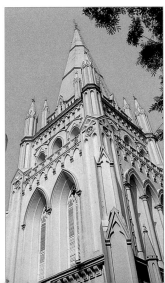

Interestingly, this is the second place of worship on the site. The original, designed in Palladian style by Coleman, was twice struck by lightning and demolished in 1852. The present cathedral, in the style of an early Gothic abbey and designed by Ronald MacPherson, was consecrated in 1862. The gleaming white exterior contrasts with the dark pews inside, with sunlight filtering through the stained-glass windows in the mornings. The cathedral served as an emergency hospital just before the fall of Singapore in 1942. The cathedral has a modern extension and a new sanctuary built below ground level, as well as an outdoor sunken courtyard/amphitheatre.

Capitol Theatre

Across the church, at the junction of North Bridge and Stamford roads lies the neoclassical **Capitol Theatre**. When it was completed in 1931, this popular icon was one of the first air-conditioned theatres in Singapore. Anti-Japanese locals bombed the building during World War II but it was rebuilt and turned into a cinema,

before it eventually closed in the late 1990s. The building now stands vacant, awaiting restoration.

Next door is the resplendent **Stamford House**, with history dating back to 1904. Designed by colonial architect R.A.J. Bidwell of Swan and Maclaren (who also designed Raffles Hotel and Goodwood Park Hotel), the elegant Venetian Renaissance-style structure now houses cafés and boutiques.

Raffles City

Towering over St Andrew's Cathedral is **Raffles City**, a silver monolith with shops, offices and hotels within as well as the busy City Hall MRT Interchange. The I.M. Pei-designed tower stands on the former site of Singapore's first school, Raffles Institution, built in 1823 and now relocated to the suburbs. The complex connects to both the 72-storey **Swissôtel The Stamford** hotel, with panoramic views from its **New Asia Bar** on the 71st floor, and the shorter but more plush 26-storey **Fairmont Singapore** hotel. Linking Raffles City and its MRT station to Suntec City (*see page 102*) is the subterranean **CityLink Mall**. The

The Singapore sling was first concocted in 1910 by barman Ngiam Tong Boon. The gin-based drink packs a punch even though it tastes so delightfully fruity.

BELOW: shoppers at Raffles City.

underground shopping strip houses a host of stores and cafés, and makes for a great rainy-day route.

War Memorial Park

To the right of Raffles City and opposite Singapore Recreation Club is the **War Memorial Park** , dedicated to 50,000 civilians from the four main ethnic groups who suffered and died in Singapore during World War II. Popularly known as the "Chopsticks Monument", the war memorial consists of four interlinked tapering columns representing each ethnic group. Beneath the 93-metre (305ft) columns are urns containing the remains of some of those who died.

Raffles Hotel

The Civic District is also the location of Singapore's most famous landmark, **Raffles Hotel** , at the corner of Bras Basah Road and Beach Road. Nearly everyone who comes to Singapore ends up at Raffles Hotel at one point or another, usually to try the world-famous Singapore Sling (invented here in 1910) at the **Long Bar** or to walk through the lush

gardens. Enter via its cast-iron porticoed entrance along Beach Road – the hotel originally faced the beach before it fell victim to reclamation – which leads into the lobby, its marbled floors embellished with plush Persian carpets. Opened in 1887 by the Sarkies brothers, the "Grand Old Lady of the East" has seen its fair share of kings and queens, presidents and prime ministers, movie actors and lions of literature, as well as ordinary people attracted to this icon of tropical elegance and style.

Having survived a chequered history – it was briefly used by the Japanese Occupation forces, when it was renamed Syonan Ryokan (Light of the South Hotel) – the Raffles underwent a major facelift in the early 1990s. Whether or not the restoration was sensitively done is contentious, but it did involve years of work, tracking down original plans and finding skilled craftsmen to repair and recreate the original fittings. For most people, the result is a resounding success, and Raffles can once again take her place among the great hotels of the world.

ABOVE: monument at War Memorial Park.
BELOW: Raffles Hotel.

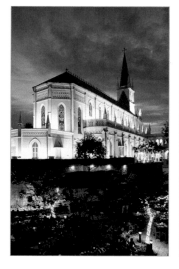

The hotel also houses the **Raffles Hotel Museum** (daily 10am–7pm; free), a shopping arcade full of luxury labels and the **Jubilee Hall Theatre**.

Mint Museum of Toys

Across from the Raffles on Seah Street, rediscover the child within at the **Mint Museum of Toys** ⓲ (tel: 6339-0660; www.emint.com; daily 9.30am–6.30pm; charge). Stuffed with 50,000 vintage toys, this eclectic museum is owned by Chang Ya Fa, who started his collection at the age of six. It includes rare and unique toys and memorabilia of Popeye the Sailor, Felix the Cat, Tintin and superheroes such as Batman and Superman. This is a definite draw for both adults and kids.

Chijmes

Beside Raffles City at the corner of North Bridge and Bras Basah roads is **Chijmes** ⓳, the former Gothic-style Convent of the Holy Infant Jesus (CHIJ), painstakingly restored with the help of Didier Repellin, the same conservationist who worked on the

Empress Place Building (tel: 6332-6277; www.chijmes.com.sg). The name Chijmes (pronounced "chimes") was adopted to incorporate the initials of the convent, church and school that had stood here since its founding in 1840 by the Sisters on the Seine from France. The convent also ran an orphanage; its Gate of Hope on Bras Basah Road was where babies would be left by their unmarried mothers.

Chijmes is today a collection of restaurants (outdoor dining in its softly lit courtyards is a delight), pubs and art and handicraft shops. Don't miss the Belgian-crafted stained-glass windows of the Chapel, renamed **Chijmes Hall** and a venue for concerts and weddings. The **Fountain Court**, flanked by pubs and restaurants with alfresco dining areas, reverberates with life when there are free outdoor concerts.

Good Shepherd Cathedral

Adjacent to Chijmes is the Roman Catholic **Cathedral of the Good Shepherd** ⓴ (tel: 6337-2036; Mon–Fri 7am–5.30pm, Sat 7am–7.30pm,

ABOVE LEFT: the Gothic-inspired Chijmes is now a nightlife venue.
ABOVE: Mint Museum of Toys.

TIP

Here's a novel way to spend your Friday night – museum-hop for less or even for free. On Friday evenings, the Asian Civilisations Museum offers half-price admission from 7 to 9pm and the Singapore Art Museum offers free admission from 6 to 9pm. For details, visit www.nhb. gov.sg.

ABOVE: Gallery 2.1 in the Singapore Art Museum. **ABOVE RIGHT:** *Love Tank,* an exhibit at the National Museum. **BELOW:** self portrait of Georgette Chen, one of Singapore's pioneer artists. Her works are part of the permanent collection of the Singapore Art Museum.

Sun 7.30am–7pm). Built in 1846 in the design of a crucifix (inspired by St Paul's in Covent Garden and St Martin-in-the-Fields in London), the cathedral is the oldest Roman Catholic church in Singapore and home to the present Archbishop of Singapore. It has Roman Doric pillars and a marble pavement imported from Antwerp. The church was gazetted as a national monument in 1973.

Singapore Art Museum

Address: 71 Bras Basah Road;
www.singaporeartmuseum.sg
Tel: 6332-3222
Opening Hrs: Sun–Thur 10am–7pm,
Fri 10am–9pm
Entrance Fee: charge
Transport: Bras Basah MRT

Further down Bras Basah Road, the former St Joseph's Institution, a school founded by the French De La Salle Order in 1852, now houses the **Singapore Art Museum** ㉑. The 19th-century building is worth visiting just to see the splendidly restored chapel and the Glass Hall, which

features a colourful glass sculpture by American artist Dale Chihuly. The museum, with a permanent collection of some 7,000 Southeast Asian pieces, showcases works by the region's leading artists. The museum also offers art from around the world; past temporary exhibitions have included works from the Guggenheim Museum in New York and the Louvre in Paris.

National Museum of Singapore

Address: 93 Stamford Road;
www.nationalmuseum.sg
Tel: 6332-5642
Opening Hrs: Singapore History
Gallery daily 10am–6pm, Singapore
Living Galleries daily 10am–9pm
Entrance Fee: charge
Transport: Bras Basah MRT

From the Singapore Art Museum, head right along Bras Basah Road and turn left at Bencoolen Street towards the neoclassical **National Museum** ㉒. A S$118-million facelift in 2006 refurbished all the internal spaces

of this 1887 jewel of a building and added a stunning modern extension in glass and steel that seamlessly connects with the older building.

Look out for the 11 national treasures in the **Singapore History Gallery**, like the 10th-century Singapore Stone and the 14th-century Majapahit gold ornaments excavated from Fort Canning Hill. The **Singapore Living Galleries** celebrate the creativity of Singaporeans through the themes of food, fashion, film and photography. Past temporary exhibitions have included Greek masterpieces from the Louvre and paintings commissioned by the British Resident William Farquhar that record the flora and fauna of the region.

The museum offers various performing and visual arts programmes, as well as audioguides to help you discover its architectural details, like the 15-metre (49ft) high Glass Rotunda that illuminates like a lantern at night, with images that depict scenes from Singapore's history.

If you thought museums were stuffy, chill out at the slick **Muse Bar** (tel: 6337-9000), serving premium cocktails and fancy bar food. Or have a fine modern European meal at **Novus** (tel: 6336-8770).

Further down, at the corner of Stamford Road and Armenian Street, is the striking Edwardian-style building that was once the Methodist Publishing House, or **MPH Building**, as it was affectionately known. Built in 1908, it was another structure designed by the colonial architect firm Swan and Maclaren.

At 45 Armenian Street is **The Substation**. With its active contemporary arts and drama calendar, it regularly attracts Singapore's young artistic talents (tel: 6337-7535; www.substation. org). The Substation also houses the 108-seat Guinness Theatre and Timbre, a bistro bar which holds regular open stage sessions for budding local artistes.

Peranakan Museum

Address: 39 Armenian Street; www.peranakanmuseum.sg

ABOVE LEFT: display at the Peranakan Museum. **ABOVE:** the museum's exterior.

In the middle of Fort Canning Park is an underground reservoir built in 1926 to feed water pipes connecting to homes in the area. The reservoir was the site of a natural spring used as baths by 14th-century Malay royalty.

TIP

Ballet by the Singapore
Dance Theatre, concerts
and other performing
arts feature regularly at
Fort Canning Park. Just
bring along a mat, a
picnic basket and your
entrance ticket, and
enjoy an open-air show.
Call the National Parks
Board, tel: 6332-1200,
or visit its website at
www.nparks.gov.sg.

Tel: 6332-7591
Opening Hrs: Mon 1–7pm, Tue–Sun
9.30am–7pm, Fri 9.30am–9pm
Entrance Fee: charge
Transport: City Hall MRT, Clarke Quay
MRT, Bras Basah MRT

Further down Armenian Street
and housed in the former Tao Nan
School is the **Peranakan Museum**
❷❸. Opened in 2008, the museum's
10 galleries showcase the fascinating
culture of the Peranakan people *(see
page 22)*. Noteworthy exhibits here
include a pair of ornate wedding
slippers with gold and silver thread
embroidery, and a richly decorated
16-piece dining table, both from
the late 19th century. Along the
same stretch are two well-known
restaurants: True Blue, which serves
Peranakan cuisine, and the modern
European Fifty Three, both housed
in old shophouses.

Fort Canning Park

Rising behind Stamford Road and
Hill Street is a tree-covered bluff, on
which sits **Fort Canning Park** ❷❹. It
was once known as Bukit Larangan
(Forbidden Hill) because no com-
moner was allowed to come up here.
During the early years of Singapore's
history, this strategic location was the
site of grand palaces protected by
high walls and swamps. The Majapahit princes who ruled Singapura in
the 14th century were buried there
– archaeological excavations in the
area have uncovered remains from
the period – and it was rumoured
that royal spirits haunted the place.
Undeterred by such superstition, the
practical Raffles built his residence
here in 1823 and renamed it Government Hill. He had chosen the site for
the same reasons as Singapore's early
rulers – it had a good vantage point
for spotting enemy movements at sea.
Later, it was renamed Fort Canning
Hill after Viceroy Canning of India.

In 1860, the British built a fort atop
the hill, from where dawn, noon and
dusk were announced each day by
cannon fire. The cannons have since
been removed to Fort Siloso on Sentosa Island *(see page 184)*. Apart from
being the first home of Singapore's
rulers and the site of the first fortress,
Fort Canning had the island's first
lighthouse, the oldest cemetery and

BELOW: Fort Canning
Park.

the island's first Botanic Garden – now the **Spice Garden**.

Today, this lovely oasis of green has been designated as a historical park. It is accessible via Canning Rise or an underpass up a flight of stairs beside Park Mall shopping centre. Enter through one of the two Gothic-style gates to the old cemetery. The cemetery, used from 1820 to 1865, was exhumed in 1970 to make way for the park. Its tombstones, now embedded in its boundary walls, contain many names associated with Singapore's history, including the colonial architect George Coleman and William Napier, the first law agent. The park also holds an older tomb purported to be where the remains of Iskandar Shah, the last ruler of pre-colonial Singapore, lie. This has been consecrated as a Muslim *keramat* (shrine).

Midway up the park is the entrance to the World War II underground bunkers, now known as the **Battle Box**, used by the British military to plan strategies against the Japanese enemy (tel: 6333-0510; daily 10am–6pm; charge). The 9-metre (30ft) deep, bombproof bunkers led to the former Far East Command Building (now The Legends Fort Canning Park). It was here that Lieutenant-General A.E. Percival, commander of the British forces, decided to surrender to the Japanese on 15 February 1942 when he realised that Singapore was running short of food and ammunition. The bunker has wax figures and film projections that recreate the events leading to Singapore's fall, while an exhibition inside the maze of tunnels details the desperate battle against the Japanese.

Fort Canning Centre is also a hub of the arts in Singapore; productions are staged at the **Black Box Theatre** by local arts groups, and the studios of the **Singapore Dance Theatre** are also found here. At the culinary academy called **at-sunrice**, you can sign up for a guided tour through the lovely Spice Garden followed by a hands-on gourmet cooking class (bookings required; tel: 6336-3307; www.at-sunrice.com).

Philatelic Museum

Address: 23B Coleman Street; www.spm.org.sg

ABOVE: old fort walls at Fort Canning Park.
BELOW: display at Philatelic Museum.

Cruise Control

The authorities have tried various approaches to reduce traffic congestion, providing excellent public transport and introducing Electronic Road Pricing (ERP)

While traffic in the rest of Asia crawls at a snail's pace during rush hour, in Singapore the problem of cars choking up the roads is kept carefully under control. Cars whizz past at a reasonable 60–70kph (37–43mph) on the expressways during peak hours – barring traffic accidents, of course. Despite having one of the highest car densities in the world, Singapore has found a solution, through a combination of regulation and technology.

The guiding principle behind traffic management in Singapore is a simple one: by government decree, the population of cars cannot grow faster than roads being built. And with the land available for road infrastructure being so limited, curbs on car ownership are considerable.

For starters, cars here are probably among the most expensive in the world:

after a hefty 45 percent tax on car imports, a registration fee of 150 percent, and an annual road tax pegged to the engine capacity of the car, a 1,600cc saloon can easily cost in excess of S$50,000. But that's not all; in 1990, the Certificate of Entitlement (COE) was introduced, without which one cannot purchase a new car. As of November 2010, the cost of a COE for a 1,600cc saloon was S$34,000, meaning the eventual price of the car is a whopping S$84,000.

Only limited numbers of COEs are available each month, and these are sold through a complex bidding system. The COE is valid for 10 years – the theory is that fewer old cars reduce breakdowns and traffic congestion – after which a new COE must be purchased. Instead of paying inflated road taxes to keep a car beyond 10 years, people would rather turn it into scrap metal and buy a new car instead.

In 1999, the authorities struck a brainwave in the form of the Electronic Road Pricing (ERP) system. With the S$200-million-dollar system in place, ERP overhead gantries stategically located in the Central Business District and expressways automatically deduct a fixed toll throughout the day from cash cards inserted in the special in-vehicle units (IU) installed in cars. While this new system has drawn a mixed response – government coffers have swelled from the fees collected via the ERP – it has succeeded in reducing traffic during peak hours. Traffic during ERP operating hours has dropped by 15 percent as motorists either pool cars or take public transport to work.

The authorities have poured millions of dollars into building, and constantly upgrading, an excellent public transportation system, a definite compensation for the expense of private motoring. ❑

LEFT AND ABOVE: traffic jams are relatively rare on the well-managed Singapore roads.

Tel: 6337-3888
Opening Hrs: Mon 1–7pm, Tue–Sun 9am–7pm
Entrance Fee: charge
Transport: City Hall MRT, Clarke Quay MRT, Bras Basah MRT

At the foot of Fort Canning Hill along Canning Rise is the **National Archives,** where written and oral records of Singapore's history are kept. Its rich archival holdings date back to the early 1800s. Further down at the corner of Armenian and Coleman streets is the **Singapore Philatelic Museum** ㉕. Completed in 1907, it was formerly part of the Anglo-Chinese School before it was restored in 1995. Although tiny, the interactive museum is a delightful treasure trove of stamps, first-day covers and postcards, and has regular exhibitions.

Armenian Church

At the corner of Coleman and Hill streets is the tiny but atmospheric **Armenian Church** ㉖, also called St Gregory the Illuminator (tel: 6334-0141; daily 9am–6pm; free). Built in 1835 and designed by Coleman, this is the oldest church in Singapore.

A cemetery in the church grounds is where the tombstones of some eminent Singaporeans are found, among them the Sarkies brothers, who founded Raffles Hotel, and Agnes Joaquim (1864–99), after whom Singapore's national flower, *Vanda Miss Joaquim*, is named. Agnes discovered the purple bloom in 1893 in a bamboo grove behind her home in Tanjong Pagar. She took the orchid to Henry Ridley, the director of the Botanic Gardens at the time, who identified the plant as a rare natural hybrid, and the rest, as they say, is history.

Central Fire Station

At No. 62 Hill Street is another architectural gem of a building, the old **Central Fire Station** ㉗, the oldest

fire station in Singapore. This distinctive red and white "blood and bandage" building was completed in 1908 and is typical of the architecture of Edwardian England, a departure from the usual Palladian and classical styles prevailing in Singapore at the time. The "blood" is exposed red brick, the "bandage" refers to the parts covered in whitewashed plaster.

The **Civil Defence Heritage Gallery** on the ground level traces Singapore's civil defence developments from the 1900s (tel: 6332-2996; www.scdf.gov.sg; Tue–Sun 10am–5pm; free). Register for a guided tour and you get to climb up the hose tower, the lookout point for firefighters in early Singapore.

The MICA Building

Also along Hill Street, near Coleman Bridge, is the **MICA Building** ㉘, which formerly housed the Old Hill Street Police Station. The more delicate features of this classical Renaissance-style building with horseshoe arches are rather overwhelmed by its startling multicoloured shutters – there are 911

ABOVE: Central Fire Station. **BELOW:** the MICA Building at night.

TIP

At nearby Magazine Road (off Merchant Road) is the ornate Tan Si Chong Su Temple, a Hokkien place of worship with well-preserved carvings, ancestral tablets and a delightful rooftop of dancing dragons and ceramic flowers (daily 7.30am–5.30pm). The temple was built in 1878 as a gathering place for the Tan clan.

altogether – but experts agree that it is one of the city's premier examples of British colonial architecture.

Built in 1934, the building was once occupied by the Japanese army during World War II. It reopened in 2000 after undergoing extensive restoration, and today houses the offices of the Ministry of Information, Communication and the Arts, the National Arts Council and the National Heritage Board. Be sure to stop by the **ARTrium** courtyard on the ground level, occupied by a number of interesting art galleries showing local artworks as well as works from Southeast Asia and China.

Clarke Quay

Clarke Quay ㉙, one of the city's hottest after-hours spots, sizzles with the trendy set in search of entertainment. The **G-Max** bungee and **GX5** swing contraptions mark the entrance to this old warehouse district, bounded by Tan Tye Place, Canning Lane, Clarke Quay and North Boat Quay. Its five buildings comprise 60 ware-

houses and shophouses that have been restored to their original 19th-century style, and are now occupied by hip clubs (Attica), bars (The Pump Room and Highlander Bar) and restaurants (Coriander Leaf).

Nearby **Read Bridge** spans the Singapore River and connects Clarke Quay with **Riverside Point**, a complex of food and drink outlets, such as Café Iguana and Brewerkz, that bears no hint of its seedier past, when it was a gathering place for secret societies, opium smokers and ladies of the night.

Robertson Quay

The residential enclave known as **Robertson Quay** lies upriver west of Clarke Quay. In the old days, European and Chinese merchants used this part of the river mostly for storage of goods. Although a few warehouses still exist along **Rodyk Street**, Robertson Quay has been taken over by some of Singapore's most exclusive riverside apartments. Several arts companies have also made this quay

SHOPPING

Although the shopping in this area is scattered over a wider area than places like Orchard Road, most of the shopping centres are connected to City Mall MRT station by a series of underground (air-conditioned) walkways.

Malls

CityLink Mall
1 Raffles Link. Tel: 6339-9913. www.citylinkmall.com p270, B3
This underground mall links City Hall to Suntec City and Esplanade.

Along the way, there are cafés, jewellery stores and mid-priced fashion boutiques.
Funan DigitalLife Mall
109 North Bridge Road. Tel: 6336-8327. www.funan.com. sg p270, A4
This IT mall has numerous outlets carrying reliable brands of the latest computers, IT accessories and electronic gadgets.
Marina Square
6 Raffles Boulevard. Tel: 6339-8787. www.marina square.com.sg p270, C4
A sprawling mall connected to the Marina Mandarin Hotel. Aside

from the stores, there is a cineplex and numerous casual eateries.
Millenia Walk
9 Raffles Boulevard. Tel: 6883-1122. www.millenia walk.com p271, C3
This mall houses boutiques, cafes, ramen eateries and Parco department store.
Raffles City Shopping Centre
252 North Bridge Road. Tel: 6318-0238. www.rafflescity. com p270, B3
One of the anchor tenants here is Robinson's department store (tel: 6216-8388). Marks &

Spencer is located within Robinson's.
Raffles Hotel Shopping Arcade
Raffles Hotel, Beach Road. p270, B3
This upscale arcade has many high-end brands such as Louis Vuitton and Tiffany & Co. CYC (The Custom Shop) is a famous store for tailor-made shirts.
Suntec City Mall
3 Temasek Boulevard. Tel: 6825-2667. www.suntec city.com.sg p270, C3
In this huge mall there's a Carrefour hypermarket and independent stores.

their home base. Among them are **Singapore Repertory Theatre** at the junction of Merbau Road and Unity Street, and the **Singapore Tyler Print Institute** on Mohamed Sultan Road. The latter, housed in a restored 19th-century warehouse, is dedicated to printmaking, paper making and paper-based art (tel: 6336 3663; www.stpi.com.sg; Tue–Sat 10am–6pm; free).

Although the nearby former nightspots of Mohamed Sultan Road have closed down and the stretch has lost its lustre over the years, Robertson Quay still has its fair share of great restaurants by the river, including Japanese *ramen* and *yakitori* outlets. Meanwhile, partygoers continue to flock to the well-known ultra-trendy **Zouk** club located further west at Jiak Kim Street.

Omar Melaka Mosque

Across the river from Clarke Quay and past Merchant Road on Keng Cheow Street is the gilded minaret of **Omar Kampung Melaka Mosque ㉚**. It stands proudly on the site as

Singapore's first mosque. Built in 1820 by wealthy Arab merchant Syed Omar Ali Aljunied, the original basic wooden structure made way for the present brick building in 1855.

Thong Chai Medical Institute

One block east across New Market Road, at the corner of of Eu Tong Sen Street and Merchant Road, stands the former **Thong Chai Medical Institute ㉛**, with its distinctive green-tiled gabled roofs shaped after clouds on the sides and its ornately decorated ridges. It was built in 1892 to serve as a free hospital, and its architecture is reminiscent of the Chinese southern style, similar to Tan Yeok Nee's house on Clemenceau Avenue *(see page 148)*. The medical institute was designed after a southern Chinese palace and has two inner courts. The institute, now restored and preserved as a national monument, served in the recent past as a nightclub and later a restaurant. It is now the headquarters of an American company. ❑

ABOVE: the GX5 swing at Clarke Quay. **BELOW:** Robertson Quay.

BEST RESTAURANTS AND BARS

American

Brewerkz
01-05/06 Riverside Point, 30 Merchant Rd. Tel: 6438-7438. www.brewerkz.com Open: Mon–Sat noon–1am, Fri–Sat noon–3am, Sun 11am–1am. **$$$** ❶ p272, C1
Handcrafted beer fresh from the on-site micro-brewery and hearty American cuisine are served in an industrial-like setting. Beers include the best-selling India Pale Ale.

Morton's of Chicago
4/F, Mandarin Oriental, Singapore, 5 Raffles Ave. Tel: 6339-3740. www.mortons.com Open: daily D. **$$$$** ❷ p270, C4
The dark-wood interiors, knowledgeable and attentive waiters, 24-ounce Porterhouse, massive crab cakes and premium wine list are all part of the Morton experience. Start the evening with a Martini at the bar.

Chinese

Golden Peony
3/F, Conrad Centennial Singapore, 2 Temasek Blvd. Tel: 6432-7488. www.conrad hotels.com Open: daily L & D. **$$$** (set lunch and à la carte) ❸ p270, C3
Refined Cantonese cuisine is complemented by good service and an elegant dining room furnished in golden pine-wood. Superb *dim sum* is available at lunchtime. There's also a special set menu paired with choice wines.

Hai Tien Lo
37/F, Pan Pacific Hotel, 7 Raffles Blvd. Tel: 6434-8338. www.singapore.pan pacific.com Open: daily L & D. **$$** (set lunch) **$$$$** (à la carte) ❹ p270, C4
This 37th-level restaurant is famous for its 360-degree views and classic Cantonese-style cuisine. The seafood dishes are always special, as is the signature barbecued Peking duck with pan-fried foie gras.

Jade
The Fullerton Hotel, 1 Fullerton Sq. Tel: 6877 8188. www.fullertonhotel.com. Open: daily L & D. **$$$** (set lunch) **$$$$** (à la carte) ❺ p273, D1
Jade serves up a sophisticated menu of Cantonese classics amid grand surroundings. Specialities include the steamed squid-ink dumplings and the new "signature soup trio". The restaurant also serves exquisite *dim sum*.

Lei Garden
01-24 Chijmes, 30 Victoria St. Tel: 6339-3822. Open: daily L & D. **$$** (set lunch) **$$$** (à la carte) ❻ p270, B3
Set amid the charming Chijmes, Lei Garden is one of Singapore's best spots for *dim sum* and Cantonese cuisine. The healthful double-boiled soups and live seafood dishes are particularly noteworthy.

My Humble House
02-27/29 Esplanade Mall, 8 Raffles Ave. Tel: 6423-1881. www.tunglok.com Open: daily L & D. **$$$** (set lunch) **$$$$** (à la carte) ❼ p270, B4
This popular, artistic Chinese restaurant serves dishes with poetic names such as "Dance of the Wind" (double-boiled seafood consommé). Alongside the sublime modern Chinese cuisine, the designer decor is both sleek and dramatic with great water views.

Peach Blossoms
5/F, Marina Mandarin, 6 Raffles Blvd. Tel: 6845-1111. www.marina-mandarin.com.sg Open: daily L & D. **$$$** (set lunch and à la carte) ❽ p270, B4
This 20-year-old restaurant with its auspicious red "eight-coloured pillar" entrance and soothing wood tones is known for its artfully presented Cantonese-style creations imbued with modern influences. You can't go wrong with specialities like baked fillet of sea perch in barbecue sauce.

Summer Pavilion
The Ritz-Carlton, 7 Raffles Ave. Tel: 6434-5268. Open: daily L & D. **$$$** (*dim sum* set lunch) **$$$$** (à la carte) ❾ p271, C4
Flanked by a lush garden with a waterfall, Summer Pavilion is like a breath of fresh air. Feast on refined Cantonese dishes such

LEFT: lobster at Equinox.
RIGHT: Raffles Grill.

as braised shark's fin with crabmeat and roe, and barbecued duckling with fresh mango and lemon sauce. The restaurant's exquisite *dim sum* are among the best in town.

European

Equinox
68–72/F, Swissôtel The Stamford, 2 Stamford Rd. Tel: 6431-5669. www.equinox complex.com Open: Mon–Sat noon–2.30pm, 3–11pm, Sun 11am–2.30pm, 3.30–5.30pm, 7–11pm. **$$$** (set lunch) **$$$$** (à la carte) ⑩ p270, B3

A complex of five restaurants and bars sits atop Southeast Asia's tallest hotel. Start with drinks at the New Asia Bar on the 71st level while taking in stunning city views from its floor-to-ceiling windows, then head over to the swanky Modern European restaurant Jaan, which has received rave reviews for its seasonal *dégustation* menus and stunning views.

Fifty Three
53 Armenian St. Tel: 6334-5535. www.fiftythree.com.sg Open: Tue–Sat L & D. **$$$$** ⑪ p270, A3

This sleek, understated restaurant by the Les Amis Group is located in a shophouse near the

Prices for a three-course dinner per person without drinks and taxes:
$ = under S$20
$$ = S$20–30
$$$ = S$30–50
$$$$ = over S$50

Peranakan Museum. The kitchen is helmed by Michal Han, who uses natural material such as stones that he collects in Scandinavia as a canvas for his dishes, which include potatoes with coffee and parmesan "soil".

Pierside
01-01, One Fullerton. Tel: 6438-0400. www.pierside kitchen.com Open: Mon–Fri L & D, Sat D. **$$$** (set lunch) **$$$$** (à la carte) ⑫ p273, D2

Seafood never looked so smart in the pared-down, quiet sophistication of this waterfront restaurant. By day stylish and by night intimate and relaxed, the modern European menu is served alongside great views of the marina. Must haves: Robin Ho's oven-roasted miso cod and Valrhona chocolate fondant.

French

Gunther's
01-03, 36 Purvis St. Tel: 6338-8955. Open: Mon–Sat L & D. **$$$** (set lunch) **$$$$** (à la carte) ⑬ p270, B3

Exquisite Modern French cuisine is rustled up by Chef Gunther Hubrechsen. He is known for giving dishes a light touch, which accentuate, instead of eclipse, the natural flavours of the ingredients.

Raffles Grill
Raffles Hotel, 1 Beach Rd. Tel: 6412-1816. www.raffles hotel.com Open: Mon–Fri L & D, Sat D. **$$$** (set lunch) **$$$$** (à la carte) ⑭ p270, B3

The timeless grace of the Raffles Hotel is captured in this handsome French restaurant, also one of the city's finest. Waiters are attentive but discreet, and chefs spare no expense when it comes to quality.

Saint Julien
3 Fullerton Rd. Tel: 6534-5947. www.saintjulien.com.sg Open: Mon–Fri L & D, Sat D. **$$$** (set lunch) **$$$$** (à la carte) ⑮ p273, D1

Frenchman Julien Bompard's CV includes Michelin-starred restaurants, though aficionados will probably remember him best from his days at Gaddi's at Peninsula Hong Kong. Now the commander of his own place, Bompard serves classical French cuisine in a quaint old boathouse by the waterfront.

Saint Pierre
01-01 Central Mall, 3 Mag-

azine Rd. Tel: 6438-0887. www.saintpierre.com.sg Open: Mon–Fri L & D, Sat D. **$$–$$$** (set lunch) **$$$$** (à la carte) ⑯ p272, B1

Belgian owner-chef Emmanuel Stroobant is as dishy as the foie gras, braised black cod and flourless choc cake he dishes up in his smart, award-winning Modern French restaurant. There are at least six varieties of foie gras on the menu, and his pan-fried version with caramelised green apple and old port sauce is simply divine.

Fusion

Coriander Leaf
02–03, 3A Merchant Court, River Valley Rd. Tel: 6732-3354. www.corianderleaf.com Open: Mon–Fri L & D, Sat D. **$$** (set lunch) **$$$** (à la carte) ⑰ p269, E4

Chef-owner Samia Ahad's food defies all categories:

calling it fusion does it no justice. Prepare to be bowled over at this eatery in atmospheric Clarke Quay, where its brilliant pan-Asian and Mediterranean menu given a Western spin (or is it the other way around?) continues to hold court.

Indian

Rang Mahal

3/F, Pan Pacific Singapore, 7 Raffles Blvd. Tel: 6333-1788. Open: Mon–Fri, Sun L & D, Sat D. **$$$** (buffet lunch) **$$$$** (à la carte) 🔞 p270, C4

The modern interiors hint at understated sophistication, befitting the classical northern, southern and coastal Indian specialities. Whether it's a new twist to a traditional dish (tandoori oyster) or a classic favourite (*murg hazari*, or stuffed

chicken), rest assured of a memorable meal.

International

Greenhouse

The Ritz-Carlton, 7 Raffles Ave. Tel: 6434-5288. www.ritzcarlton.com Open: daily 6.30am–11.30pm, Sun brunch 11.30am–3pm. **$$$** 🔞 p271, C4

Its famed Sunday champagne brunch is a must for anyone who wants to indulge in a non-stop flow of vintage Moët & Chandon, fresh Boston lobsters, oysters, roasts, pan-fried foie gras, over 50 varieties of farmhouse cheeses and other delicacies. International buffet lunches are served on weekdays.

Italian

Garibaldi

01-02, 36 Purvis St. Tel: 6837-1468. www.garibaldi.com.sg Open: daily L & D.

$$$** (set lunch) **$$$$ (à la carte) 🔞 p270, B3

This sleek restaurant is synonymous with Italian fine dining in the city. Heading the kitchen is Chef Roberto Galetti, who uses only the best seasonal ingredients from Italy. His specialities include the perfectly *al dente* angel hair pasta with half spicy lobster, sweet peas and tomato sauce.

Ristorante Bologna

4/F, Marina Mandarin, 6 Raffles Blvd. Tel: 6845-1111. www.marina-mandarin.com.sg Open: Mon–Fri L & D, Sat D. **$$$** (semi-buffet lunch) **$$$$** (à la carte) 🔞 p270, B4

Established in 1987, this was one of the first Italian restaurants to open in Singapore. Helming the elegant venue is the affable Chef Carlo Marengoni, who ensures that diners leave utterly satisfied. Must-tries are the home-made pastas, oven-baked rack of lamb with rosemary and red wine sauce, as well as the classic tiramisu.

Japanese

Inagiku

3/F, Fairmont Singapore, 80 Bras Basah Rd. Tel: 6431-6156. www.fairmont.com/singapore Open: daily L & D. **$$$$** (set lunch and à la carte) 🔞 p270, B3

Dine on beautifully executed Japanese creations made of premium ingredients air-flown from

LEFT: New Asia Bar.

Japan. The hotel hires a team of talented Japanese chefs who cleverly combine time-honoured traditions with contemporary techniques.

Japanese Dining SUN

02-01 Chijmes, 30 Victoria St. Tel: 6336-3166. Open: daily L & D. **$$$** (set lunch) **$$$$** (à la carte) 🔞 p270, A/B3

Features a contemporary setting with calligraphy splashed across the walls. Tuck into authentic dishes alongside beautifully presented modern Japanese creations and delicate desserts at prices that won't burn a hole in your wallet. Ask about the chef's special seasonal menu, which changes every three months.

Keyaki

4/F, Pan Pacific Hotel, 7 Raffles Blvd. Tel: 6434-8335. www.singapore.panpacific.com Open: daily L & D. **$$$$** (à la carte) 🔞 p270, C4

To get to the restaurant, you stroll past a Zen garden and fish pond before smiling, soft-spoken waitresses greet you at the entrance. Once inside, take your pick from *kaiseki*, *robatayaki*, sashimi, *teppanyaki* and *shabu-shabu*. Round off with sake.

Shinji

1 Beach Road, Raffles Hotel #02-20. Tel: 6338-6131. www.shinjibykanesaka.com Open: Mon–Sat L & D. **$$$$** (set lunch and dinner) 🔞 p270, B3

This is the first and only

outpost of two-Michelin-starred chef Shinji Kanesaka's famous Edomae-style sushi restaurant in Tokyo. Exquisite menus of perfectly executed sushi and pristine seafood are served. Watch the chefs prepare them right in front of you at the counter seats.

Local

Kopi Tiam
2/F, Swissôtel The Stamford, 2 Stamford Rd. Tel: 6431-6221. www.singapore-stamford.swissotel.com Open: daily B, L & D. **$$$** ㉖ p270, B3
Make a beeline for tasty local dishes such as the Hainanese chicken rice, *rojak* and *laksa*. Catch the chef flipping *roti prata*, an Indian bread, on a griddle, at weekends.

Princess Terrace
Lobby Level, Copthorne King's Hotel, 403 Havelock Rd. Tel: 6318-3168. www.millenniumhotels.com.sg Open: daily L & D. **$$$** ㉗ p272, A1
The Princess Terrace's famous authentic Penang-style buffet has been attracting locals for the past three decades. Expect a tempting spread of favourites such as *char kway teow* (flat rice

Prices for a three-course dinner per person without drinks and taxes:
$ = under S$20
$$ = S$20–30
$$$ = S$30–50
$$$$ = over S$50

noodles fried in sweet soy sauce), *Hokkien mee* and Penang *laksa* (which are both kinds of noodle soup), chicken curry, and delicious multicoloured *nonya* desserts – all prepared by experienced chefs from Penang.

Peranakan

True Blue
47/49 Armenian St. Tel: 6440-4548. www.trueblue cuisine.com Open: Tue–Sat L & D. **$$$** ㉘ p270, A3
Appropriately located just two doors away from the Peranakan Museum, this eatery is adorned with the owner Benjamin Seck's personal collection of Peranakan antiques and artefacts. The dishes are just as impressive, although portions are small. Try favourites like spicy beef *rendang* and *ayam buah keluak* (chicken stewed with Indonesian black nuts) – all lovingly prepared by Benjamin's mother, Daisy.

Thai

Yhing Thai Palace
36 Purvis St. Tel: 6337-1161. Open: daily L & D. **$$** ㉙ p270, B3
There's nothing palatial about this place; In fact, the decor is uninspiring and it can get noisy. But it pleases with a bill of Thai-Chinese fare at reasonable prices. The olive fried rice and Thai fish cakes are favourites, as is the grilled squid salad bathed in a piquant sauce.

Bars

Brewerkz
01-05/06 Riverside Point, 30 Merchant Road. Tel: 6438-7438. www.brewerkz.com ❶ p272, C1
A microbrewery, pub and restaurant rolled into one. To taste all six types of beer, try a six-beer sampler, then go for a 12-, 16- or 24-ounce glass of your favourite; the India Pale Ale is a local favourite.

Café Iguana
01-03 Riverside Point, 30 Merchant Road. Tel: 6236-1275. www.cafeiguana.com ❷ p272, C1
You can sample over 100 different tequilas here – just not all at once. Their margaritas are recommended and wine is available too, along with a Tex-Mex menu.

Highlander Bar and Restaurant
01-11 Clarke Quay, 3B River Valley Road. Tel: 6235-9528. www.highlanderasia.com ❸ p269, E4
The staff all wear tartan, the manager is from Aberdeen, and the Highlander attempts to recreate the atmosphere of a Scottish castle with wood panelling and barrelheads mounted on a stone wall. A glass display lined with its collection of 200 types of whiskies is a sight to behold.

Long Bar
1 Beach Road, Raffles Hotel. Tel: 6412-1229 ❹ p270, B3
The Raffles Hotel bar still serves the famous Singapore Sling, which was

invented here in 1915. No one cares about Singapore's anti-litter laws here: patrons are expected to toss empty shells of peanuts onto the floor!

Muse Bar
01-01 National Museum, 93 Stamford Road. Tel: 6337-9000 ❺ p270, A3
This is the place for chill-out music, premium cocktails, and fancy bar food.

New Asia Bar
Level 71, Swissôtel The Stamford, 2 Stamford Road. Tel: 6837-3322. www.equinoxcomplex.com ❻ p270, B3
This is one of the best spots from which to enjoy views of the city – and in clear weather as far as Malaysia – while sipping cocktails and champagne, particularly at dusk. A lift zips you up to the top level of the complex.

Post Bar
The Fullerton Hotel, 1 Fullerton Square. Tel: 6877-8135 ❼ p273, D1
The former post office turned luxury hotel is where the city's hip come to be seen.

Lantern
80 Collyer Quay. Tel: 6333-8388. www.fullertonbayhotel.com ❽ p273, D2
Lantern is an outdoor rooftop bar with great views of the marina and beyond. Sink into one of the curvaceous lounge chairs to sip champagne and indulge in gourmet snacks, while a Cuban band plays in the background.

THE ASIAN CIVILISATIONS MUSEUM

Religious statuary, calligraphic art, textiles and architecture that span several centuries are all housed in the historic Empress Place Building

If you're wondering how the multi-ethnic culture of Singapore originated, this museum holds the key. Even visitors who are not history buffs will find the interactive zones, innovative virtual hosts and in-gallery videos highly entertaining. With 11 galleries spread out over three floors, you can easily spend half-a-day at this excellent museum.

Start with the Southeast Asia collection on level two. From prehistoric agricultural tools to fabric displays and artefacts, the exhibits reveal the diversity of the region. On the same level are the China and West Asia galleries: the Chinese deities, fragile Dehua porcelain and Qu'ran-inspired calligraphic art are highlights.

Visit more Southeast Asia and West Asia galleries on level three, then head down the central staircase to level one, the South Asia galleries, dominated by religious statuary and architectural motifs.

To fully appreciate the museum, take the free one-hour guided tour (Mon 2pm, Tue–Fri 11am and 2pm, Sat–Sun 11am, 2pm and 3pm).

ABOVE: over 1,300 artefacts from the ancient civilisations of Asia are housed within the Empress Place Building, a grand national monument whose history dates back to 1864 *(see page 80)*. With hands-on activities for children, ongoing talks and workshops, and changing special exhibitions, a trip here is no boring history excursion.

BELOW: this late 19th-century batik piece from Java is part of the fabric collection of the Southeast Asia gallery. The patterns and motifs are inspired by various rituals and taboos, and the ideas are said to come to the weavers in dreams sent by the gods. The gallery displays mainly textiles from the Malay-Indonesian world.

The Essentials

Address: 1 Empress Place, www.acm.org.sg
Tel: 6332-2982
Opening Hrs: Mon 1–7pm, Tue–Sun 9am–7pm, Fri until 9pm
Entrance Fee: charge
Transport: Raffles Place MRT

EXPLORING ISLAM

The main subject of the West Asia galleries is Islam, with a section focusing on the Qu'ran. The Qu'ran is the holy book that forms the foundation of any Islamic education, and it means "to read" or "to recite". It is also admired as a calligraphic art form, and the various styles of calligraphy can be seen in these galleries – on paper, textiles, metalwork and even ceramics. Look out for a quaint mosque-like setting (it faces towards Mecca, the direction of prayer) where images of mosque architecture from around the world are projected for viewing. The gallery here also showcases achievements of Islamic scholars since ancient days. For instance, work of Islamic scientists from the 9th to 16th centuries in areas such as medicine, chemistry and mathematics paved the way for the development of modern western science. Learn about Islamic astronomy in this section too; exhibited are precision astrolabe instruments that assisted ancient travellers. By using stars for navigation, Muslim traders were able to get to Southeast Asia in the 9th century.

BELOW: this impressive gateway, characteristic of provincial Mughal architecture, leads to the gallery of Medieval India where a collection of exhibits from the 13th to 19th century showcases the period's culture.

ABOVE: in this re-created scholar's studio are a traditional 19th-century wooden couch bed from Fujian, with a zither (stringed instrument) on it. Painting and music were some of the main pursuits of the Chinese literati.

RIGHT: Naga Muchalinda, the King of Mythical Serpents, shelters a sandstone figure of Buddha from the floods. This 11th- to 12th-century artefact from Cambodia is similar to stone images that were placed in Khmer temples for worship. Theravada Buddhism is the main religion in Cambodia, Burma, Thailand and Laos.

CHINATOWN, THE CENTRAL BUSINESS DISTRICT AND MARINA BAY

Beneath the gleaming glass and steel skyscrapers of Singapore's financial district lies the colourful hubbub of Chinatown, with old temples, restored shophouses and busy markets. The new leisure complex of Marina Bay completes the contrast

The area south of the Singapore River comprises two distinct neighbourhoods – Chinatown and the Central Business District, set against a backdrop of towering banks and office buildings, one of the tallest skylines in Southeast Asia. Flanking the bay to the east is the shiny new mega-casino and entertainment complex of Marina Bay.

CHINATOWN

It may seem strange to have a Chinatown in a place that has a predominantly Chinese population anyway, but the oddity can be traced back to Raffles, who subdivided his new town into various districts and according to racial lines in the early 1820s. He used two rivers as dividing lines. The marshy area at the mouth of the Singapore River was designated a commercial area, while the area directly west was given to Chinese immigrants who did much of the manual labour. Kampung Glam, between Rochor River and the sea, was zoned off for Arab traders and Malay merchants.

Despite urbanisation, Chinatown, huddled on the south bank of the Singapore River and stretching inland as far as Cantonment Road,

still has pockets of narrow streets and shophouses. In the past, it was divided into different areas as the early immigrants tended to congregate in certain neighbourhoods according to the dialect they spoke and their village origins. This distinction is blurred today.

The entire quarter may be hemmed in by soaring high-rises today but Chinatown, thankfully, is still dominated by exotic sights and smells, albeit amid mountains of gaudy tourist junk. Frogs await

LEFT AND RIGHT: candlestick detail and worshippers at Chinatown's Thian Hock Keng Temple.

skinning in the local wet markets, while in the medical halls there are pearls to be ground and ginseng roots to rejuvenate the tired. At certain times of the year the pungent aroma of the seasonal durian fruit permeates the air.

Past and present

The Singapore Tourism Board spent S$97.5 million on a project to evoke a sense of the past and recreate Chinatown's rich heritage that was lost in the process of urban renewal. Traditional trades, street hawkers and performers have been revived and people are encouraged to live in Chinatown again. Critics, however, fear that this new Chinatown might turn into an artificial theme park for visitors, losing its gritty edge and ambience in the process.

But even without such deliberate planning, a stroll in Chinatown still reveals contrasting vignettes that make the district a fascinating blend of the past and the present. It is not uncommon to see executives with briefcase in one hand and mobile phone in the other pass temples where elderly women in *samfoo* (Chinese traditional blouse and trousers) toss wooden sticks from a tin can at temples as they pray for "lucky numbers" in the lottery.

Beautifully refurbished shophouses that are now home to trendy advertising agencies and fashionable bars stand shoulder to shoulder with decaying shophouses selling an assortment of antiques and bric-a-brac. And in the shopping centres and on the streets that thread through Chinatown, handmade puppets, opera masks, silk clothing, herbs and traditional Chinese furniture are sold alongside computers and other electronic goods.

Chinatown has its fair share of Buddhist and Taoist temples. But one of the most curious things about the neighbourhood is that it harbours

ABOVE: shops specialising in traditional Chinese medicinal herbs can be found around Sago Street and South Bridge Road.

Chinatown, the Central Business District and Marina Bay

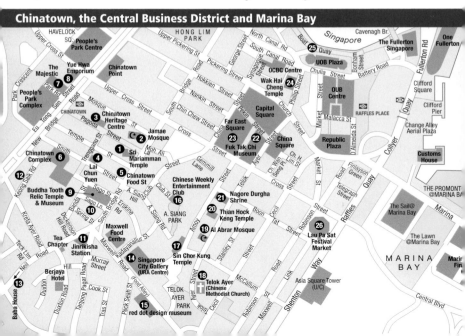

some of the island's best-known Hindu and Muslim shrines. Chinatown, like Singapore's other ethnic enclaves, reflected a healthy eclecticism that has survived to this day.

The Chinatown MRT station at New Bridge Road/Eu Tong Sen Street allows easy access to this area.

Sri Mariamman Temple

Towering above the shophouses along South Bridge Road are the brightly painted figures on the *gopuram* (tower) entrance of the **Sri Mariamman Temple ❶** (tel: 6223-4064; daily 7am–noon, 6–9pm). Dedicated to the goddess Mariamman – who is known for curing serious illnesses – it's the oldest and most important Hindu shrine in Singapore. Here, devotees perform *pujas* (prayers) amid gaudy statues and vivid ceiling frescoes.

Built during the 1820s, this is the annual site of Thimithi *(see page 59)*, the Hindu fire-walking festival that takes place in October. In an elaborate ceremony that honours the goddess Draupathi, the faithful work themselves into a frenzied trance and walk over burning embers to fulfil their vows. Curiously, it's a ritual that also draws participation from a small number of Chinese devotees.

Eu Yan Sang Medical Shop

Across the same street at No. 269 is **Eu Yan Sang**, a traditional Chinese medicine shop with over 70 branches in the region (tel: 6225-3211; www.eu yansang.com). The original shop was founded in Malaysia over a century ago by Eu Kong, a Chinese immigrant who used traditional Chinese medicine, instead of opium, to alleviate the pains tin miners suffered from. Today, you can walk into its Chinatown store and consult a *sinseh*, or Chinese doctor, who will prescribe the correct herbs for your ailment. But even if you are in the pink of health, the bottled bird's

TIP

Eu Yan Sang Medical Centre shop also contains the intriguing Bird's Nest Gallery, which will tell you all you ever wanted to know about this key Chinese ingredient – from how difficult it is to harvest to good it is at boosting the immune system and keeping you looking youthful.

BELOW: Sri Mariamman Temple detail.

Map labels:
Art Science Museum 29
Skating Rink
Theatres
Marina Bay (freshwater reservoir)
Helix Bridge
Events Plaza
Sands Casino
28
BAYFRONT (U/C)
30
MARINA BAY SANDS
Sands Expo and Convention Centre
Bayfront Avenue
Marina Bay Sands Hotel and SkyPark
Marina Bay Sands Promenade
★ Mist Walk
Marina Bay City Gallery
...ulevard
East Coast Pkwy
GARDENS BY THE BAY
0   200 m
0   200 yds

nest, herbal candies and ginseng wines make interesting souvenirs.

Jamae Mosque

Adjacent to the Sri Mariamman Temple across on Pagoda Street is the lovely **Jamae Mosque** , with its distinctive pagoda-like minarets rarely seen in Muslim mosque architecture (tel: 6221-4165; daily 9.30am–6pm). Its unique design was perhaps a gesture of deference to the predominantly Chinese neighbourhood. The mosque was constructed in 1826 by Muslim Chulia immigrants who came from South India's Coromandel Coast.

Chinatown Heritage Centre

Address: 48 Pagoda Street;
www.chinatownheritagecentre.sg
Tel: 6325-2878
Opening Hrs: daily 9am–8pm
Entrance Fee: charge
Transport: Chinatown MRT

Chinatown, like most old areas in Singapore, is in danger of losing its character. Temple Street's old tradesmen for instance – the pavement barber, idol-carver and calligrapher

ABOVE: Chinese opera costumes are on display at the Chinese Opera Teahouse. **BELOW:** display at the Chinatown Heritage Centre.

– have all gone, their places taken up by sometimes nondescript restaurants, pubs and offices.

For this reason the **Chinatown Heritage Centre** ❸ was introduced to give Chinatown a sense of history. Occupying three restored shophouses on Pagoda Street, the museum showcases the lifestyles, traditions and rituals of the people who lived and worked there. The dark and cramped living quarters of early Chinatown are realistically recreated, and one of the centre's highlights is the home of a Chinatown tailor and his family. Using authentic furniture, utensils and other paraphernalia, the living conditions of the Chinatown of yesteryear are brought to life.

In addition, there are 11 exhibition galleries, which take visitors through a journey to discover the evolution of Chinatown. There are depictions of Chinese clan associations and gambling dens, festivals, food and culture, as well as multimedia displays of famous Chinatown personalities.

Trengganu Street

The heart of Chinatown is an area off South Bridge Road that embraces

Pagoda, Temple, Trengganu and Sago streets. Linking Pagoda Street is atmospheric **Trengganu Street**, which, not so long ago, was lined with street stalls selling live snakes, turtles and other exotic wildlife destined for the dinner table. The only exotica to be found these days are arts and crafts from Asia and wild herbs from China. Trengganu Street is in fact Chinatown's main hub because it's the neighbourhood's only full cross street.

Many of the elegantly restored shophouses in the area now play host to a colourful assortment of restaurants, cafés and teahouses as well as Chinese "medical halls", antiques and handicrafts stores.

Chinatown Night Market

In the evenings, Pagoda, Trengganu and Sago *(see page 129)* streets are closed to traffic and transformed into the lively **Chinatown Night Market** (Sun–Thur 5–11pm, Fri–Sat 5pm–1am). With a host of stalls selling traditional Chinese goods like calligraphy, paper fans and lanterns as well as contemporary items like funky jewellery, bags and shawls, the market deserves a leisurely trawl.

Lai Chun Yuen

At the corner of Trengganu Street and Smith Street is a striking building with gleaming wooden floors and carved banisters – look up at the balcony running along its upper level. The building was formerly called **Lai Chun Yuen** ❹, a Cantonese opera house that packed in fans in its heyday. Famous opera stars performed here in the 1920s. If there is a faint similarity between the facade of the theatre and that of the Raffles Hotel, it's because both were designed by R.A.J. Bidwell. The ground level of the building is occupied by Chinese art and handicrafts shops. There are plans to convert the building into a boutique hotel.

Along Smith Street

Smith Street is home to several arts associations. Often, in the afternoons, you can follow the sound of a Chinese fiddle, wander up a narrow staircase and find old folks honing their art. They are always delighted to play to an appreciative audience – but it's polite to ask first. The **Chinese Opera Teahouse** (tel: 6323-4862; www.ctcopera.com.sg) on Smith Street offers performances every Friday and Saturday from 7pm to 9pm. Pay S$35 and you will get to enjoy a set Chinese dinner, Chinese tea and dessert.

This is also a chance to relieve the hustle and bustle of 1960s street hawking – with 21st-century sanitation standards – when the street is closed to traffic in the evenings and at weekends. A mix of hawker stalls ply a range of local culinary staples at **Chinatown Food Street** ❺ (Mon–Thur, Sun and public holidays 5–11pm, Fri–Sat 5pm–1am). Tuck into *satay*, fishball noodles and *poh piah* (local-style spring rolls).

ABOVE: shoppers on Smith Street.

EAT

Amid the traditional shophouses in Chinatown's bustling night market is a unique, not-to-be-missed stall called Erich's Wuerstelstand (Kiosk 2 & 3, corner Trengganu and Sago streets; tel: 9627-4882). Run by an Austrian chef who has lived in Asia for about two decades, the stall serves up a range of savoury grilled sausages, including traditional bratwurst, from 3pm until late.

Along Smith Street, the higher floors of **Chinatown Complex** ❻ have a spectrum of stalls offering a tempting array of local food. The basement is also worth exploring for the unusual ingredients on sale – from live fish and poultry to bean curd, fresh fruit, flowers and vegetables. The best time to visit this "wet" market is in the morning. Be privy to the constant banter between housewives and fishmongers, although the faint-hearted may just find the sight of skinned frogs a tad too grisly. On weekend afternoons, old folks spread their treasures – old stamps, dusty crockery, bronze Buddhist statues – on blankets. If something catches your fancy, remember to bargain.

Eu Tong Sen Street

At the end of Smith Street, the pedestrian bridge (also known as Garden Bridge) across New Bridge Road and Eu Tong Sen Street leads to **People's Park Complex**, a local favourite for its mix of shops, offices and cinemas. If looking for Chinese silk and textiles, be sure to visit this place. Next door is **The Majestic** ❼. Once known as Tin Yin Dance Stage, a venue for Cantonese opera, this former Art Deco-style cinema hall was recently restored and converted into another sterile shopping mall. The facade has been kept intact, but the interior is almost unrecognisable in its new reincarnation – filled with mostly ho-hum clothing shops and beauty salons.

The 45-year-old **Yue Hwa Emporium** ❽ (tel: 6538-4222; www.yue hwa.com.sg) is just next door, a good one-stop shop for all things Chinese, from silk products, cheongsams and handicrafts to tea and health tonics. The emporium occupies the 1900 building of the former Great Southern Hotel, once considered the Grand Old Lady of Chinatown.

Across the street is **People's Park Centre** with a motley assortment of shops, while opposite, at the corner of New Bridge Road and Upper Cross Street, is **Chinatown Point**; the revamped mall is a good place to shop for Chinese speciality food and trinkets. There are also goldsmith jewellers and travel agencies here.

ABOVE: Yue Hwa Emporium is a treasure trove of Chinese arts and crafts. **BELOW AND BELOW RIGHT:** Buddha Tooth Relic Temple.

Sago Street

Back at the heart of Chinatown proper, Trengganu Street meanders left into **Sago Street**, named after the numerous *sago* (a pearl-like starch) factories that used to be here. These days you are more likely to find restored shophouses housing Chinese bakeries, restaurants and herbal shops. **Fong Moon Kee** at No. 16A (tel: 6223-0940) sells traditional healing oils to help common ailments and citronella oil, made from lemongrass, that repels mosquitoes when rubbed on the skin. Traditional, too, are the delicious Chinese pastries at **Leung Sang Hong Kong Pastries** at No. 18 (tel: 6221-1344).

Buddha Tooth Relic Temple and Museum

Address: 288 South Bridge Road; www.btrts.org.sg
Tel: 6220-0220
Opening Hrs: daily 7am–7pm
Entrance Fee: free
Transport: Chinatown MRT

Right in between Sago Street and Sago Lane is a new structure, the **Buddha Tooth Relic Temple and Museum** ❾. Inspired by the Tang dynasty, the temple has sacred objects such as an intricately carved 5-metre (16ft) wooden image of the Maitreya Buddha (or Future Buddha). Religious artworks, Buddhist texts and other cultural artefacts can be found on the upper floors.

The temple's centrepiece is one dogged by much controversy – a sacred tooth belonging to the Buddha. Kept on the fourth floor in a golden stupa and only taken out for viewing on Vesak Day and Chinese New Year, the tooth's authenticity has been questioned by several Buddhist scholars. Curtains obscuring the stupa from view are unveiled twice a day (9am and 3pm). On the roof, you can admire the blooms of the *Dendrobium Buddha Tooth*, an orchid hybrid specially named after the temple's most sacred relic.

Opposite is **Sago Lane** ❿, once known as the "Street of the Dead" as it was here that Chinese families brought their aged to die. Beds were rented out in macabre deathhouses for the elderly to wait out their last days. The lane also had

BELOW: you can learn about Chinese tea at Neil Road's Tea Chapter. Window detail from a Keong Saik Road shophouse.

Chinese Teahouses

Savour fragrant tea while you learn about the finer points of the complicated art of Chinese tea-brewing in the traditional settings of teahouses in Chinatown and Tanjong Pagar. **Tea Chapter** at 9/11 Neil Road offers a wide range – more than 50 varieties – that may be savoured in tiny teacups (daily 11am–11pm; tel: 6226-3026; www.tea-chapter.com.sg). It also offers tea appreciation workshops. **Yixing Xuan Teahouse** at 30/32 Tanjong Pagar Road pampers its regulars by storing their tea leaves in containers with the customers' names written on the sides (Mon–Sat 10am–9pm, Sun and public holidays 10am–7pm; tel: 6224-6961; www.yixingxuan-teahouse.com).

ABOVE: Baba House.

shops selling coffins, joss sticks and miniature houses and cars made of paper, which were routinely burned for the dead to serve them in their afterlife. In the old days the street resounded to a constant cacophony of sounds from funeral bands and chanting from priests performing the last rites. The death-houses of Sago Lane are long gone, replaced by an empty field that is now used for religious festivals and Chinese opera performances.

Tanjong Pagar district

From Sago Street (or Lane), turn right and walk to the corner of Tanjong Pagar and Neil roads, where the **Jinrikisha Station ⓫** stands. Rickshaw coolies once parked their two-wheeled vehicles here. The station, built in 1903 in the classical style, is crowned by a dome. The first *jinriks* (rickshaws) arrived in Singapore in the 1880s from Shanghai. They were the main means of transport in Singapore in the early 1900s before they were replaced by the three-wheeled

trishaws in the 1940s. The rickshaw coolies found it convenient to live around the station, renting bed space in tiny Chinatown cubicles. Sometimes the same bed space was rented out to two coolies working different shifts.

Once a decrepit part of town, the **Tanjong Pagar** district has been restored into a haven for all kinds of businesses, as well as cosy restaurants and pubs. Recently, a number of discreet gay and lesbian clubs and saunas have also moved in here.

The area has a long and interesting history. Once a Malay fishing village known as Tanjong Pagar (Cape of Stakes), legend has it that this part of the coast was afflicted by schools of sharp-toothed garfish, which attacked people on shore. As a result, a barricade of plantain stems was erected along the coast to trap the fish. In the 1830s, the land around Tanjong Pagar was turned into a nutmeg plantation. The area became a thriving commercial hub, but by the 1960s the neighbourhood fell into disrepair and would have met the wrecker's ball if the government had not started its big conservation drive. Tanjong Pagar soon became an archetype and a testing ground for how the remainder of historic Singapore would be restored.

The 190 shophouses were renovated for "adaptive reuse", in architectural speak, as restaurants, shops and offices. The first units were put up for tender in 1987 and almost overnight Tanjong Pagar became a drawcard for creative people in search of office and restaurant space. The area takes on a magical glow at night when the lights come on and people unwind in the pubs and restaurants lining Tanjong Pagar, Craig, Neil and Duxton roads. The two-storey structures – narrow yet deep – lend themselves perfectly to romantic dining with their ornate plaster facades and wooden window shutters, pastel hues, teak floors,

wooden stairways, high-beamed ceilings and red-tiled roofs.

Keong Saik Road

Further down along Neil Road past Kreta Ayer Road is the once notorious **Keong Saik Road** ⑫, a red-light district that has now been gentrified. Many of its splendid examples of shophouses in the Chinese Baroque architectural style *(see pages 176–7)* have been restored and converted into boutique hotels such as Chinatown Hotel in the adjoining Teck Lim Road and the the über-cool **Hotel 1929** (www.hotel1929.com), which is partly responsible for making this once seedy strip hip. Almost parallel with Keong Saik Road is Bukit Pasoh Road, whose old buildings have been nicely spruced up thanks to trendy boutique hotel New Majestic, by the same folks behind Hotel 1929, and several top restaurants such as Absinthe, Oso and Andre.

Baba House

Address: 157 Neil Road; www.nus.edu.sg/museum

Tel: 6227-5731
Opening Hrs: by appointment only
Entrance Fee: free

Located near the Singapore General Hospital is **Baba House** ⑬. This little gem of a museum offers visitors the rare opportunity to step back in time and experience the domestic lifestyle of a Peranakan family living in the year 1928. Nestled among a cluster of conserved terrace houses, the three-storey dwelling has unique architectural features and intricate ornamentation that bear the trademark Peranakan style. On the third floor is a gallery for temporary exhibitions. Dedicated to the research and study of the Peranakans *(see page 22)*, the house was donated by Agnes Tan, the daughter of well-known Baba public figure Tun Tan Cheng Lock.

Singapore City Gallery

Address: 45 Maxwell Road, URA Centre; www.ura.gov.sg/gallery
Tel: 6321-8321
Opening Hrs: Mon–Sat 9am–5pm

ABOVE: streetside calligrapher at work – a rare Chinatown sight.
BELOW: window detail from a Keong Saik Road shophouse.

BELOW: ornate painted doors mark the entrance to Fuk Tak Chi Museum at Far East Square.

Entrance Fee: free
Transport: Tanjong Pagar or Chinatown MRT

Returning to the Jinrikisha Station, Tanjong Pagar Road forks right into Maxwell Road. At the corner with Kadayanallur Street is **Maxwell Food Centre**, one of Singapore's oldest hawker centres. Snaking queues are a regular sight at lunchtime, and at night, when many clubbers head over for supper after a night out. Popular items to try here are the *rojak* (a type of mixed salad), fish noodles and chicken porridge.

Across Kadayanallur Street is the Urban Redevelopment Authority's **Singapore City Gallery** at the **URA Centre**, where the key attraction is a massive and detailed scale model of central Singapore. Spread over two storeys are permanent exhibits, interactive displays and touch-screen terminals, as well as video and audiovisual programmes that offer an insight into the workings of this efficient city. The displays succinctly tell how Singapore grew from a fishing village into a thriving modern metropolis. You can also read about URA's ambitious Concept Plan, a blueprint for the physical development of the city in the 21st century.

red dot design museum

Address: www.red-dot.sg
Tel: 6327-8027
Opening Hrs: Mon, Tue and Fri 11am–6pm, Sat–Sun and public holidays 11am–8pm
Entrance Fee: charge
Transport: Tanjong Pagar MRT

Further along Maxwell Road on the right is **red dot design museum** ⓯. Located in the old Traffic Police building, this is the second red dot design museum in the world (the first is in Germany) and is run by the German body that presents the prestigious red dot design awards. Its stark interior is a fitting background for the interactive installations and exhibits of some very slick product designs from around the world. MAAD (Market of Artists and Designers), a unique flea market featuring original works by designers, is held at this venue the first weekend of every month.

Chinatown Spas

Chinatown has several boutique spas which are great for a few hours of pampering. Whether you want a traditional Chinese massage or a relaxing treatment, you'll find it here. **Kenko** (199 South Bridge Road; tel: 6223-0303) offers Chinese-style reflexology. **Afond Spa** (293/293A South Bridge Road; tel: 6836-0676; www.afondspa.com), in a three-storey old shophouse, offers interesting treatments such as chocolate body wrap or Javanese herbal wrap. At 83A Club Street, **Qi Mantra** (tel: 6221-5691; www.qimantra.com) dispenses traditional Chinese acupuncture massage. **Spa Haven** (45/46 Amoy Street; tel: 6221-2203; www.spahaven.com.sg) is best known for its beauty treatments.

Club and Amoy streets

Kadayanallur Street leads uphill into Ann Siang Road, which joins up with **Club Street**. This street and the one down the hillside, **Amoy Street**, were once the strongholds of the Hokkien community whose members lodged here once they got off the boat from China. These streets used to hum with the activities of various *kongsi* (clan associations), which catered to the needs of immigrants who came from the same village in China, shared the same surnames, dialects and often occupations.

Camaraderie still thrives on Club Street, but present-day clans are more likely to be trendy professionals from nearby advertising and design firms who convene in the restaurants and bars lining the street.

A dead-end road on the right of Club Street leads to the members-only **Chinese Weekly Entertainment Club ⑯**, after which the street took its name. This Victorian-style mansion was the social club for prominent members of the Chinese community, who met here for regular card games. Founded by a wealthy Peranakan in 1891, a number of its

members later went on to establish some of Singapore's leading banks.

Back on Ann Siang Road, go past Batey House and arrive at a dead-end occupied by the **Ann Siang Hill Park**. A staircase leads downhill to Amoy Street and the **Sin Chor Kung Temple ⑰** (daily 7.30am–5.30pm). Built in 1869 and dedicated to the Tua Pek Kong deity, the temple is popular with the Teochews. Despite its diminutive size, the temple is always thronged with people and filled with smoke from the joss sticks burned by worshippers. Just next door is the Amoy Street Food Centre, another popular place for lunch with nearby office workers.

Telok Ayer Chinese Methodist Church

Parallel to Amoy Street is **Telok Ayer Street**, where the red and white **Telok Ayer Chinese Methodist Church ⑱** stands diagonally opposite the Amoy Street Food Centre (tel: 6324-4001; www.tacmc.org.sg; Mon–Fri 9am–5pm, Sat 9am–1pm). Completed in 1925, its unusual architecture is a blend of East and West – a flat-roofed Chinese pavilion and a ground floor graced

ABOVE: red dot design museum. **BELOW:** the entrance of Thian Hock Keng Temple.

with European-style columns – and a testament to the British Protestant missionary effort in Singapore. The national monument was a refugee shelter during World War II.

Al Abrar Mosque

Further north on Telok Ayer Street, past McCallum Street, is the brown and white **Al Abrar Mosque** N. It was constructed between 1850 and 1855 by the Muslim Chulia community from South India (tel: 6220-6306; daily 5–7am, 11.30am–9pm). The earlier mosque that used to stand here in the 1830s was a mere thatched structure known as Kuchu Palli (or hut mosque).

Thian Hock Keng Temple

Telok Ayer Street, meaning "Water Bay" in the Malay language, once bordered Singapore's original shoreline. Today the reclaimed land is blocked from the sea by a wall of gleaming skyscrapers. It was here that seafarers and immigrants from the Fukien Province set up a joss house in the 1820s in gratitude for their safe arrival after their long voyage from China. By 1842 the joss house had become

ABOVE: the courtyard of Wak Hai Cheng Temple is hung with numerous burning spirals of incense. **BELOW:** Far East Square has gates dedicated to each of the five elements.

the **Thian Hock Keng Temple** N or Temple of Heavenly Happiness (tel: 6423-4616; daily 7.30am–5.30pm). The temple is dedicated to Ma Cho Po, Goddess of the Sea, who could reputedly calm rough waters and rescue those in danger of drowning.

The temple is visually extravagant, built with materials imported from China and Europe but without a single nail. Dragons, venerated for protection on sea voyages, leap along the roof and curl around solid granite pillars. Incense wafts from great brass urns in front of altars laden with fruit offerings. During renovations in 1999, a silk scroll bearing the handwriting of Qing Emperor Guang Xu (1871–1908) was found in the temple. The scroll, inscribed with four large Chinese characters saying *bo jing nan ming* ("the wave is calm in the South Seas") was a gift from the emperor to the Thian Hock Keng Temple in 1906 to mark the completion of its first major restoration. It is considered a rare piece of calligraphy by the emperor, who gave similar pieces to just two other temples in the region – the Wak Hai Cheng Temple on Phillip Street (*see*

page 136) and a temple on Malaysia's Penang island.

Nagore Durgha Shrine

Further down, past **Telok Ayer Green** on the same street is the **Nagore Durgha Shrine ㉑**, also called Masjid Chulia, an architectural companion to Jamae Mosque on South Bridge Road. The shrine, built in 1818, is an interesting marriage of the classical style, typified by moulded arches, with Indian-Muslim motifs such as the perforated grilles at roof level. The building also incorporates Western architectural elements like Doric columns and Palladian doors. It reopened in 2008 as an Indian-Muslim heritage centre.

Far East Square

North along Telok Ayer Street, past Cross Street on the left, is **Ying Fo Fui Kun** at No. 98, the first Hakka Clan Association founded in 1822 by the Hakka people from China.

Further down at No. 76 is **Fuk Tak Chi Museum ㉒**, previously the Fuk Tak Chi Temple, dedicated to Tua Pek Kong the Earth God (tel: 6532-7868; daily 10am–10pm; free). Dating from 1824, it is Singapore's oldest temple, set up by the Hakkas and Cantonese. The museum has a collection of 200 artefacts, including a Chinese gold belt, abacus board and even a rental expiry notice from early Chinatown residents.

Far East Square ㉓, opposite China Square, is a conservation area bounded by Cross Street, Telok Ayer Street and China Street. The square blends the new with the old to provide a vast commercial space taken up by offices, restaurants, bars and shops. The area encompasses the four kinds of shophouse styles prevalent in Chinatown (Early, First Transitional, Late and Second Transitional) from the 1840s to the 1960s *(see pages 176–7)*. Look out for the five gates that mark the main entrances into Far East Square, each one representing one of the five elements that make up the Chinese universe: metal, wood, water, fire and earth. Its buildings of historical significance, apart from the Fu Tak Chi Museum, include the **Chui Eng Free School**, one of Singapore's first Chinese schools, established in 1854 to give the poor a chance to be educated. The school closed in 1954.

TIP

Chinatown is located close to the financial district, which means that office staff from the surrounding office towers descend on food centres in droves at lunchtime. For a leisurely meal, avoid the peak hours of noon–1.30pm.

BELOW: Wak Hai Cheng Temple.

Pekin Street – now closed to traffic – is noted for its remittance houses, where the early immigrants sent money back to their families in China. Look out for the plaster relief signs on the columns of No. 42. It once belonged to signmaker Seng Huat, who made similar signs for his clients in Chinatown to advertise their businesses.

Wak Hai Cheng Temple

Opposite **Capital Square**, a modern office block with a sheet of water cascading off a wall on its side, is the dark and incense-filled **Wak Hai Cheng Temple ㉔** (tel: 6533-8537; daily 6am–6pm). Tucked away at the corner of Church and Phillip streets, it huddles beneath the shadow of the towering I.M. Pei-designed **OCBC Centre**.

The temple was built in the 1830s by the local Teochew community for the protection of traders travelling between Singapore and China. The temple, which combines the worship of Buddhism and Taoism, has an ornately decorated roof that depicts scenes from Chinese village

Those shapes that look like wire or Christmas trees hanging up in the courtyard of Wak Hai Cheng Temple are actually incense spirals. You can find them all over Chinatown, filling the air with their characteristic, slightly acrid smell. The large ones can take up to 10 days to burn.

life, including an opera stage and houses. In the courtyard is a large terracotta furnace where paper money is burned to assist the deceased in their journey to the netherworld.

CENTRAL BUSINESS DISTRICT

The core of "Singapore Inc" runs along the waterfront from the Singapore River to Keppel Road and the massive Tanjong Pagar Container Terminal. The commercial area centres on **Raffles Place**, which has been transformed into an open-air plaza with the busy Raffles Place MRT interchange station below.

The two main thoroughfares are Shenton Way and Robinson Road, but Cecil Street and Battery Road also brim with skyscrapers. The tallest buildings are clustered around the Raffles Place area, which adjoins the neighbouring **Civic District** *(see page 97)*: **OUB Centre, UOB Plaza** – both designed by Japanese architectural maestro Kenzo Tange – and **Republic Plaza**, by the famous Japanese architect Kisho Kurokawa, all reach a height of 280 metres (919ft) – the maximum allowed by local aviation rules. The atrium outside UOB Plaza, with its large bronze statue of Salvador Dalí's *Homage to Newton*, is always filled with smartly dressed executives with ears permanently plugged to their mobile phones. The buzz, and the seething mass of humanity, especially at lunchtime, is quite incredible. Art-lovers can look out for other sculptures dotted around the area. A highlight on the riverbank is the voluptuous bronze *Bird* by Colombian artist Fernando Botero, which was inspired by the dove, the universal symbol of peace.

Boat Quay

On one side of UOB Plaza is the Singapore River, with **Boat Quay ㉕** sitting immediately left of the building. For a century until the late 1960s, Boat Quay reverberated to the clamour of coolies loading and unloading sacks of rice, coal and other cargo between lighter-boats huddled at the bottom of the steps and shophouses connected precariously by narrow gangplanks. When the fervour of urban renewal gripped Singapore in the 1970s, this crammed south side of the river was deemed unsightly.

The lighter-boats were banned from the river, flotsam and jetsam resulting from the loading activities were cleared from the waters, and the shophouses of Boat Quay were refurbished and converted into a Latin Quarter of sorts with bars and restaurants. Today, Boat Quay echoes to the clink of wine glasses at dusk, when executives descend from surrounding office towers to unwind at drinking holes like Penny Black, Molly Malone's and Harry's Bar, with their open-air terraces overlooking the river. Although recent competition from similar waterfront areas has taken its toll on this entertainment district, dining options are still plentiful – local and international cuisines can be found all along this riverfront strip.

Lau Pa Sat

In the CBD's maze of steel and glass, the distinctive **Lau Pa Sat Festival Market ㉖** (whose Hokkien name translates into "old market") stands out (daily 24 hours). Bounded by Shenton Way, Robinson Road, Cross Street and Boon Tat Street, this Victorian octagonal structure was built from cast iron in Glasgow and shipped in 1894 to Singapore, where it was reassembled on the waterfront. The national monument, once a produce market, was restored in the 1980s, and is now filled with some 100 food stalls selling a variety of hawker fare, from fried noodles and rice to Indian-Muslim specialities. This is another place that gets very crowded during lunchtime with office workers from the CBD. In the evenings, **Boon Tat Street** on one side is closed to traffic and transformed into an al-fresco dining area filled with hawkers grilling *satay*.

MARINA BAY

The reclaimed Marina Bay area bordering the waterfront is Singapore's exciting new downtown. When

ABOVE: cruise boat in front of Boat Quay.
BELOW: casino floor at Marina Bay Sands.

completed, it will be a focal point on the island, with fabulous water views and landscaped parklands. Planned to be ready in phases, it will be anchored by an extension of the CBD called **Marina Bay Financial Centre ㉗**. This upcoming development will include three office towers, two residential towers, Marina Bay Link Mall and new food and drink outlets such as LeVeL 33, a multi-concept restaurant, lounge and microbrewery perched on the 33rd floor.

Marina Bay Sands

Complementing the Financial Centre is the massive S$5 billion "integrated resort" **Marina Bay Sands ㉘** – the most expensive ever built by the American casino-resort giant Las Vegas Sands. Since its opening in 2010, Marina Bay Sands has been the talk of the town and continues its development in different stages. The casino has four levels of gaming

ABOVE: Helix Bridge crosses from Marina Bay Sands to the Marina Bay Promenade.

and 500 tables. There are six varieties of games on offer: baccarat, roulette, sic-bo, Singapore stud poker, non-commission baccarat and money wheel.

Besides a casino, this mega leisure, entertainment and hospitality complex includes a luxury hotel, convention facilities, and restaurants helmed by celebrity chefs from America, Australia, France, Spain and Japan. Gourmands can look out for big names like Wolfgang Puck, Daniel Boulud, Tetsuya Wakuda, Guy Savoy, Santi Santamaria and Hide Yamamoto. The resort also has two world-class 2,000-seat theatres, where the world famous Broadway musical *The Lion King* and renowned shows like *Riverdance* will be showcased.

It's not just about entertainment here – the resort also has an **Art Science Museum ㉙**. The enormous lotus-shaped building features galleries exhibiting art, science, media,

SHOPPING

Chinatown is a place to shop for souvenirs, arts and crafts and all kinds of products from China. Head to Club Street and Ann Siang Road for unique labels and independent boutiques. Over in the Marina Bay area you can find a host of well-known luxury brands.

Art galleries

Chinatown Point
133 New Bridge Road. Tel: 6877-8359. p272, C2
There are several antique shops and art galleries located in this shopping centre. When you are done, enjoy an Indian

vegetarian meal at Annalakshmi.

Clothing

Style: Nordic
39 Ann Siang Road. Tel: 6423-9114. www.style nordic.com p272, C2/3
Come here for trendy Scandinavian clothing and furniture. Exclusive brands include Nudie Jeans, Pour, Rodebjer and Designhouse Stockholm.

Food

Leng Sang Hong Kong Pastries
18 Sago Street. Tel: 6221-1344. p272, B2

A traditional Chinese pastry shop selling old-school walnut biscuits and some of the best egg-custard tarts in Chinatown.

Mall

Marina Bay Shoppes
www.marinabaysands.com p273, E2
This is one of the latest places to window-shop or splurge at swanky boutiques such as Hermès, Hugo Boss, Louis Vuitton and Max Mara. Most of these brands are also available on Orchard Road, but if you are staying in the area, this is a convenient place to shop.

Music and books

Asylum
03-01, 69 Circular Road. Tel: 6324-2289. www.the asylum.com.sg p273, C1
This store stocks experimental music, books on culture and design, limited-edition fashion and contemporary art.

Souvenirs

Yue Hwa Emporium
70 Eu Tong Sen Street. Tel: 6538-9233. www.yue hwa.com.sg p272, B2
This traditional emporium has everything imaginable from China, including silks and cheongsams.

technology, design and architecture. The galleries cover both permanent and touring exhibitions. Architecturally, this structure has an inventive roof that allows rainwater to cascade through the central atrium of the building in a beautiful waterfall.

There are many wonders of engineering in this new area. The 200-metre (650ft) high Sands Sky-Park, a unique structure designed by architect Moshe Safdie, crowns the three Marina Bay Sands hotel towers. Perched on top of these soaring towers, the sweeping 1.2-hectare (3-acre) tropical park with landscaped gardens stretches further than the Eiffel tower would if laid flat, and the space is large enough to fit three football fields. This incredible cantilever can hold hundreds of people and is a one-of-a-kind observation deck with amazing views. There is also an infinity pool where people can do laps up in the sky. There will be new eating and drinking concepts too, including the renowned hotspot Ku De Ta restaurant and Sky Bar as well as The Sky on 57 restaurant, helmed by the Singaporean chef Justin Quek.

Helix Bridge

Another engineering masterpiece is the pedestrian **Helix Bridge** ⓾, the world's first double-helix curved bridge, which was opened in 2010. It crosses from Marina Bay Sands to the other side of the waterfront and the cluster of five-star hotels there.

The elegant structure is made of stainless-steel tubes forming a major and minor helix that spiral around each other. At night, the bridge comes "alive" when the lighting is programmed to match different festivities. It is located just next to Singapore's first art park, the Youth Olympic Park, and near the floating platform where the opening and closing of the inaugural Youth Olympic Games took place in August 2010. There are five viewing platforms along the path to give pedestrians superb vistas of both bays and the city skyline. The nearest MRT station to the bridge is Promenade, and there is also a new vehicular bridge, the Bayfront Bridge, next to it. The double-helix bridge together with Marina Bay Promenade forms a 3.5km (2-mile) pedestrian loop around the entire bay. ❑

BELOW: Marina Bay Sands.

Safer Gambling

In an attempt to control gambling problems, the government has introduced a casino entry levy. Singapore citizens or permanent residents must have a valid entry levy to enter the casino, and it expires after 24 hours. If they fail to pay up or overstay, they will be fined. Foreigners must show their passports and enter and exit via the "Foreigners" lane. Meanwhile, to assist with any potential gambling problems, the National Council for Problem Gambling (NCPG) introduced a website and 24-hour hotline for those people who "experience difficulty in controlling their gambling or have a gambling addiction, which could lead to serious personal, financial and family issues".

BEST RESTAURANTS, BARS AND CAFÉS

Restaurants

Australian

Broth
21 Duxton Hill. Tel: 6323-3353. www.broth.com.sg
Open: Mon–Fri L & D, Sat D.
$$$ ㉚ p272, B3
Tucked at the end of a cobblestoned path between a row of shop-houses, it feels like you're a world away from everything else. Chef-owner Steven Hansen makes scrumptious salads and lamb loin in mint sauce.

Moomba
52 Circular Rd. Tel: 6438-0141. www.themoomba.com
Open: Mon–Fri L & D, Sat D.
$$$** (set lunch) **$$$$ (à la carte) ㉛ p273, D1
The city's first Australian restaurant is still among

the best. Expect good service, an extensive collection of boutique Australian wines and excellent contemporary Australian cuisine. Over 90 percent of the produce it uses is imported from Australia.

Chinese

Beng Hiang
112 Amoy St. Tel: 6221-6695. Open: daily L & D.
$$$ ㉜ p273, C2
Established more than 30 years ago, this place is jam-packed with regulars every night. This is one of the few restaurants in town which serves authentic Hokkien dishes. The *kong bak* – slabs of fatty pork steeped in thick soy sauce and served with soft and fluffy

mantou buns – is a top-seller.

Majestic Restaurant
1/F, New Majestic Hotel, 31–37 Bukit Pasoh Rd. Tel: 6511-4718. Open: daily L & D. **$$$$** (à la carte) ㉝ p272, B3
The stylish New Majestic Hotel's restaurant pairs modern Cantonese cuisine with an idiosyncratic decor. Savour elegant fare such as grilled rack of lamb in Chinese honey sauce and braised lobster in a creamy milk & lime sauce, while you contemplate the view of swimmers in the pool above through portholes in the ceiling.

Qun Zhong Eating House
21 Neil Rd. Tel: 6221-3060.
Open: Thur–Tue L & D. **$**
㉞ p272, B3
A queue forms outside the restaurant even before mealtimes. Disregard the surly staff and drab decor, and order the reasonably priced Beijing fare – simple yet satisfying. Do what the rest do, and go for the *xiao long bao* (steamed pork dumplings), noodles and red bean pancake.

Silk Road
2/F, Amara Hotel, 165 Tanjong Pagar Rd. Tel: 6227-3848. www.silkroadrestaurants.com Open: daily L & D. **$$** (set lunch) **$$$$** (à la carte) ㉟ p272, B4

Everything about Silk Road is refined, be it the warm, contemporary decor, the delicious Chinese provincial cuisine – Beijing, Liaoning, Shanxi and Sichuan – prepared by the bevy of chefs, or the tea master who pours the aromatic Eight Treasure Tea from a copper kettle with a metre-long spout.

Spring Court
52–56 Upper Cross St. Tel: 6449-5030. www.springcourt.com.sg Open: daily L & D.
$$$ ㊱ p272, C2
This successful family-run restaurant has been in operation since 1929. Singapore-style Cantonese cuisine is served in a four-storey heritage building. Crowd-pleasing classics include the crisp roast chicken and golden cereal prawns. *Dim sum* is available for lunch.

Swee Kee Fishhead Noodle House
96 Amoy St. Tel: 6224-9920. www.ka-soh.com.sg
Open: daily L & D. **$$** ㊲
p273, C2
Value-for-money, simple home-cooked Cantonese food is dished out at this well-known restaurant, whose menu apparently hasn't changed since the 1940s. Authentic fishhead soup with rice noodles, painstakingly cooked until thick and creamy, is the mainstay. Other house specialities include the prawn paste

LEFT: Australian dining at Moomba.

chicken deep-fried until crispy.

European

Absinthe

48 Bukit Pasoh Rd. Tel: 6222-9068. www.absinthe.sg Open: Mon–Fri L & D, Sat D. **$$$$** ⑱ p272, B3

Run by a couple of highly experienced French personalities – chef François Mermilliod and general manager Philippe Pau – this restaurant presents impressive modern French meals with top-notch service. The restaurant is set in an old conservation building in Chinatown.

Andre

41 Bukit Pasoh Rd. Tel: 6534-8880. www.restaurant andre.com Open: Tue–Fri noon–2pm, 7–11pm, Sat–Sun 7–11pm. **$$$$** ⑲ p272, B3

The Bukit Pasoh enclave's hip quotient was raised when media darling chef Andre Chiang opened his highly anticipated restaurant here. Taiwanese-born Chiang, formerly of Swissotel's Jaan par Andre, has trained with some of the best French chefs, including Pierre Gagnaire, so you can expect only the finest southern French nouvelle cuisine menu injected with heaps of inventiveness.

Prices for a three-course dinner per person without drinks and taxes:
$ = under S$20
$$ = S$20–30
$$$ = S$30–50
$$$$ = over S$50

Ember

Hotel 1929, 50 Keong Saik Rd. Tel: 6347-1928. www.hotel1929.com Open: Mon–Fri L & D, Sat D. **$$$** (set lunch) **$$$$** (à la carte) ⑳ p272, B3

Chef-owner Sebastien Ng's Modern European cuisine is delightfully robust yet refined, and sometimes comes with wonderful Asian accents. Everything is good really, but you should definitely try the pan-seared foie gras and slow-roasted lamb loin.

Guy Savoy

Marina Bay Sands, 10 Bayfront Avenue, Level 2 Casino. Tel: 6688-8513. www.marinabaysands.com Open: daily 6–10.30pm. **$$$$** ㊶ p272, E2

A dining experience at Guy Savoy promises impeccable service, superb wines, great views and classy French cuisine. Standouts include the artichoke and black truffle soup and pigeon served two ways. At the end of the meal, the dessert trolley filled with sweet treats is a temptation too far for the sweet-toothed.

Magma

2 Bukit Pasoh Rd. Tel: 6221-0634. www.magmatc.com Open: Mon–Thur noon–11pm, Fri noon–midnight, Sat 11am–midnight, Sun 11am–11pm. **$$$** ㊷ p272, B3

For homey and authentic German fare, Magma is

RIGHT: desserts at Guy Savoy.

the place to head. The mammoth Bavarian pork knuckle with crackling skin is served with a generous portion of pea mash and sauerkraut. Delicious too are the grilled bratwurst and *flammkuchen* (the German version of pancakes). Check out, too, the huge range of German wines and beers.

The Screening Room

12 Ann Siang Rd. Tel: 6221-1694. www.screeningroom.com.sg Open: Mon–Sat L & D. **$$$$** ㊸ p272, C2

Film buffs can expect a feast for the senses at this eatery owned by Samia Ahad (who runs Coriander Leaf restaurant in Clarke Quay; *see page 117*). The restaurant serves tapas and meze platters as well as steaks, grills and gourmet burgers. Have a nightcap at the rooftop bar before leaving.

Waku Ghin

Marina Bay Sands, 10 Bayfront Avenue, Level 2 Casino. Tel: 6688-8504. www.wakughin.com Open: daily 6–8.30pm, 8.30–10.30pm (two seatings). **$$$$** ㊹ p273, E2

Diners don't have to wait for months to score a seat at Tetsuya Wakuda's restaurant in Sydney now that he has opened Waku Ghin in Singapore. His highly lauded European cuisine with Japanese influence is exquisite, as are the fine wines and sparkling views of Marina Bay. Expect to pay at least S$400 for his *dégustation* menu filled with the freshest seasonal ingredients.

Indian

Annalakshmi

B1-02 Chinatown Point, 133 New Bridge Rd. Tel:

6339-9993. Open: Mon 6–10pm, Tue–Sun 11am–10pm. **$–$$$$** ㊺ p272, C2
Few restaurants manage to look stately yet remain unpretentious. Annalakshmi is one of those. Exquisite Indian vegetarian cuisine is served by friendly staff members who are volunteers. The menu has no prices, and diners pay as they wish – the money funds artistic and charitable activities.

Kinara
57 Boat Quay. Tel: 6533-0412. www.thekinaragroup.com Open: daily L & D. **$$$** ㊻ p273, D1
Warm, friendly staff serve hearty Punjabi cuisine by the Singapore River in a beautiful space decorated with antique furniture from Rajasthan. The roasted leg of lamb, marinated for over 24 hours, is a must-try.

Indonesian

House of Sundanese Food
55 Boat Quay. Tel: 6534-1602. www.sundanesefood.com Open: Mon–Fri L & D, Sat–Sun D. **$** (set lunch) **$$** (à la carte) ㊼ p273, D1
Busy but charming place with delicious West Java-inspired fare such as spicy prawns, grilled chicken and *sayur lodeh* (vegetables in coconut milk). Their charcoal-grilled fish is legendary; the secret lies in the traditional Sundanese sauce.

Italian

Buko Nero
126 Tanjong Pagar Rd. Tel: 6324-6225. Open: Tue–Sat L & D. **$$$** (set lunch) **$$$$** (à la carte) ㊽ p272, B3
Run by an Italian husband and Singaporean wife team, the menu reflects this Italian-Asian marriage. Signatures include the tofu and vegetable tower, spaghetti with spicy crabmeat and prawns, and Horlicks ice cream. There are just seven tables, and the restaurant is perennially full. Diners call in advance – sometimes a month ahead – for dinner.

Oso Ristorante
46 Bukit Pasoh Rd. Tel: 6327-8378. www.oso.sg Open: Mon–Fri L & D, Sat–Sun D. **$$$$** ㊾ p272, B3
Italian partners Diego Chariani and Stephane Colleoni relocated Oso from Tanjong Pagar to a historic building in Bukit Pasoh, next to Absinthe. The restaurant has a separate cheese room and cigar room. Diego is famous for his regional Italian cuisine, including his home-made pastas, all perfectly matched with Italian wines.

Pasta Brava
11 Craig Rd. Tel: 6227-7550. Open: Mon–Sat L & D. **$$** (set lunch) **$$$** (à la carte) ㊿ p272, B3
A real taste of Italy in a converted old Singapore shophouse. If you don't find the sauce you want for your pasta on the menu, chatty chef-owner Rolando Luceri will prepare anything that his available ingredients will allow. Check out his southern Italian signatures, including the grilled vegetable-based antipasti and ravioli filled with pumpkin.

Senso
21 Club St. Tel: 6224-3534. www.senso.com.sg Open: Mon–Fri L & D, Sat–Sun D. **$$$$** (51) p272, C2
Drinks at the sleek bar should precede dinner at Club Street's handsomest restaurant. And if the weather permits, dine alfresco at the lovely courtyard. Classic Italian dishes, such as Milanese *osso bucco* and hand-made pasta with lobster, are ready items on the menu.

Spizza for Friends
29 Club St. Tel: 6224-2525. Open: daily L & D. **$$** (52) p272, C2
Spizza's winning formula: ingredients imported

Prices for a three-course dinner per person without drinks and taxes:
$ = under S$20
$$ = S$20–30
$$$ = S$30–60
$$$$ = over S$60

from Italy, a thin and crispy crust and a wood-fired oven. Try the Quinta Pizza – tomato, mozzarella and black truffles topped with a cracked egg; or the very special Isabella – mozzarella, parma ham and *rucola* (rocket). End with a sweet pizza – Zara comes dressed in melted chocolate, bananas and almond flakes.

Local

Lau Pa Sat Festival Market

18 Raffles Quay. Open: 24 hours. **$** ⑤ p273, D3
The cast-iron structure in the heart of the financial district has been here since 1894. Now a gazetted national monument, the restored food centre boasts 60 stalls selling delicious local fare and a side street peddling *satay* in the evening.

Maxwell Food Centre

Maxwell Rd, next to URA Ctr. Open: daily B until late. **$** ⑤ p272, C3
Join any of the long queues at one of Singapore's oldest food centres. Try the fish noodles, chicken rice or porridge and other local delights. Tip: Avoid lunch hours – executives arrive in droves from the nearby CBD offices.

Peranakan

The Blue Ginger

97 Tanjong Pagar Rd. Tel: 6222-3928. www.theblue ginger.com Open: daily L & D. **$$** ⑤ p272, B3

This authentic Peranakan restaurant has been around for more than 10 years, satisfying customers with tasty offerings such as *ayam buah keluak* (stewed chicken with black nuts), *otak otak* (spicy fish mousse), beef *rendang* (dry beef curry) and the must-have durian *cendol* (a dessert with green jelly).

Spanish

Santi

Marina Bay Sands, 10 Bayfront Avenue, Level 2 Casino. Tel: 6688-8501. www.marinabaysands.com Open: daily 6.30–10.30pm. **$$$$** ⑤ p273, E2
Chef Santi Santamaria's contemporary cuisine with Catalan origins and creative Asian interpretation has won over sophisticated diners. Seasonal ingredients and fresh seafood are delivered to your table with much flair. The restaurant also has a tapas bar at the entrance.

Thai

Thanying

2/F, Amara Hotel, 165 Tanjong Pagar Rd. Tel: 6222-4688. http://singapore.amara hotels.com Open: daily L & D. **$$$** ⑤ p272, B4
Thanying means "Thai noble lady". Indeed, this madam has cultivated a loyal following with her refined Thai cuisine. Whether it's the green

LEFT: Lau Pa Sat Festival Market. **RIGHT:** The Penny Black.

Bars

Harry's Bar

28 Boat Quay. Tel: 6538 3029. www.harrys.com.sg ⑨ p270, D1
Harry's Bar is an institution with the pin-striped investment crowd, who gather to cut business deals and to take in the moody jazz and blues sessions performed nightly.

Molly Malone's Irish Pub

56 Circular Road. Tel: 6536-2029. www.molly-malone.com ⑩ p270, C1
a traditional bar that oozes quaint cosy charm, Molly Malone's is always busy with those inclined towards Irish-style dark beers.

The Penny Black

26/27 Boat Quay. Tel: 6538-2300. www.pennyblack.com.sg ⑪ p270, D1
Popular with the financial district crowd, this pub serves great lunches of sandwiches and steaks, meat pies, and fish and chips – all washed down with English ales like Ruddles and Old Speckled Hen.

Sky Bar

Marina Bay Sands North Tower, 1 Bayfront Avenue. Tel: 6688-7688. www.kudeta.com.sg ⑫ p273, E2
Perched on top of the new Sands SkyPark is this stylish circular bar. Sip at a cocktail while enjoying the sensational skyline.

curry or crispy boneless grouper, every dish in the elegant teak-panelled dining room is beautifully presented. The extensive menu is complemented by a Thai dessert buffet.

FENG SHUI PRINCIPLES

Is it science, art or just plain superstition? *Feng shui* **is widely practised in Singapore, even by Westerners not easily swayed by unseen forces**

ABOVE: auspicious Water Gate at Far East Square *(see page 135)*.

The Chinese believe that success or failure in a career or business, the state of a person's health, wealth and even relationships are all governed by *feng shui*. *Feng* (wind) *shui* (water) is a means of creating harmony between man and his surroundings to achieve balance and well being. It refers to the art of placing a building in relation to other structures in the area to create a balance. But it's not just orientation that counts: how a person's home or office is designed internally and how the furniture is arranged within also has an effect on the occupants' well-being.

This coincides with the Chinese concept of *yin* (negative/feminine) and *yang* (positive/masculine). Each cannot exist without the other. In life, if the *yin* and the *yang* are in balance, there will be harmony. The Chinese believe that *qi* – an invisible energy – flows through the universe and also the human body. The key to *feng shui* is effectively harnessing the flow of this *qi* (pronounced "chi").

ABOVE: the curve of Boat Quay represents the belly of the carp, an auspicious shape.
LEFT: the *luo pan*, used by feng shui masters to determine the most favourable alignment.

THE TOOLS OF FENG SHUI

Bad *feng shui* can be countered by simple solutions such as hanging a mirror to deflect bad *qi* or energy, or by reorienting a door so that good *qi* will flow in. *Feng shui* tools abound to assist the masters in giving advice. Apart from the *luo pan* (compass) which calculates a person's most favourable direction, the *ba kua*, or eight-sided Chinese trigam with a mirror in the middle, is another means of deflecting bad *qi*. If the *ba kua* has a *yin* and *yang* symbol in the middle, it is used like a *luo pan* – as a means to identify problem areas and to rectify them.

Other principles which bring about harmonious *feng shui* include the use of the right colour, round shapes or symbolic "good luck" symbols such as a water fountain or pond. Crystals and wind chimes placed at certain strategic locations within the house or office are also used to enhance the flow of *qi*.

Others may prefer to turn to prayers at altars which pay homage to the the Fu Lu Shou, the Gods of Wealth, Health and Longevity *(pictured above)*.

ABOVE: the waters of the Fountain of Wealth *(see page 102)* in Suntec City supposedly bring good fortune to the person who touches it. In fact the entire Suntec City development – based on the human hand – was inspired by *feng shui* principles: its four 45-storey towers are the fingers, while a shorter 18-storey building is the thumb. The fountain is held in the palm of the hand, and since water symbolises wealth, the significance is clear. Interestingly, the massive bronze fountain, which covers 1,683 sq metres (18,177 sq ft), is listed in *Guinness World Records* as the world's largest.

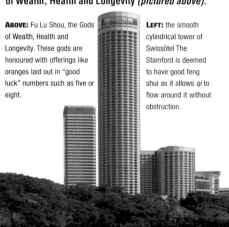

ABOVE: Fu Lu Shou, the Gods of Wealth, Health and Longevity. These gods are honoured with offerings like oranges laid out in "good luck" numbers such as five or eight.

LEFT: the smooth cylindrical tower of Swissôtel The Stamford is deemed to have good feng shui as it allows *qi* to flow around it without obstruction.

ABOVE: the direction of rotation of the Singapore Flyer, the world's biggest observation wheel, was reversed after feng shui masters said it was taking good fortune away from the city.

ORCHARD ROAD AND SURROUNDS

International retailers jostle with home-grown stores
along the ultra-modern malls of Orchard Road.
And when the shopping palls, the lush Botanic
Gardens offer a leafy retreat

O rchard Road is to Singapore what Fifth Avenue is to New York and the Champs-Elysées is to Paris – one long stretch of shops, shopping centres and hotels, spanning from the top of the road where Plaza Singapura stands to the other end where Tanglin Road begins. But there is more to Orchard Road than just shops. It has a presidential palace, Botanic Gardens, sidewalk cafés, and a charming residential enclave filled with some of Singapore's finest examples of Chinese Baroque shop- and terrace houses.

Orchard Road derives its name from the sprawling orchards of nutmeg and pepper that dominated the area in the 19th century. Plagued by frequent floods because of their location in a valley, the plantations were finally wiped out by a mysterious disease at the turn of the 20th century almost overnight. Stamford Canal – part of which runs below the pathway fronting Wisma Atria – was widened in 1965 to alleviate the flooding, and from then Orchard Road took off. Today the area is one of Singapore's most coveted business and residential addresses, full of swanky shopping complexes and multimillion-dollar condominiums. The only vestiges of

the past are found in the street names – inspired by plantation owners like Scotts, Cairnhill and Cuppage.

Around Dhoby Ghaut

Orchard Road starts at the junction of Bras Basah and Handy roads. **Dhoby Ghaut MRT Station** marks the beginning of the road, once an area of grassy fields covered with linen left to dry in the sun by Indian-owned *dhoby* (laundries) that used to operate along the banks of the former Bras Basah Canal.

LEFT: shoppers on Orchard Road.
RIGHT: Peranakan Place.

ABOVE: sentry on duty at Istana, the official residence of the President. A "changing of the guards" ceremony takes place here on the first Sunday of each month at 6pm.

Facing the MRT station is the ageing redbrick **MacDonald House** ❶, built in 1949 for the Hongkong and Shanghai Bank and one of the first high-rise office buildings in the area. Most of the Victorian buildings that once lined this street have been bulldozed to make way for shopping malls. In stark contrast, next door are the shimmering office tower blocks of **Atrium @ Orchard**, connected to Dhoby Ghaut MRT Station.

Next door to the Atrium is **Plaza Singapura**, home to French hypermart Carrefour as well as the Golden Village Cineplex. Across the street at Penang Road is **Park Mall**, which specialises in furniture and hip home decor.

The Istana

Just beyond Plaza Singapura is the **Istana** ❷, the official residence of Singapore's president. The palace and its sprawling gardens are strictly off limits to the public, except on National Day and certain public holidays, when

the gates are thrown open to curious sightseers. The Istana was built in 1869 by the colonial architect J.F.A. McNair, and it served as the residence of the British governor until the island became self-governing in 1959.

Facing the Istana squarely is **Istana Park** ❸, dominated by an imposing steel sculpture flanked by garden courtyards of heliconia and lotus-filled ponds, a pleasant place to stop for a drink at the park's café.

House of Tan Yeok Nee

Behind the park, at the corner of Clemenceau Avenue and Penang Road, is an old Chinese-style house. Now known as the **Chicago Graduate School of Business**, this was the former **House of Tan Yeok Nee** – a name more descriptive of its origins. Teochew cloth pedlar turned wealthy gambier and pepper merchant, Tan Yeok Nee built his elegant house in 1885. It is a rare example of a typical Chinese southern-style courtyard

TIP

Watch the "changing of the guards" ceremony that takes place on the first Sunday of each month at 6pm. Forget about getting a glimpse of the palace building from the gates though: the grounds are so huge, all you can see is a never-ending expanse of greenery.

Map:

0 — 200 m
0 — 200 yds

Anderson Road
Ardmore Park
Orange Grove Road
Grove Road
Nassim Road
Seton Close
Seton Walk
St Martin's Dr.
Tomlinson Road
Tanglin Road
Tanglin Mall
Botanic Gardens ⓫
Tourism Court
Grange Road
Claymore Road
Claymore Rd
Delfi Orchard
Orchard Towers
Claym. Dr.
Palais Renaissance
Thai Embassy
International Building
Hill
Royal Plaza on Scotts
DFS Plaza
Pacific Plaza
Shaw Centre
Shaw House
Scotts Road
Far East Plaza
Grand Hyatt Hotel
Scotts Square
Tangs Department Store ❾
Lucky Plaza
Goodwood Park Hotel ❿
Mount Elizabeth
Jln.
Elo
Jln. Jintan
Jln. Lada Puteh
Jln. Kay Manis
Nutmeg R
Para
Orchard Road
Orchard
Hilton
Forum
Liat Towers
Far East Shopping Centre
Wheelock Place
ION Orchard
Anguilla Park
ORCHARD
Wisma Atria
Ngee Ci
Orchard Road
Turn
Orchard Boulevard
Orchard
Cuscaden Walk
Anguilla Park
Paterson Road
Cuscaden Walk
Boulevard
Tupai
Jalan
Tree Hill
Jalan Kelawar
Jalan Arnap
Paterson Road
Grange R
Leonie Hill

house, with a grand entrance and sloping roofs with spiral ornamentation. The national monument, after undergoing extensive restoration work, was taken over by the school in 2000; however, it is not open to visitors.

Church of Sacred Heart

Further up Clemenceau Avenue on the right is **Tank Road**, where three institutions stand in testimony of Singapore's polyglot character. First is the **Church of the Sacred Heart** ❹, one of the oldest Roman Catholic churches in Singapore (tel: 6737-9285; daily 7am–7pm). Founded in 1910 by a French priest, the whitewashed building is constructed in the French Baroque style. Just next door is the four-storey **Teochew Building**, which has a green-tiled Chinese roof and a design that is likened to the *gong dian*, or imperial courts, of China. It is the headquarters for the Teochew-speaking Chinese clan in Singapore.

Chettiar Temple

Further down the road is the **Sri Thandayuthapani Temple** ❺, better known as the Chettiar Temple (tel: 6737-9393; daily 6am–noon, 5–9pm). The temple, built in 1859 by the Chettiars, an Indian caste of moneylenders, is one of the Hindu community's most important monuments. Take a good look at the 48 glass panels on the roof, designed to capture the rays of the rising and setting of the sun. It is also here, during the annual Thaipusam festival, that hundreds of pilgrims, their bodies pierced by hooks, spears and spiked steel structures called *kavadi*, end their walk from the Srinivasa Perumal Temple *(see page 168)* on Serangoon Road.

Chesed-El Synagogue

Just off Tank Road on Oxley Rise is the grandiose-looking **Chesed-El Synagogue** ❻, the second synagogue to be built in Singapore *(see page 174)*.

SHOP

All of Singapore (and the region) comes out to shop during the Great Singapore Sale from the end of May to early July. It even has its own dedicated website: www.greatsingapore sale.com.sg.

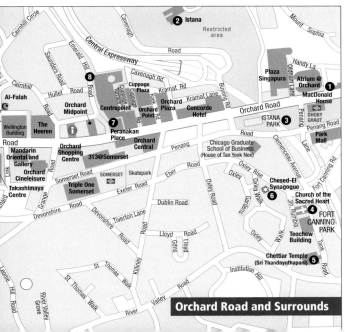

Orchard Road and Surrounds

ABOVE: Cuppage
Terrace.

Orchard Central

The Orchard Central site has an interesting history. From the mid-1960s to 1970s it was called Glutton's Square, a popular open-air street-dining spot. It served as a car park by day and was transformed into a hawker centre in the evening. In its heyday, there were as many as 80 stalls selling local fare, such as *char kway teow* (fried rice noodles) and oyster omelette. The government eventually closed Glutton's Square in 1978 because of poor hygiene conditions and relocated most of the stalls to Newton Circus hawker centre. The food stalls were revived during the 2004 Singapore Food Festival, but have since been relocated to the Esplanade and renamed Makansutra Glutton's Bay.

It dates back to 1905 and was funded by Manasseh Meyer, a prominent Jewish businessman (tel: 6732-8862; open only Monday service 7.30am). The Jewish population in Singapore today only numbers a few hundred, having shrunk from a high of 2,500 in the 1930s. At one time, it is said they owned half of the rental property on the island.

Concorde Hotel to Centrepoint

Back on Orchard Road, a block from the Istana is Concorde Hotel (formerly Le Meridien Hotel), with an outdated shopping arcade and a food court on the lower level. Past the nondescript **Orchard Plaza**, filled with equally tired-looking shops, is **Orchard Point**, with department store **OG** as the anchor tenant. Flanking it is **Cuppage Terrace**, with restored shophouses turned into bars and restaurants. In the vicinity is another old shopping centre, **Cuppage Plaza**. Its many small but superb Japanese eateries and karaoke bars are frequented by Japanese businessmen.

Further along is **Centrepoint**, home to Cold Storage supermarket and **Robinson's**, a large department store with a history dating back to the 1850s – its original location was at Raffles Places until a fire broke out in 1972. Robinson's has some of the nicest sales staff in Singapore, and its eagerly awaited biannual sales are a big attraction.

Peranakan Place

Next door is charming **Peranakan Place** ❼ a complex of ornate Peranakan-style shophouses that have been transformed into a commercial hub. At its outdoor cafés and bars patrons can sip iced lemon tea and beer under a canopy while people-watching. More bar options (Alley Bar and Acid Bar) can be found in the adjoining shophouses.

Emerald Hill

Further down from Peranakan Place is another stretch of shophouses, housing a string of popular bars (including No. 5, Que Pasa and Ice Cold Beer). Take time to explore the

DRINK

All along Orchard Road, there is no shortage of open-air terrace cafés where you can stop for coffee. Most are located on street level or within shopping centres. They are also great places for people-watching.

lovely old restored terrace houses further up the slope on **Emerald Hill ❽**. Once belonging to wealthy Peranakan families, the 30 or so homes on the slightly curved road were built between 1901 and 1925 in the so-called Chinese Baroque style *(see pages 176–7)*, typified by ornamental mouldings, shuttered wooden windows, pastel colours and colourful ceramic tiles. These houses were also the first to be given conservation status in 1981, which meant the owners could not alter their facades.

Look out for the four terrace houses, numbering 39 to 45, with forecourts and gates topped with an ornate Chinese roof. No. 45, designed by M.T. Moh in 1903, is particularly striking – it features a Chinese grand entrance that was carefully restored by Chinese craftsmen. Keep an eye out, too, for the richly carved door of No. 127.

Mega-malls galore

Across the road are two new shopping malls. **Orchard Central**'s layout is a little difficult to navigate, but the "super" escalators are designed

to zip you up from the ground level to the different "clusters": fashion, active lifestyle, food and so on. If you're tired of shopping, there's also a loft climbing wall here. Within shouting distance is the busier **313@ Somerset**, which is linked to Somerset MRT. The main tenants include Zara, Forever 21 and Japanese brand Uniqlo, and there's a massive Food Republic food court. The mall has a sheltered walkway-terrace called Discovery Walk, lined with cafés and bars like Brotzeit.

At the corner of Orchard and Grange roads, just behind the Meritus Mandarin Hotel, is **Orchard Cineleisure**, comprising a cineplex and entertainment arcades. Diagonally opposite Orchard Cineleisure on Somerset Road is Triple One Somerset, a quieter mall with a good line-up of eateries, beauty spas and salons. Back on Orchard Road, Meritus Mandarin Hotel's swish shopping arcade, Mandarin Gallery, has a retail concept featuring designer labels and lifestyle offerings. Across the road is **The Heeren,** where the younger set can find funky street fashion. One block down is the Grand Park

ABOVE: shophouses at Peranakan Place. **BELOW LEFT:** Orchard Road poseurs. **BELOW:** Peranakan Place.

Orchard Hotel's Knightsbridge shopping destination, offering more luxury goods to well-heeled shoppers.

Further along the same side of the road as Meritus Mandarin is the massive brown granite facade of **Ngee Ann City**, with its twin towers. One of Southeast Asia's largest shopping malls, it has the Japanese **Takashimaya** department store and boutiques selling designer labels. The Louis Vuitton and Tiffany flagship stores are here, as well as a Harrods store from London and half a dozen excellent restaurants on its upper floors. Singapore's largest bookstore, **Kinokuniya**, is found on the third floor. Linked to it by an underground tunnel is **Wisma Atria**, which houses the Japanese department store **Isetan**, as well as independent boutiques, eateries and another massive Food Republic food court.

Next to Wisma Atria is **ION Orchard,** its facade lined with double-storey flagship stores of swanky brands like Prada, Louis Vuitton, Dior and others. The mall is also crammed with other top retail brands, from Miu Miu to Muji. The complex is the tallest building on Orchard Road, with 48 floors of luxury residences above it. After browsing the many stores, head up to ION Sky on levels 55 and 56 to drink in the 360-degree city view.

Opposite Ngee Ann City is **The Paragon**, noted for luxury designer boutiques like Gucci and Escada, and other top brands like Banana Republic and Karen Millen. On the top floor are stores selling high-end kids' clothes and Toys 'R' Us. The mall's basement has a gourmet supermarket, the **Paragon Market Place**.

In contrast, across Mt Elizabeth Road is the dowdy **Lucky Plaza**, a complex of shops offering cameras, watches, luggage and cheap accessories. This happens to be a Sunday hangout for hundreds of Filipino domestic workers on their day off work.

Tangs

Adjacent to Lucky Plaza is **Tangs Department Store ❾**, below the high-rise pagoda-roofed Marriott Hotel, at the corner of Scotts and Orchard roads. The store was founded by C.K. Tang, a Chinese Teochew who made his fortune in the early 1900s by cycling from house to house selling China-made lace to English families. Tang built his first store in 1932 at nearby River Valley Road, offering oriental treasures and household goods. In 1958, Tang bought the land on which his store now sits for a song. The presence of a Chinese cemetery opposite his store didn't faze him, even though his friends warned him about the bad *feng shui*.

His gamble paid off. Business outgrew the old building, and the new store, which kept the ornate roof, styled after Beijing's Imperial Palace, is a well-loved Orchard Road icon. The five-storey store is particularly noted for its collection of skincare labels and useful kitchen gadgets.

Scotts Road

On the other side of the street, at the corner with Scotts Road, is **Shaw House** – home to another branch of **Isetan** department store and the **Lido Cineplex**. Next door is the quieter **Pacific Plaza**, with beauty care outlets and a yoga studio. Past the Royal Plaza on Scotts Hotel is the striking red **DFS Galleria Scottswalk**, a duty-free haven.

On the other side of the street is the **Grand Hyatt Singapore**. The entrance to the hotel is set at an angle that is supposed to usher in good luck and prosperity, according to *feng shui* experts *(see pages 144–5)*. The grand staircase in the lobby has 32 steps – a number that sounds like the phrase for "life is easy" when said in Cantonese. Pop into the hotel to have a Martini or cocktail at the Martini Bar, followed by a meal at **mezza9**.

Next door is **Far East Plaza**, a bit tatty around the edges but still popular. Its basement-level shops are filled with teen-friendly stores, while upstairs are a handful of tattoo and body-piercing shops.

Perched at the top of a gentle rise is the castle-like **Goodwood Park Hotel ⑩**, built in 1900 as the Teutonia Club for German residents in Singapore. Designed by R.A.J. Bidwell, this luxury hotel has had a long and interesting history: during World War II, the Japanese used the building as a military headquarters, and, in 1945, the British turned its premises into a war-crime court.

The lower end of Orchard

Back at Orchard Road proper, across from Shaw House is a stunning glass pyramid – **Wheelock Place**, a complex of offices and restaurants designed by Japanese architect Kisho Kurokawa. American bookstore chain Borders fills the entire ground floor, and **Marks & Spencer** is in the basement. Wheelock Place is linked to ION Orchard and Orchard MRT via an underground walkway.

Next to Wheelock Place is **Liat Towers**, mostly noted for its Hermes and Zara stores. Starbucks, on the ground level, is always abuzz with people. Give tired Far East Shopping Centre a miss and head for the **Hilton Hotel** next door, whose shopping gallery is another designer label haven.

TIP

Art fans can head to ION Orchard's Level 4, touted as the largest art space in a mall. After that, head straight up via high-speed elevators to the ION Sky observatory on the 55th and 56th levels overlooking the bustling shopping belt. This is also where the new Salt Grill restaurant by celebrity Aussie chef Luke Mangan is located.

BELOW: Tangs Department Store.

Across the road is **Palais Renaissance**, where the well-heeled shop and get their hair styled at the famous Passion hair salon by celebrity stylist David Gan. Another ultra-chic P.S Cafe outlet is located here.

Just next door again is the infamous **Orchard Towers**. Besides sundry shops selling jewellery, silk and clothing, this place is most known for its many floors of shoddy bars and nightclubs. Going on again, you get to **Delfi Orchard**, with mainly beauty salons and bridal boutiques. Opposite is family-oriented **Forum The Shopping Mall**, with a Toys 'R' Us outlet as well as other children-friendly stores and creative learning and activity centres. Those looking for stylish kids' clothes can head to Guess Kids, DKNY Kids and Ralph Lauren Kids.

Tanglin Road

Tanglin Road marks the end of Orchard Road, but the dividing line has blurred somewhat, and Tanglin is often treated as an extension of Orchard Road. Just past Orchard Parade Hotel is **Tanglin Shopping Centre**, a great place to rummage for antiques and arts and crafts. Next to it is the upscale St Regis Hotel and across the road is the quaint Tudor Court, housing shops selling Asian artifacts and the French gourmet store Hediard. At the end of Tanglin Road is **Tanglin Mall**, which has an excellent Market Place supermarket frequented by expats.

Singapore Botanic Gardens

Address: 1 Cluny Road; www.sbg.org.sg
Tel: 6471-7138
Opening Hrs: daily 5am–midnight
Entrance Fee: free

From Tanglin Mall, walk past the British, American and Australian embassies and Gleneagles Hospital along Napier Road and wind down at the **Singapore Botanic Gardens ⓫**.

SHOPPING

Stretching from Dhoby Ghaut to Tanglin, Orchard Road is renowned as a shopping paradise. There is something for everyone here, from massive department stalls and upscale fashion boutiques to funky streetware. For more information, see www.orchardroad.sg.

313@Somerset
313 Orchard Road.
Tel: 6496-9313/6496-9300.
www.313somerset.com.sg
p269, D2
This mall just above Somerset MRT has mid-range shops, fashion stores like Zara and Forever 21, and plenty of reasonably priced eateries. Mac and

iPhone users can find all they need at the EpiCentre store.
Centrepoint
176 Orchard Road.
Tel: 6737-9000. www.centre point.com.sg p269, D1
Shoppers love Centrepoint for its Robinson's sale and Cold Storage for groceries.
ION Orchard
2 Orchard Turn. Tel: 6238-8228. www.ionorchard.com p268, B4
This mall has an excellent range of retail outlets, both high-end and mid-range, plus a good mix of restaurants and cafés. It also has an observation deck on the 55th and 56th levels.

Mandarin Gallery
333A Orchard Road. Tel: 6831-6363. www.mandarin gallery.com.sg p269, C1
Linked to Meritus Mandarin Hotel, this shopping arcade houses renowned brands such as D&B and Marc by Marc Jacobs, as well as home-grown labels like Ashley Isham.
Ngee Ann City
391A Orchard Road #08-05.
Tel: 6733-0337. www.ngee anncity.com.sg p269, C1
This is still one of the most frequented spots along this shopping belt, thanks to anchor tenant Takashimaya, Kinokuniya bookstore, and its many great restaurants and cafés.

The Paragon
290 Orchard Road. Tel: 6738-5535. www.paragon.sg p269, C1
The Paragon is known for its luxury brands such as Prada, Tod's and Gucci on the first level, and stylish children's stores on the top level. Metro, the home-grown department store, is here too.
Tangs Orchard
310 & 320 Orchard Road.
Tel: 6737-5500. www.tangs. com p268, B4
This well-established store offers a great range of cosmetics, clothing, shoes and accessories, and has an excellent kitchenware and lifestyle section in the basement.

Singapore's oldest national park was set up in 1859 and today is known worldwide as a living museum of tropical plants, with over 2,000 species of trees and shrubs, and a centre for botanical research. Beautifully landscaped, with walkways winding around the expansive greenery, the gardens cover a sprawling 64 hectares (158 acres). It is the second patch of primary forest left in Singapore – Bukit Timah Nature Reserve *(see page 223)* is the other. Henry Ridley, its first director (1888–1912), developed the method of tapping the rubber tree here.

The gardens make up three sections. The main **Tanglin Core** features lush rainforest, Swan Lake, an 1860s bandstand and bronze sculptures by the British sculptor Sydney Harpley. The **Central Core** has the **National Orchid Garden** (daily 8.30am–7pm; charge) – with more than 1,000 species of orchid *(see pages 160–1)* – and also **Palm Valley**, where there are regular open-air musical performances. The **Bukit Timah Core** features the Ecolake and

a spice garden. There is an astonishing range of bird life, and you may also spot squirrels and green crested lizards. Here, families can also visit the Jacob Ballas Children's Garden, designed to help kids below 12 discover more about plants and nature through fun-filled play and exploration. They can learn about photosynthesis in an interactive exhibit, climb up a tree house and get "lost" in a maze garden. Back at the **Visitor's Centre** (tel: 6471-7361), pick up a gift at the souvenir shop or have a bite at the alfresco café, Casa Verde. Within walking distance from the visitor's centre is the beautiful fine-dining restaurant Au Jardin by Les Amis.

About 10 minutes' walk from the Botanic Gardens is the lush **Dempsey Hill** (Dempsey Road), a retail and dining enclave housed in an 1860s former British army barracks. Within three clusters are different blocks – some filled with stores selling antique furniture, fine teak works, carpets and art pieces, others occupied by popular restaurants, cafés and bars, including the famous Samy's Curry.   ❑

ABOVE: Botanic Gardens. **BELOW:** Tanglin Road Shopping Mall at Christmas.

BEST RESTAURANTS, BARS AND CAFÉS

Restaurants

Contemporary

Blu
24/F, Shangri-La Hotel, 22 Orange Grove Rd. Tel: 6213-4598. www.shangri-la.com Open: Mon–Sat D. **$$$$** (set dinner and à la carte) ⑤⑧ p268, A3
Blu presents innovative cuisine topped with stunning city views. Soothing live jazz, snazzy touches such as the Philippe Starck lamps, Danny Lane's glass art and cheongsam-clad female bartenders all contribute to Blu's success.

Hard Rock Café
02-01 HPL House, 50 Cuscaden Rd. Tel: 6235-5232. www.hardrock.com.sg Open: Tue–Thur 11am–2am, Fri–Sun 11am–3am. **$** (set lunch) **$$$** (à la carte) ⑤⑨ p268, A/B4
It's the same hard-rocking formula that's amazingly still relevant today: American-sized portions, fun staff and a live band that brings the house down daily. The set lunch is a bargain, and the fajitas and burgers are always good bets. Don't forget the sinful brownie for dessert.

Chinese

Crystal Jade Palace
04-19 Ngee Ann City, 391 Orchard Rd. Tel: 6735-2388. Open: daily L & D. **$$** (set lunch) **$$$** (à la carte) ⑥⓪ p269, C1
Crystal Jade is famous for its consistently good food. Feast on excellent roast meat and "live"

seafood such as the delicious baked prawns. The group also runs noodle and dumpling joint Crystal Jade La Mian Xiao Long Bao (tel: 6238-1661) and the more casual dining spot Crystal Jade Kitchen (tel: 6238-1411), all in the same building.

Din Tai Fung
B1-03/06 Paragon, 290 Orchard Rd. Tel: 6836-8336. Open: Mon–Fri 11am–10pm, Sat–Sun 10am–10pm. **$$** ⑥① p269, C1
You notice the flurry of activity at the open concept kitchen before you realise diners are watching the chefs in action and lining up for their xiao long bao, or steamed pork dumplings, which have exactly 18 pleats each. Fans sing praises of the chicken soup and humble fried rice, too.

Hua Ting
2/F, Orchard Hotel, 442 Orchard Rd. Tel: 6739-6666. www.millenniumhotels.com.sg Open: daily L & D. **$$$$** ⑥② p268, B4
This stalwart serves traditional and innovative Cantonese delicacies created by well-known master chef Chan Kwok. Popular items include double-boiled shark's bone cartilage soup with three treasures and baked silver codfish with

honey. The dim sum is also a highlight. Artefacts from Thailand, Burma, Vietnam and China lend a classy touch to this elegant restaurant.

Imperial Treasure Nan Bei Restaurant
05-12/13 Ngee Ann City, 391 Orchard Rd. Tel: 6738-1238. Open: daily 11am–11pm. **$$$** ⑥③ p269, C1
Former managing director of the successful Crystal Jade group of restaurants Alfred Leung started his own restaurant chain based on similar lines. His Imperial Treasure restaurant empire has grown rapidly in a short period, and this outlet boasts top-grade Cantonese dishes, from roast goose to the comforting double-boiled chicken soup.

Orchard Lei Garden
03-00 Orchard Shopping Centre, 321 Orchard Rd. Tel: 6734-3988. Open: daily L & D. **$$$** ⑥④ p269, D2
This restaurant is famous for its superbly made dim sum, including prawn dumplings and steamed Shanghai dumplings. The Peking duck is also commendable, with its utterly crispy skin and wrapped with the thinnest pancakes. A good place for lunch in between shopping.

Soup Restaurant
02-01 DFS Scotts Walk, 25 Scotts Rd. Tel: 6333-8033. www.souprestaurant.com.sg

LEFT: Hard Rock Café.

Open: daily L & D. **$$** ⑥⑤
p268, B4
The restaurant is modelled after a traditional Chinese home, with water features and a canopy of faux frangipani trees. Kitsch decor aside, Soup is famous for its healthy Chinese food. Menu highlights include double-boiled herbal soups and Samsui ginger chicken – steamed chicken dipped in ginger sauce and wrapped in fresh lettuce.

European

Iggy's
The Hilton Hotel, 581 Orchard Rd. Tel: 6732-2234. www.iggys.com.sg Open: Mon–Fri noon–1.30pm, 7–9.30pm, Sat 7–9.30pm. **$$$$** (set lunch & dinner) ⑥⑥ p268, B4
Ranked number 28 under the S. Pellegrino World's 50 Best Restaurants list, Iggy's has moved from its small space at the Regent Hotel to a much bigger venue at the Hilton. Savour *dégustation* menus of inventive dishes crafted from the freshest ingredients, such as cappellini in scampi oil.

French

Au Jardin
EJH Corner House, Singapore Botanic Gardens, 1

Prices for a three-course dinner per person without drinks and taxes:
$ = under S$20
$$ = S$20–30
$$$ = S$30–50
$$$$ = over S$50

Cluny Rd. Tel: 6466-8812. www.lesamis.com.sg Open: Mon–Thur, Sat D, Fri L & D, Sun B & D. **$$$$** (set dinner) **$$$$** (à la carte) ⑥⑦ off p268, A4
"Au Jardin", meaning "in the garden" in French, is appropriately set in a restored 1920s bungalow in the Botanic Gardens. At this highly acclaimed (and very expensive) restaurant, contemporary French flavours are as peerless as they should be. Request the *dégustation* menus if you want to sample a good range of the exquisite dishes.

Les Amis
02-16 Shaw Centre, 1 Scotts Rd. Tel: 6733-2225. www.lesamis.com.sg Open: Mon–Sat L & D. **$$$$** (set lunch and à la carte) ⑥⑧ p268, B4

ABOVE: Crossroads Café at the Marriott.

This sophisticated stalwart draws well-heeled diners who appreciate its exquisite French cuisine, which is both light and contemporary, with a focus on the ingredients' natural flavours. The award-winning wine list is just as outstanding. The minimalist chic main dining room is illuminated by stunning chandeliers.

Indian

Samy's Curry
Blk 25, 01-03 Dempsey Rd. Tel: 6472-2080. Open: daily L & D. **$** ⑥⑨ off p268, A4
A tenant at Dempsey Road's former civil service club before any of the other trendy outlets were opened, this 30-year-old restaurant specialises in fiery South Indian cuisine served on banana leaves. Signatures include the fish-head curry, masala chicken and prawns and

Mysore mutton. Wash down the heat with some chilled lime juice if you must.

Indonesian

The Rice Table
02-09/10 International Bldg, 360 Orchard Rd. Tel: 6835-3783. Open daily L & D. **$** ⑦⓪ p268, B4
For one price, you order as many Indonesian dishes as your stomach can allow. Try the *tahu telor*, a tower of bean-curd with shredded cucumber and sweet sauce, the tender spicy beef *rendang* (dry beef curry) and grilled chicken. Don't be afraid to ask for seconds.

International

Crossroads Café
Marriott Hotel, 320 Orchard Rd. Tel: 6831-4605. www. singaporemarriott.com Open: Sun–Wed 7am–1am, Thur–

Sat 7am–3am. **$$$** **71**
p268, B4
Whether nursing a juice or tucking into grilled Tasmanian salmon or prawn and chorizo risotto, this ever-bustling sidewalk café is the best place to watch Orchard Road pass by.

The Line
Lower Lobby, Tower Wing, Shangri-La Hotel, 22 Orange Grove Rd. Tel: 6213-4275. www.shangri-la.com. Open: daily B, L & D. **$$$$** **72** p268, A3
The Line exudes loud, exuberant New York chic, thanks to the masterly touches of renowned interior designer Adam D. Tihany. Sixteen culinary stations serve a wide range of international cuisines – from aromatic tandoori chicken to fresh sashimi, all manner of seafood and a lovely dessert spread.

mezza9
Grand Hyatt, 10–12 Scotts Rd. Tel: 6732-1234. http:// restaurants.singapore.hyatt.com Open: Mon–Sat noon– 11pm, Sun 11.30am–11pm. **$$$$** **73** p268, B4
This well-known restaurant features show kitchens for sushi, *yakitori*, seafood, Western and Chinese dishes as well as deli and dessert counters, walk-in wine cellar and a Martini bar. You can order from the various show kitchens and watch the chefs in action. The champagne brunch is especially popular.

One-Ninety
Lobby Level, Four Seasons Hotel, 190 Orchard Blvd. Tel: 6831-7250. www.four seasons.com Open: daily 6.30am–11pm. **$$$$** **74** p268, B4
The open kitchen, communal dining and warm

lighting set the stage for this lively restaurant. The small but scrumptious menu includes an amazingly juicy *wagyu* burger, a healthy cod with soy vinaigrette, and a sprinkling of local dishes.

PS Café at Paragon
03-41/44 Paragon, 290 Orchard Rd. Tel: 9297-7008. www.pscafe.sg Open: daily 9.30am–10.30pm. **$$** **75** p269, C1
This trendy and perennially busy café serves inspired East-West fusion dishes, sandwiches and scrumptious desserts. The favourites are cold tofu salad, *laksa* pesto pasta and banana and mango crumble. Its other must-visit outlets, PS Café at leafy Tanglin Village (tel: 9070-8782) and Palais Renaissance (tel: 9834-8232), are hotspots with the expats and yuppies.

Thai

Sabai
391B Orchard Road, 04-23 Ngee Ann City Tower B. Tel: 6333-8491. Open: daily L & D. **$$$** **76** p269, C1
Dine on exquisite Royal Thai cuisine prepared by a team of veteran Thai chefs. The menu includes specialities like crunchy wing bean salad with roasted coconut, chilli jam and lime juice, as well as a range of Thai curries and fresh seafood. Service is outstanding and gracious.

Soht & Baay
1 Orchard Turn, 04-11/05-01 ION Orchard. Tel: 6509-6058. www.sohtandbaay.com Open: Mon–Thur 11.30am–2.30pm, 6.30–10pm, Fri–Sun 11.30am–10.30pm. **$$$** **77** p268, C1
The highlights at this fine Thai restaurant are its fresh seafood and superb organic ingredients

sourced from the best suppliers in Thailand, as well as perfectly balanced flavours. Celebrated Chef Apasara (who owns a 25-year-old restaurant in Chonburi, Thailand) whips up outstanding dishes here, such as steamed crabs and charcoal-grilled sea bass.

Japanese

Sun with Moon Japanese Dining & Café

501 Orchard Road, Wheelock Place, 03-15/16/17. Tel: 6733-6636. Open: daily L & D. **$$** 78 p268, B4

This wildly popular restaurant offers reasonably priced and satisfying sushi, sashimi, rice and *ramen* sets for lunch. The à la carte menu includes a good ranged of cooked dishes too, such as *wagyu* beef and tempura.

Local

Chatterbox

Meritus Mandarin, 333 Orchard Rd. Tel: 6831-6291. www.mandarin-singapore.com Open: Sun–Thur 5–1am, Fri–Sat and eve of public holidays 24 hours. **$$** 79 p269, C1

The iconic coffee house is most famous for its (expensive) chicken rice. Check out, too, the other delicious local fare, such as *nasi lemak* (coconut rice with condiments), lobster *laksa* and *bak kut teh* (pork rib soup).

Newton Circus

Bukit Timah Rd (near Newton MRT). Open: daily L until

LEFT: The Line.

late. **$–$$** 80 p266, A3 Best visited at night. Ignore the touts, make sure you choose somewhere where prices are posted prominently, and you've got one of Singapore's best local food experiences. Good bets include barbecued seafood, grilled chicken wings, fishball noodles and fried carrot cake.

Mexican

Margarita's

Block 11, 01-19 Dempsey Rd. Tel: 6471-3228. Open: Tue–Sun 11.30am–3pm, 6–10pm. **$$$** 81 off p268, A4

A good option in Tanglin Village. Ask for a table at the terrace and chill out with a margarita while waiting for your meal to arrive. A must-try is the signature enchiladas or chilli con carne.

Peranakan

House of Peranakan Cuisine

Pan Pacific Orchard, 10 Claymore Rd. Tel: 6733-4411. Open: daily L and D. **$$** 82 p268, B4

One of Singapore's best Peranakan restaurants, this establishment has recipes that are three generations old. Good choices are the Nonya flowercrab, braised duck, stewed pork and *ayam buah keluak* (stewed chicken with Indonesian black nuts).

Spanish

Don Quijote Block 7

01-02 Dempsey Rd. Tel:

Bars

Alley Bar

180 Orchard Road, Peranakan Place. Tel: 6738-8818. 13 p269, D2

Many bars have come and gone, but Alley Bar seems to have the right formula, with its hip setting and acid jazz tunes and funk beats. This former alley has a 15-metre (50ft) long bar, high ceilings and a huge gilt-framed mirror right at the end. Next door is **Acid Bar** (tel: 6738-8828), a spot for nightly acoustic sessions of blues and jazz.

Brotzeit

01-27, 313@Somerset, 313 Orchard Rd. Tel: 6834-4038. 14 p269, D2

Brotzeit (German for 'bread time") gets crowded in the evenings, when expats and executives in the area come here for German beers and Bavarian bites.

Hacienda

13A Dempsey Road. Tel: 6476-2922. www.hacienda. com.sg 15 off p268, A4

A delightful Tanglin Village setting to chill out in. Relax on the open-air deck or in a

6476-2811. www.don-quijote-restaurants.com Open: Mon–Sun 6–10pm, Fri–Sat 11.30am–2.30pm, Sun à la carte brunch buffet 11.30am–2.30pm. **$$$** 83 off p268, A4

Don Quijote's tapas-style titbits and the hearty paellas are probably the best in town. The bread and butter pudding or fried milk with cinnamon syrup is a perfect sweet

leafy courtyard while you sip a watermelon Martini.

Ice-Cold Beer

Emerald Hill. Tel: 6735-9929. www.emeraldhillgroup.com 16 p269, D1

The name says it all – Ice-Cold Beer is the place to chug down literally ice-cold beer. The lip-smacking chicken wings are a perfect accompaniment.

Muddy Murphy's Irish Pub

B1-04 Orchard Hotel Shopping Arcade, 442 Orchard Road. Tel: 6735-0400. www.gaelic inns.com.sg 17 p268, B4

Muddy Murphy's is a thriving Dublin-styled pub, where taps flow with Guinness and Kilkenny ale. It's standing room only on most Friday nights.

Que Pasa

7 Emerald Hill. Tel: 6235-6626. 18 p269, D1

Just next door to Ice-Cold Beer, this venue, reminiscent of a wine bar in Spain, is always full. Premium wines, sangria and tapas are served in this atmospheric setting lined with crates and barrels.

ending to the meal. Besides refreshing sangrias, there are plenty of excellent Spanish wines to choose from.

Prices for a three-course dinner per person without drinks and taxes:

$ = under S$20
$$ = S$20–30
$$$ = S$30–50
$$$$ = over S$50

ORCHIDS IN A GARDEN CITY

Singapore helped the orchid industry bloom, and commercial producers in Southeast Asia now export millions of dollars' worth of flowers each year

Singapore owes its success in orchid-growing to a tropical climate and the pioneering orchid hybridisation work of the Botanic Gardens *(see page 154)*. The seeds of Singapore's orchid industry were sown in 1893 when Agnes Joaquim showed Henry Ridley, the gardens' first director, a mauve orchid bloom in her garden. It was a new natural orchid hybrid – a cross of *Vanda hookeriana* and *Vanda teres*. The Botanic Gardens began producing the hybrid *Vanda* Miss Joaquim (above) and distributed it to growers in Singapore and Malaya.

It was under Eric Holttum, the garden's director (1925–49), that the orchid industry bloomed. The popularity of *Vanda* Miss Joaquim convinced him that orchids of similar quality could be produced by hybridising. In 1928, he set up a laboratory and experimented with the asymbiotic method of culture, which involved germinating orchid seedlings from a single pod. The first *Spagthoglottis* hybrids flowered in 1931, and soon other orchid hybrids were produced, starting a thriving cut-flower industry.

Today, the Botanic Gardens have a sprawling National Orchid Garden with over 1,000 species of orchids and 2,000 hybrids bred over the last 70 years. It frequently produces orchid hybrids named after VIPs on state visits; in the VIP Orchid Garden, visitors can gaze at *Dendrobium* Margaret Thatcher or *Vandaenopsis* Nelson Mandela.

BELOW: a giant cage display fille[d] orchids at the Singapore Orchid S[how] section of the Singapore Garden f[estival]

LEFT: orchids are part of Singaporean culture. Local batik artist, Sakasi Said, sits next to his completed batik painting of orchids on a piece of fabric measuring 100 meters (330 feet) in length.

ABOVE: *dendrobium* hybrids are the most common type of orchids, with well over 1,000 species. It produces pretty flowers that are diverse in colour and form. Vandaceous hybrids are the second-most common hybrids, mainly used for breeding: they are showy plants and are frequently used in landscaping and in the cut-flower trade. Most of the hybridisation work that the National Orchid Garden undertakes involve these two main groups of orchids. Pictured here is the vandaceous hybrid *Aranda* Noorah Alsagoff.

ABOVE: some newly created hybrids are named after state visitors, such as the *Dendrobium* Margaret Thatcher pictured. Other VIP orchids include *Dendrobium* Memoria Princess Diana and *Vandaenopsis* Nelson Mandela.

TEST TUBE ORCHIDS

The National Orchid Garden's well-regarded hybridisation programme takes place in the temperature-controlled Tissue Culture Laboratory. The key to successful hybridisation is in creating sterile conditions for the seedlings to grow. A single pod placed in a flask germinates more effectively than it would if left to nature, resulting in several healthy seedlings. A pod yields about 20 orchid plantlets in each flask. When the tiny plants are over 3cm (1¼ inches) in height and have developed roots, they are ready to be transferred from the flask to the pot. Amateur horticulturists can buy these flasks and bring them home to grow their very own orchids. Detailed instructions are given with each purchase.

Another major centre for orchid cultivation in Singapore is the Mandai Orchid Garden *(see page 226)* in the north of Singapore. An amazing variety of blooms are grown here, both for the local market and for export. Visitors frequently buy a box of orchid sprays to bring home; with proper care, the blooms will last for several weeks.

RIGHT: seedlings in a flask at the orchid breeding lab run by the Singapore Botanical Gardens. These tiny plants are sold in convenient ready-to-take-home flasks like this.

LITTLE INDIA AND KAMPUNG GLAM

To experience the sensory impact of the subcontinent,
take a stroll along Little India's Serangoon Road,
then step south into a slightly different world,
that of the Malay enclave of Kampung Glam

Most Asian cities grew in ramshackle fashion, but Singapore was planned from the very start. Sir Stamford Raffles, on his second visit to the island in 1822, sketched a masterplan for his trading entrepôt that divided urban Singapore into various ethnic districts.

LITTLE INDIA

Little India was a later addition, a suburb that grew up around a camp for Indian convict workers. It was never intended to be an enclave for Indian migrants, who had Kampung Chulia (an area now marked by Chulia and Market streets in the CBD) designated to them by Raffles. But the abundant grass and water that had made the Serangoon area an attractive place for cattle-breeding attracted both Indian proprietors and labourers in the 1840s. Some of the cattle owners even brought labourers from their hometowns in India to work for them. One of them was I.R. Belilios, a Venetian Jew from Calcutta who brought nearly all his Bengali staff with him.

Cattle trading soon took off. The animals were also used for driving machines and for transportation, which in turn spawned a spectrum of economic activities, such as wheat grinding, and pulled in even more Indians to the area. Retail and commercial activities developed to cater to the burgeoning population's needs, and by the turn of the 20th century, the area began to take on the character of an Indian neighbourhood.

Today, visitors who step into **Serangoon Road** – the main road that runs into the heart of Little India – immerse themselves in the area's vibrant sights, sounds and smells.

LEFT: Little India fabric vendor.
RIGHT: shopping on Serangoon Road, the heart of the neighbourhood.

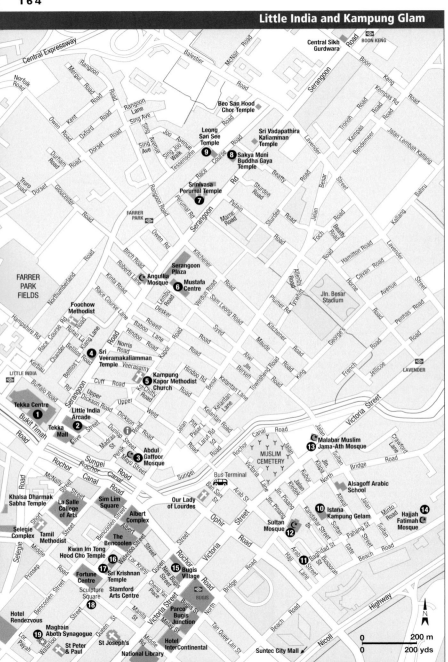

Central Expressway

Norfolk Road

Mergui Road

Rangoon Road

Kent Road

Oxford Road

Owen Road

Dorset Road

Durham Road

Truro Road

Gloucester Road

Dorset Road

Race Course Road

Rangoon Lane

Sing Ave

Joo Avenue

Sing Joo Walk

Sing Avenue

Tessensohn Road

Balestier Road

McNair Road

Serangoon Road

BOON KENG

Boon Keng Road

Central Sikh Gurdwara

Beo San Hood Chor Temple

Leong San See Temple **9**

Sakya Muni Buddha Gaya Temple **8**

Sri Vadapathira Kaliamman Temple

Race Course Rd

Petain Road

Beatty Road

Sturdee Road

Marne Road

Srinivasa Perumal Temple **7**

Perumal Rd

Serangoon Rd

Owen Rd

FARRER PARK

FARRER PARK FIELDS

Northumberland Road

Hampshire Rd

Race Course Rd

Foochow Methodist

Kinta Road

Birch Road

Roberts Lane

Serangoon Plaza

Angullia Mosque

Serangoon Road

Kitchener Road

Verdun Road

Sam Leong Road

Mustafa Centre **6**

Lembu Road

Desker Road

Rowell Road

Baboo Lane

Hindoo Road

Rotan Lane

Chander Road

Belilios Road

Rotan Lang Lane

Kerbau Road

LITTLE INDIA

Sri Veeramakaliamman Temple **4**

Norris Road

Veerasamy Road

Cuff Road

Buffalo Road

Upper Dickson Road

Serangoon Road

Kampung Kapor Methodist Church **5**

Hindoo Rd

Kelantan Lane

Weld Road

Klang Lane

Syed Alwi Road

Maude Road

Jln Berseh

Townshend Road

Kitchener Road

Jln Besar

Jln. Besar Stadium

George's Rd

Allenby Road

Tyrwhitt Road

Hamilton Road

Cavan Road

Foch Road

Beatty Road

Kallang Road

Lavender Street

Horne Road

Penhas Road

Jellicoe Road

King

French

LAVENDER

Tekka Centre **1**

Bukit Timah Road

Little India Arcade

Tekka Mall

Clive St

Madras St

Perak Road

Dunlop Street

Upper Dickson Road

Mayo Street

Abdul Gaffoor Mosque **3**

Rochor Canal Road

Sungei Road

Rochor Canal

McNally Street

Short Street

Khalsa Dharmak Sabha Temple

La Salle College of Arts

Selegie Complex

Selegie Road

Tamil Methodist

Prinsep Street

Middle Road

Sim Lim Square

Bencoolen Street

Albert Complex

The Bencoolen

Waterloo Street

Kwan Im Tong Hood Cho Temple

Fortune Centre **17**

Sri Krishnan Temple **16**

Sculpture Square **18**

Stamford Arts Centre

Hotel Rendezvous

Maghain Aboth Synagogue **19**

St Peter & Paul

St Joseph's

Queen St

Waterloo St

Manila St

Victoria Street

National Library

Middle St

Bugis St

Bencoolen St

Prinsep St

Pitt St

Pasar L

Latif Rd

Sungei Road

Jalan Pisang

Jln Pisang

Bus Terminal

Bali Lane

Arab St

Our Lady of Lourdes

Ophir Road

Rochor Road

Canal Road

Victoria Lane

MUSLIM CEMETERY

Jalan Kubor

Jln Kubor

Jln Klapa

Jln Kledek

Jalan Sultan

Jln Sultan

Kandahar Street

Istana Kampung Gelam **10**

Sultan Mosque **12**

Aliwal Street

Baghdad St

Beach Road

North Bridge Road

Malabar Muslim Jama-Ath Mosque **13**

Crawford Lane

Bridge Road

Alsagoff Arabic School

Minto Rd

Pahang St

Sultan Gate

Bussorah St

Kandahar St

Hajjah Fatimah Mosque **14**

Arab St

Bali Lane **11**

Bugis Village **15**

Cheng Yan Place

Queen St

New Bugis St

Bugis Junction

BUGIS

Parco Bugis Junction

Tan Quee Lan St

Bugis St

Middle Road

North Bridge Road

Beach Road

Nicoll Highway

Highway

Hotel InterContinental

Lor Payah

Queen St

Suntec City Mall

N

0   200 m

0   200 yds

At street corner stalls, jasmine flowers perfume the air as they are deftly strung into garlands for use in Hindu temples in the neighbourhood. In restaurants, people eat curried rice off banana leaves with their fingers, and you may chance upon the *roti prata* man, twirling lumps of dough into the air in ever-increasing circles and then pan-frying them on a hot griddle. Dunked in curry, *roti prata* makes for a delicious breakfast.

Tekka Centre

Just at the corner of Serangoon Road and Bukit Timah Road lies **Tekka Centre ❶**. Tekka means "bamboo shoot" in Teochew, and a profusion of bamboo grew here in the past. Stalls selling Malay, Chinese and Indian food draw sizeable crowds for breakfast. Tekka also has a newly renovated "wet market" with an amazing array of produce, including fresh seafood, meats, vegetables, grated coconut, herbs such as coriander, basil and kaffir lime leaves, as well as all manner of dried goods. Upstairs are clothing, brassware and antiques shops.

The market once occupied a sprawling site on Serangoon Road and was known as Kandang Kerbau ("cattle pen" in Malay) Market, after the cattle station that marked the site. In fact Tekka Centre is sometimes referred to by this old name. Modernisation today encroaches on this largely low-rise ethnic quarter with newer structures like the unremarkable six-storey shopping complex, **The Verge** (formerly Tekka Mall), opposite Tekka Centre, which houses a supermarket, food court, fast-food outlets and shops.

Little India Arcade

Opposite is **Little India Arcade ❷**, flanked by Hasting Road and Campbell Lane. Located in a restored Art Deco-style shophouse built in 1913, the arcade houses one of Singapore's most famous Indian restaurants, the

Banana Leaf Apolo. Souvenir stalls abound in an open courtyard selling incense sticks, Ayurvedic herbal oils and handicrafts from India. Sweet snacks such as *gulab jamun* (milk balls in sweet syrup) and *halwa*, a bright orange-coloured pudding, are also sold at counters at the arcade's Serangoon Road entrance.

Around Serangoon Road

Serangoon Road and the side streets that lead off it, like Campbell Lane, Dunlop Street, Clive Street and Upper Dickson Road, are lined with shops spilling over with spices, fabrics, brassware and glittering jewellery. Here you can buy home-made yoghurt wrapped in a plastic bag for a dollar on the "five-foot way" (the mandatory five-foot-wide corridor that fronts all shophouses – as decreed by Raffles), maybe see an old man wrapping areca nut, gambier, tobacco and lime in *seray* (betel nut leaf) to be chewed for a narcotic-like effect, or a green parakeet choosing tarot cards based on Hindu mythology for S$3 (outside Komala Vilas Restaurant at 76 Serangoon Road).

ABOVE: for a small fee, you can have your fortune told by a green parakeet – with the help of its able-bodied human assistant, of course. **BELOW:** the Tekka Centre.

In the handful of jewellery shops run by Indian goldsmiths (most are now owned by Chinese), take a closer look at the silver amulets depicting body parts, such as arms, legs or feet, in the display cabinets. The Hindus will buy the amulet representing the limb or organ that is suffering, and present it as an offering in the hope that the gods will get the message and relieve their pain.

Streets such as Dickson, Dunlop and Clive once led to the private residences of Europeans who settled near the Race Course when it was completed in the 1840s, while streets like Belilios and Desker reflect the names of former cattle owners. Wanderlust and Moon @ 23 Dickson are two new boutique hotels that have been launched along Dickson Road.

ABOVE: Little India is a vegetarian's fantasy come true – there are heaps of shops doling out "thosai", a rice-flour based pancake eaten with a selection of vegetable curries.
BELOW: henna tattoos.

Be sure to explore **Campbell Lane**, which bursts into colour at the first light of day, with stalls offering floral garlands and jasmine flower bunches, which Indian women use as hair adornments. **Jothi Music Corner** on this street is popular with local Indians for its selection of Bol-

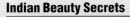

Indian Beauty Secrets

Thanks to Hollywood celebrities, Indian beauty practices never looked so hip. Whether you're looking for a henna tattoo or Ayurvedic massage, Little India is your one-stop beauty spot – the Indian way, of course. Call at **Vanessa Beauty Salon & Henna Artwork Creations** for henna body art and henna hair colouring (22 Buffalo Road; tel: 6291-0977). **Susiee House of Beauty** swears by its secret herbal formula that halts hair loss after a few treatments (32-A Buffalo Road; tel: 6292-6720). Threading is an art, and if your therapist does it right, removing facial hair with a thread is painless. Try **Rupini's Beauty** (24/26 Buffalo Road; tel: 6291-6789; www.rupinis.com.sg).

lywood VCDs and Bhangra music CDs. Further on the right, **Dunlop Street** has shops selling all manner of Indian goods. **Royal Saree Palace** is a good place to shop for silk saris, as is the fabric emporium **Haniffa Textiles**.

Abdul Gaffoor Mosque

Address: 41 Dunlop Street
Tel: 6295-4209
Opening Hrs: daily 7am–noon
Entrance Fee: free
Transport: Little India MRT

Little India is famous not just for Hindu temples but for shrines representing the spectrum of faiths practised in Singapore. The lovely old **Abdul Gaffoor Mosque** ❸ was originally built in 1859 and named after a South Indian lawyer's clerk. This Arabian- and Renaissance-style mosque is an oasis of calm. The prayer hall, decorated with Moorish arches, has a tableau tracing the origins of Islam. Outside prayer times, the mosque is occupied by devotees who drop by to spend time to read the Qu'ran or to chat.

Sri Veeramakaliamman Temple

Address: 141 Serangoon Road;
www.sriveeramakaliamman.com
Tel: 6295-4538
Opening Hrs: daily 5.30–12.30pm,
4–9pm
Entrance Fee: free
Transport: Little India MRT

Return to Serangoon Road, and you will find **Sri Veeramakaliamman Temple ❹**, one of the oldest temples in Singapore. It is dedicated to the multi-armed Goddess Kali, the manifestation of anger in the face of evil. In one of her images, she is shown ripping a hapless victim apart. As consort to Shiva, the goddess is also known as Parvati in her benign form; therefore she is both loved and feared. Dating back to 1855 and built by indentured Bengali labourers, the temple's main shrine has a striking statue of Kali, with her sons – Ganesh the Elephant God and Murugan the Child God – depicted on either side. Tuesdays and Fridays are considered sacred days, and are especially busy with

devotees streaming in to pray and ask for blessings.

Kampung Kapor Church

On the opposite side of Serangoon Road, a walk down Veerasamy Road leads to the corner where it connects with Kampung Kapor Road. Here stands a gem of a little church – the **Kampung Kapor Methodist Church ❺** with Dutch-style gabled roofs (call ahead to view; tel: 6293-7997; www.kkmc.org.sg). Formerly known as the Straits Chinese Methodist Church, it was built in 1930 to cater to a largely Peranakan congregation from Melaka. Its history dates back to 1890, when Methodist missionary Sophia Blackmore started the first Malay-language church service in Singapore.

Mustafa Centre

Back on Serangoon Road, a 15-minute stroll past the Moorish-style **Angullia Mosque** on the left takes you to a decidedly secular temple to consumerism. Located on the left along Syed Alwi Road, the sprawling **Mustafa Centre ❻** is a six-storey shopping

ABOVE: worshippers at
Sri Veeramakaliamman
Temple.

TIP

Little India heaves on Sunday nights with migrant workers who descend on the area in droves. The streets and sidewalks spill over, and the crowds of mainly men (on their only day off work) can seem daunting to a first-timer. Avoid visiting Little India at this time, as it won't be a pleasant experience.

complex that is hugely popular with bargain hunters (tel: 6295-5855; daily 24 hours). It's also the only department store in Singapore that offers retail therapy round the clock, thanks to its far-sighted Indian owner, who is dubbed Singapore's Retail Raja.

Tourists and "foreign workers" from India often come here to shop for goods to take home to the subcontinent. There is a mind-boggling range of goods – from household appliances and luggage to computers, cameras and food items (daily 10.30am–11.30pm).

Srinivasa Perumal Temple

Address: 397 Serangoon Road, www.heb.gov.sg
Tel: 6298-5771
Opening Hrs: daily 6.30am–noon, 6–9pm
Entrance Fee: free
Transport: Farer Park MRT

Further along Serangoon Road, the great *gopuram* (tower) of the **Srinivasa Perumal Temple** ❼, built in 1855, is visible, showing the different incarnations of Vishnu. The *gopuram* graces the entrance of a Hindu temple and consists of an odd number of tiers, the actual configuration depending on the money contributed to build it. Perumal Temple's five-tier *gopuram* was a donation from P. Govindasamy Pillai, one of the earliest Indian migrants who made good. He ultimately set up a chain of popular general goods stores in Little India and was known for his philanthropic work, a legacy continued by his sons today.

Perumal Temple is at the centre of the Hindu trinity made up of Brahma the Creator, Vishnu the Preserver and Shiva the Destroyer. The temple is dedicated to Krishna, one of the incarnations of Vishnu. Perumal is another name for Krishna, and statues of him – coloured blue to signify blue blood – are everywhere in the temple. There are also statues of his two wives, Lakshmi and Andal, the goddesses of Beauty and Wealth respectively, and of his mount, the mythical Garuda bird. The temple ceiling is dominated by a colourful circular pattern depicting the nine planets of the universe.

The annual Thaipusam procession sets off from here. Devotees, their tongues and cheeks pierced by metal skewers and carrying *kavadi* (cage-like constructions decorated with wire and peacock feathers), make their way to the Sri Thandayuthapani Temple in Tank Road (*see page 149*).

Petain Road houses

A little further from Perumal Temple, on the opposite side of Serangoon Road, is **Petain Road**, which, like many of the nearby roads that were built after World War I, was named after men who had distinguished themselves in World War I battles. Petain Road was named after the Marshal of France, Henri-Philippe Pétain (1856–1951).

The street was once a swampland filled with vegetable gardens. In 1916, the swamps were drained, the farmers forced out, and the area was converted into a residential neigh-

bourhood. It is here that architecture typical of 1920s can be seen at its best. Called Chinese Baroque or Singapore Eclectic *(see pages 176–7)*, it is a blend of European, Malay, Indian and Chinese influences.

The row of 18 ornate terrace houses share the same characteristics – carved wooden eaves found in Malay houses, Indian-style stucco pillars, classical-inspired columns and pilasters, facades made up largely of colourful Spanish floral tiles and Chinese symbols in the bas-relief plaster work depicting animals and flowers. Look out for the beautifully tiled covered "five-foot" walkway linking the houses.

Sakya Muni Buddha Gaya

Race Course Road, running parallel to Serangoon Road behind Srinivasa Perumal Temple, may have lost its glamour as a racing track and its horses, but there is a pair of very different Chinese temples here worth visiting. At 366 Race Course Road is the stunning **Sakya Muni Buddha Gaya Temple ❽**, also known as the Temple of 1,000 Lights. A 15-metre (50ft) high Buddha image sits under

a halo of lightbulbs, on a base depicting scenes from the life of Prince Siddharta Gautama (tel: 6294-0714; daily 8am–4.45pm). Worshippers may illuminate the lights around the statue for a small donation or have their fortune told by spinning a wheel on the left of the prayer hall.

The temple began as a wooden shelter in 1927 by Thai monk Vutthisasara. Its immense popularity saw a grander building constructed in the 1930s, with funds from Aw Boon Haw and Aw Boon Par, the brothers behind the Haw Par Villa in Pasir Panjang Road *(see page 196)*. Guarding the entrance of the temple are a pair of ferocious-looking tigers.

Leong San See Temple

The richly carved and ornately decorated **Leong San See Temple ❾** (Dragon Mountain Temple) at 371 Race Course Road just across the street is dedicated to Kuan Yin, the Chinese Goddess of Mercy (tel: 6298-9371; daily 6am–6pm).

The temple, dating back to the late 1800s, bears the image of Confucius at its altar and is popular with many

ABOVE: at Leong San See Temple in Race Course Road, joss sticks are burnt as supplication to the ancestral gods.
BELOW: giant Buddha statue at Sayka Muni Buddha Gaya Temple.

ABOVE: an Arab Street shop spilling over with all manner of baskets.

TIP

When in Arab Street, do what Arabs do – try smoking fruit-flavoured tobacco through water, better known as *shisha*. This Middle Eastern tradition can be experienced at Café Le Caire (39 Arab Street, tel: 6292-0979; www. cafelecaire.com).

parents, who bring their children here to pray for success at examinations and filial piety. Established by Reverend Chuan Wu as a lodge for the sick in 1926, it is now an elaborate temple built on funds donated by prominent merchant and philanthropist Tan Boon Liat. Note especially the dragon sculptures on top of its roofs. At the back is a courtyard with old ancestral tablets.

KAMPUNG GLAM

Raffles allocated this area, a neighbouring district of Little India, to Sultan Hussein, the Malay ruler of Singapore who signed two treaties in 1819 and 1824, ceding the island to the British. Here the sultan built a palace for his family and homes for his royal retainers, who had followed him from Riau.

Today the sleepy neighbourhood is landlocked, but in former times it ran along the shore (hence the name Beach Road), with many of the houses built on stilts above the tidal mud flats. Much of Kampung Glam was

mangrove swamp when it was drained in the 1820s. The name means "Village of the *Gelam* Tree" in Malay. The bark of these trees (*Melaleuca leucadendron*) had medicinal value and was used by the Malays to caulk their ships, although it would be difficult to find a *gelam* tree in the area today.

Istana Kampung Gelam

At the very heart of the district, at 85 Sultan Gate, is **Istana Kampung Gelam** ⑩, the old royal palace, built in the early 1840s by Sultan Ali Iskandar Shah on the site of the original wooden palace built by his father, Sultan Hussein. Erected on stilts, the original building was styled after a Malay palace, with a veranda on the upper floor. Istana Kampung Gelam was said to have been designed by George Coleman, who combined traditional Malay motifs with the Palladian style, though there is no concrete proof that he was its architect.

The palace has been converted into a **Malay Heritage Centre** (tel: 6391 0450; www.malayheritage.org.sg; grounds daily 8am–9pm; museum Mon 1–6pm, Tue–Sun 10am–6pm; free except for museum and cultural shows). In the grounds is a museum housing nine galleries chronicling Malay history and culture. The exhibits include artefacts unearthed during the restoration period, such as rifles belonging to Malay soldiers during World War II and earthen pots that were used for burying the placentas of newborn babies. The adjacent canary-yellow two-storey **Gedung Kuning** (Yellow Mansion), built for Tengku Mahmoud, grandson of Sultan Hussein, is now the **Tepak Sireh Restoran** *(see page 175)*.

Arab Street

Arab traders, together with Bugis, Javanese, Boyanese, Banjarese, Sumatrans, Malays and people from the Riau Islands, eventually settled in the area, transforming Kampung Glam

into a commercial hub, especially along **Arab Street** ⓫, four blocks away, which still draws those looking for bargains in textiles, lace, basketware and haberdashery.

In Arab Street you can shop for batik cloth, either in sarong lengths or fashioned into clothes, table linen and paintings. Baskets of every shape, size and colour are piled on the pavement. There's leatherware and ethnic jewellery, too, as well as gold and silver, embroidered *songket* fabric and alcohol-free perfumes.

Sultan Mosque

Dominating the *kampung* (village) skyline is the golden dome of **Sultan Mosque** ⓬, dating back to 1924 (tel: 6293 4405; Mon–Thur, Sat–Sun 9am–4.30pm, Fri 9am–noon, 2.30–4.30pm).

Swan and Maclaren, the architectural firm responsible for the mosque, adopted the design of the Taj Mahal and combined it with Persian, Moorish, Turkish and classical themes. It is the largest mosque in Singapore, where the muezzin calls the faithful to prayer five times a day – the women to their enclave upstairs, and the men to the main prayer hall. With its striking golden domes and soaring minaret, this is one of the loveliest and most important places of Muslim worship in Singapore.

Bussorah Street

The most enchanting view of the mosque is from the corner of Bussorah Street and Baghdad Street. Part of **Bussorah Street**, whch is lined with charming 19th-century restored shophouses, has been closed to traffic.

The street was once part of the "Pilgrims Village" in the early days when steamships plied the sea. Bussorah and other nearby streets used to house *haj* pilgrims travelling to Mecca from East Asia. Today, however, the colourful streets have been transformed into a delightful shopping area, peppered with Arabic-style cafés and restaurants serving Middle Eastern cuisine.

Two streets down, on **Haji Lane**, the hip quotient is maintained with

ABOVE: Sultan Mosque seen from Bussorah Street. **BELOW:** inside the mosque.

Religious Tensions

Although a peaceful country with no significant social unrest, Singapore has experienced occasional racial tension in the years since independence

Singapore's enviable record of religious and ethnic harmony was not won lightly. The country has twice been wrecked by communal riots, once in 1950, when the British still ruled Singapore, and again in 1964 during the brief period when Singapore was part of an ill-fated union with Malaysia. These sobering experiences convinced the government that inter-religious peace in a multiethnic society like Singapore was fragile and needed to be cultivated through even-handed state policies.

Government policies aside, a live-and-let-live attitude of religious tolerance and the belief that each religion has its merits help Singaporeans cope with each other's religious practices in close proximity. This, however, does not imply the complete absence of religious tension – in fact, the potential for religious friction is ever present. In the early 1980s, for example, a Christian charismatic offshoot in Singapore actively converted huge numbers of Chinese from the Buddhist and Taoist faiths. These new converts in turn began to engage in aggressive proselytisation, and by the late 1980s started to target the Malays, causing considerable religious and ethnic tension. Because Islam is central to their identity, the Malays perceived these efforts as an attack on their community as well as their religion. The stress this caused was considered sufficiently serious for the state to intervene and pass a Maintenance of Religious Harmony Bill in 1990, which empowers the state to place a restraining order on individuals who engage in aggressive evangelism.

The geopolitics of religion, too, influences the state's perceptions of certain ethnic groups, in this case the Malay community. Singapore has always perceived itself and been viewed by others as a "Chinese state" because of its Chinese majority, yet geopolitically it is situated in a Malay- and Muslim-dominant region. This has given Singapore's Malays a political significance in excess of their size, both as the indigenous minority and in the larger context of the region they live in.

Yet at the same time, the prevailing perception has been that the Malays' loyalty to religion is at times greater than their loyalty to the nation. When the Allied forces attacked Iraq in 1991 following its invasion of Kuwait, a local newspaper poll indicated that six out of 10 Malays disapproved of the attack, compared to three out of 10 Singaporeans. The 9/11 terrorist attacks in America raised similar concerns. Because the Malays' loyalty is perceived to be divided, they have in the past been consciously disadvantaged in national service and employment in the armed forces. Although the government maintains that the situation has improved, many Malays still feel that they are institutionally discriminated against.	❑

BELOW: attractive Abdul Gaffoor Mosque dates back to 1859.

independent stores run by young local designers. The cool vibe continues on adjoining **Bali Lane**, where cafés like **Blu Jaz** (11 Bali Lane) feature jam sessions by local musicians in the evenings.

Malabar Jama-Ath Mosque

Kampung Glam has several other beautiful mosques. At the corner of Jalan Sultan and Victoria Street is the humble **Malabar Muslim Jama-Ath Mosque ⑬** in blue-coloured mosaic, a quiet place of worship with a bygone ambience that harkens back to the era when the *kampung* was founded (tel: 6294-3862; daily 10am–noon, 2–4pm). The mosaic tiles were only added after the mosque opened in 1963. The island's oldest Muslim cemetery lies beneath fragrant frangipani trees a little further along Victoria Street opposite Jalan Kledek.

Hajjah Fatimah Mosque

Behind Jalan Sultan and off Beach Road is the lovely **Hajjah Fatimah Mosque ⑭**, built by a British architect in 1846 (tel: 6297-2774; daily 9am–9pm). The structure is named after a faithful Muslim woman, who, after her husband's death, ran his shipping business so well that the proceeds enabled her to build the mosque on the site of their home, which had been demolished after it was ravaged by a fire. Its Gothic-style spire, which tilts at six degrees, is a neighbourhood curiosity.

Bugis Village

Leaving Kampung Glam behind, head down Beach Road towards the corner of Rochor Road and Victoria Street to reach **Bugis Village ⑮**. The name is inspired by the former **Bugis Street**, arguably Singapore's most infamous attraction and known for its street food, raucous entertainment and uninhibited transvestites in days gone by – until it was demolished years ago to make way for an MRT

station. Some of the old Bugis Street attractions are back in its new guise as Bugis Village, but it is a pale imitation of its former self. The old shophouses have been restored and some of the original hawkers have returned. Rows of tightly packed stalls peddling clothes, bags and watches lend a bazaar-like atmosphere, but this sterile impostor cannot match the buzz of the original Bugis Street.

Across Bugis Village is **Bugis Junction**, a mall that features a glass-covered air-conditioned "street" with boutiques and cafés. Forming part of the complex is the Intercontinental Singapore, using shophouse architecture as its theme.

Kwan Im Tong Hood Temple

At nearby Waterloo Street, Buddhists and Hindus are equally comfortable praying at the **Kwan Im Tong Hood Cho Temple ⑯** (tel: 6337-3965; daily 6.15am–6.15pm) or at Sri Krishnan Temple, perhaps for double assurance. The Chinese temple was rebuilt in 1895 and again in 1982 to cater to the increasing number of devotees who come here to pay their respect to the deities. Chief among them is Kuan Yin, or the Goddess of Mercy,

ABOVE: colourful pyjamas for sale at Bugis Village's streetside vendors.
BELOW: Arab Street shoppers in Islamic dress and headscarf *(tudung)*.

sitting in a heavily gilded altar. Outside the temple are fortune tellers and a motley collection of vendors selling traditional medicine and flowers.

Sri Krishnan Temple

Just next door, even Chinese worshippers offer incense sticks to Lord Krishnan (the Hindu equivalent of Kuan Yin) and other Hindu deities at **Sri Krishnan Temple** (tel: 6337-7957; daily 6am–noon, 5–9.30pm). Although it wasn't until the 1980s that the present elaborate carved tower entrance was added, the temple has been on the same site since the 1870s.

Sculpture Square

Address: 155 Middle Road; www.sculpturesq.com.sg
Tel: 6333-1055
Opening Hrs: Mon–Fri 11am–7.30pm, Sat–Sun 11am–6pm
Entrance Fee: free
Transport: Bras Basah MRT

Across Sri Krishnan Temple is a designated arts strip near the Singapore Art Museum. The area is home to local arts groups like Action Theatre, Young

ABOVE: detail from the Sri Krishnan Temple at Waterloo Street depicting Hanuman, the Monkey God.

Musicians' Society and Stamford Arts Centre, where artists work on disciplines ranging from Indian music to Chinese dance and Italian opera. The arts hub is also home to the Nanyang Academy of Fine Arts and the LaSalle College of the Arts, housed in a striking matt-black building.

The lovely **Sculpture Square** at the junction of Waterloo Street and Middle Road was constructed in 1870 as a church and a girl's school. The chapel, with its 19th-century arc windows and circular vents, is one of the few Gothic-style buildings still standing in Singapore today. Restored and opened in 1999, it's the only space in Singapore dedicated to three-dimensional art.

Maghain Aboth Synagogue

At 26 Waterloo Street stands yet another institution that is testimony to Singapore's multiracial society: the Victorian-style **Maghain Aboth Synagogue** . Erected in 1878, this was the first synagogue to be built for the Jewish community in Singapore (viewing by appointment only; tel: 6337-2189). ❑

SHOPPING

Little India is great for picking up quality saris or for a 24-hour shopping spree. Over at Kampung Glam, the narrow Haji Lane is lined with independent stores by local designers.

Music

Jothi Music Corner
48 Serangoon Road. Tel: 6299-5528. p267, C4
Popular with local Indians for its selection of Bollywood VCDs and Bhangra music CDs.

Clothing

Haniffa Textiles
60 Serangoon Road. Tel: 6299-3709 p267, C4
Another fabric emporium selling vibrant silk saris.

Know it Nothing
51 Haji Lane. Tel: 6392-5475. www.knowitnothing.com. p270/1, C1/2
A two-storey boutique selling locally designed men's clothing as well as independent cult labels from all over the world. Shoes and accessories are available too.

Pluck
31–33 Haji Lane. Tel: 6396-4048. www.pluck.com.sg. p270/1, C1/2
This small store sells vintage dresses, bags and quirky accessories. There is a fabulous ice cream parlour next to the boutique.

Royal Saree Palace
132 Dunlop Street. Tel: 6336-885. p267, C4
This a good place to shop for gorgeous silk saris.

Silk Fabric House
115 Arab Street. Tel: 6293-6083. p270, C1
This shop sells sequined and embroidered textiles.

Malls

Bugis Junction
200 Victoria Street. Tel: 6557-6557. www.bugis junction-mall.com.sg. p270, B2
This complex has a glass-covered shopping street, a huge department store, Cineplex, trendy boutiques and cafés.

Mustafa Centre
145 Syed Alwi Road. Tel: 6295-5855. www.mustafa. com.sg. p267, D3
This 24-hour department store will meet most of your retail needs, from electronics and clothing to groceries.

BEST RESTAURANTS

Indian

Ananda Bhavan
01-10, Blk 663 Buffalo Rd. Tel: 6291-1943. www.ananda bhavan.com Open: daily 7am–10pm. $ **34** p266, C4 Also at 58 Serangoon Rd. Tel: 6297-9522

You order, take a queue number and wait for your number to be called before collecting your scrumptious South Indian meal.

Banana Leaf Apolo
54–58 Race Course Rd. Tel: 6293-8682. www.bananaleaf apolo.com Open: daily 10.30am–10.30pm. $$ **35** p266, C4 Also at 01-32 Little India Arcade, 148 Serangoon Rd. Tel: 6297-1595. Open: daily 6.30am–10.30pm.

This perennially busy restaurant fills up quickly and is busy even in the period between lunch and dinner. It's the place for spicy South Indian food served on banana leaves. Top menu choices include masala prawns and chicken.

Kashmir
52 Race Course Rd. Tel: 6293-6003. www.kashmir. com.sg Open: daily L & D. $$ **36** p266, C4

Prices for a three-course dinner per person without drinks and taxes:

$ = under S$20
$$ = S$20–30
$$$ = S$30–50
$$$$ = over S$50

This elegant restaurant serves Kashmiri delicacies. The fish tikka and mutton kebab are superb, as are the fluffy naans and basmati rice.

Komala Vilas
76–78 Serangoon Rd. Tel: 6293-6980. www.komalavilas. com.sg Open: daily 7am–10.30pm. $ **37** p267, C4 Also at 82 Serangoon Rd. Tel: 6294-3294, and 12–14 Buffalo Rd. Tel: 6293-3664.

This boisterous Little India institution is the place for saffron rice and an array of vegetable curries, vadai (savoury fritters) and Indian breads such as whole-wheat bhattura and chapati, and rice flour-based dosai.

Muthu's Curry
138 Race Course Rd. Tel: 6392-1722. www.muthuscurry. com Open: daily 10am–10pm. $$ **38** p267, C3

The locals are passionate about their fish-head curry, and Muthu's Curry inevitably comes up as one of the top places to sample this dish. It has been serving its award-winning fish-head curry since 1969. The chicken, mutton and prawn dishes are always good bets too.

Singapore Zam Zam Restaurant
697–699 North Bridge Rd. Tel: 6298-6320. Open: daily 8am–11pm. $ **39** p270, C1

A rough-and-ready place serving Indian-Muslim specialities. The fragrant mutton or chicken briyani

(with saffron rice) is robustly spicy, as are the flaky breads, called murtabak when stuffed with minced mutton or chicken, and prata when eaten plain and dipped in curry.

Malay

Hajjah Maimunah Restaurant
11 & 15 Jalan Pisang. Tel: 6291-3132. Open: Mon–Sat 11am–9pm. $ **90** p270, C1

Self-service Malay restaurant that's always packed to the gills: just point to the dish and it will be served with fluffy rice. The tender and spicy beef rendang and sotong bakar (grilled squid) are heavenly.

Tepak Sireh Restoran
73 Sultan Gate. Tel: 6396-4373. www.tepaksireh.com.sg Open: daily L & D. $ (buffet lunch and dinner) **91** p271, C1

This resplendent mustard-coloured building next to the Istana Kampung Gelam was originally built for Malay royalty. Its recipes, reportedly handed down for generations, live

up to expectations. The buffet spread includes tender beef rendang and chicken curry.

Middle Eastern

Alaturka
6 Bussorah St. Tel: 6294-0304. Open: daily 11am–11pm. $$ **92** p271, C2

Charming Turkish eatery serving authentic meze plates, fluffy pide (the Turkish version of pizza), lavash (balloon bread with sesame seeds), a variety of kebabs, and desserts like baklava and sütlaç, a milky Turkish rice pudding.

Café Le Caire
39 Arab St. Tel: 6292-0979. Open: daily 10am–5am. $$ **93** p271, C2

Le Caire's charming ambience is reminiscent of a homey eatery in Cairo. Downstairs is more casual, with tables spilling onto the sidewalk, while upstairs is more elaborately furnished. The fare is mainly Middle Eastern; expect reasonable prices and generous portions.

SINGAPORE SHOPHOUSES

Of all the architectural styles in Singapore, none is as distinctive as the lavishly decorated shophouses found in the city's older neighbourhoods

Known as Chinese Baroque or Singapore Eclectic architecture, these shophouses sport a rich mix of Malay, Chinese and European architectural details, all giving a distinctive look to Singapore's urban landscape. The shophouse was so called because the lower floor was used for business while the upper level served as living quarters. The design, initiated by Raffles, had detailed specifications to achieve conformity. They were arranged in a linear form and built of masonry with tile roofs. Linking the shophouses was a covered path called the "five-foot way" because the width between the building and the street had to be exactly five feet. The style later evolved to two-storey residential terrace houses with occupants on both floors. Over the years, five distinct shophouse styles developed: Early, First Transitional, Late, Second Transitional and Art Deco – many of which have been restored to their original splendour.

ABOVE: Boat Quay was where *coolies* (labourers) once lugged sacks of rice, spices and other goods on their backs from "bumboats" along the Singapore River to the shophouses on the shore. Today, its restored shophouses have been turned into a thriving nightlife hub.
BELOW: a rare "English" facade shophouse in Chinatown, dating from 1910.

SHOPHOUSE STYLES

Early: This was the style of the first shophouses, erected in the 1840s. With their squat upper levels and simple lines unadorned of detail, they resemble dolls' houses.

First Transitional: Dating back to the early 1900s, these shophouses takes on an extra floor in order to maximise space. Once dilapidated and shunned, many old shophouses are much sought-after properties these days because of their unique facades and historical value. Strict guidelines govern the restoration of shophouses, many of which have been turned into chic restaurants, bars and boutique hotels as well as offices.

Late: Dating from 1910 to the late 1930s, this is the most florid of all shophouse styles, with lavishly decorated facades and the most ornate details.

Second Transitional: This style, from the late 1930s onwards, was a little less florid than its predecessor. It combined Asian and European architectural influences, including Malay-style wooden eaves, Corinthian columns and pilasters, French windows with timber louvres and semicircular fanlights as well as European glazed ceramic tiles and bas-reliefs depicting motifs from Chinese mythical tales, and flowers and animals.

Art Deco: This is the most recent of styles, mainly built between 1940 and 1960. It is probably the least common of the styles and the most European in character. The private forecourt area with a gate and a balcony on the upper floor are typical features. The shophouse is not unique to Singapore: it can be found in Melaka and Penang in Malaysia, known as the Straits Settlements in the colonial era.

ABOVE: a fine example of the Second Transitional Shophouse Style on Petain Road in Little India.
BELOW LEFT: the Early Shophouse Style is best seen at Kampung Glam and Little India.
BELOW MIDDLE: the First Transitional Shophouse Style lines Telok Ayer Street near Chinatown.
BELOW RIGHT: the Second Transitional style of the late 1930s onwards can be seen at Cuff Road, Little India.

SENTOSA AND
THE SOUTHERN ISLANDS

It's easy to escape from the frenzied city to Sentosa,
a playground of attractions and lovely beaches.
The other southern islands, in contrast,
are tiny specks of sand visited by few people

The most popular of Singapore's outlying islands is **Sentosa**, which has become a major resort and recreation area after its previous life as a military base. Several other islands can be easily reached from the mainland, ranging from tiny specks, like the Sisters' Islands, to larger ones, like St John's.

SENTOSA

Sentosa was once called Pulau Blakang Mati, which means "island at the back of which lies death" in Malay, because the frequent outbreaks of disease there had claimed the lives of many of its islanders. It was also a refuge for pirates in the 19th century before it was turned into a military fortress by the British – who positioned guns towards the sea, thinking this would best protect their colony of Singapore. But history proved them wrong, and during World War II Singapore succumbed to the Japanese, who came overland through the peninsula of Malaya (now Malaysia).

When the British withdrew their military presence in Singapore in 1968, the government decided to transform the former garrison island of 395 hectares (976 acres) into a leisure resort. But first, a more appealing name had to be found. The name Sentosa ("Isle of Peace and Tranquillity" in Malay) was picked in a naming contest, and, in 1972, Sentosa welcomed its first visitors.

Getting to Sentosa

The island can be reached by cable car or land. The more scenic option is by cable car, shuttling 65 metres (213ft) above the water from stations

at Mount Faber *(see page 191)* and the HarbourFront Centre to Sentosa. The lofty ride offers a bird's-eye view of the city and the busiest container port in the world (cable cars run daily 8.30am–10pm: packages, including admission fees and a guided tour of Sentosa, are available).

From HarbourFront Centre, you can take a taxi, bus or walk across the 710-metre (2,329ft) causeway that links Sentosa to Singapore. Most visitors take the train to the HarbourFront MRT station and walk to the nearby HarbourFront Centre Bus Terminal to catch the Sentosa Bus to the island (Sun–Thur 7am–10.30pm, Fri–Sat and holidays 7–12.30am; charge).

A more convenient way to get to Sentosa is by the Sentosa Express, a light rail system that began operations in early 2007 (daily 7am–midnight; charge). Board at the third floor of VivoCity. Once on the island, you can alight at either the Beach or Imbiah stations, then walk or take the shuttle bus or tram services to the various attractions. Since January 2011, visitors have been able to

ABOVE: the Sentosa Express. **BELOW:** dolphin show at Underwater World.

get to Sentosa on foot via the Sentosa Boardwalk, parallel to Sentosa's vehicular bridge. This sheltered boardwalk, which starts from VivoCity's waterfront promenade, will eventually be lined with lush tropical landscapes and lookout points where people can enjoy the view along the way.

The admission fee to the island varies according to the times and mode of transport. It includes access to all the beaches and unlimited bus rides on Sentosa. If you take a taxi directly to the drop-off point at the Resorts World casino, there is no admission fee. All the major attractions on the island, however, have separate admission charges, which can all add up. The best deals are package tickets which include transportation and entry to multiple attractions on Sentosa (tel: 1800-736-8672 or visit www. sentosa.com.sg for more information).

Resorts World Sentosa

Sentosa is undergoing a massive S$8-billion redevelopment, with most of the new amenities and attractions already in place. In 2010, the **Sentosa Cove**, an upmarket residential project

Universal Studios

Spend an entire day at Universal Studios Singapore (tel: 6577-8888; www.rwsentosa.com; Mon–Sun 10am–7pm, Fri–Sat 10am–7pm). There are seven zones – the Lost World, Far Far Away, Sci-Fi City, New York, Hollywood, Ancient Egypt and Madagascar – and 24 themed rides, of which 18 were designed exclusively for Singapore. Highlights include Shrek's 4-D Adventure; Jurassic Park Rapids Adventure, a thrilling raft ride; Lights, Camera, Action, simulating a hurricane blowing away New York; and the Universal Studios' signature ride, the Battlestar Galactica duelling rollercoaster. In the evenings you can come and watch a stunning firework show set to music in the Hollywood zone.

with a marina, and the S$6.59-billion **Resorts World Sentosa ❶ (RWS)** were launched. RWS, operated by Genting Singapore, a subsidiary of Malaysia's Genting Group, is one of Singapore's two "integrated resorts", a term coined by the government for these mega-complexes housing casinos and various attractions. The other is in Marina Bay *(see page 138)*.

The vast RWS complex is home to Southeast Asia's first and only Universal Studios theme park, a casino, several hotels, as well as restaurants helmed by celebrity chefs (including world-famous chef Joel Robuchon's first outpost, to be launched in February 2011). Besides Universal Studios, there are other attractions, such as the upcoming Marine Life Park, touted as the world's largest oceanarium. It will also boast the world's longest man-made rainforest river, the Maritime Xperiential Museum and the world's first 4D multi-sensory typhoon theatre. Other entertainment offered by the resort includes the Voyage de la Vie show at the Festive Grand theatre, featuring performance by an international a group of circus stars, topped

with energetic music, stunts, vibrant costumes and amazing sets. While Marina Bay Sands is targeted at higher-end clientele, RWS is seen as a place for the family with kids in tow. A whole day should be set aside for a visit to Sentosa; in fact, there is probably enough to keep visitors busy for a few days, especially at RWS.

Underwater World

Address: 80 Siloso Road; www.underwaterworld.com.sg
Tel: 6275-0030
Opening Hrs: daily 9am–9pm
Entrance Fee: charge
Transport: Take the blue line bus service from Beach Station

On the western side of the island is **Underwater World ❷**, one of Asia's best aquariums and a must-see while at Sentosa. One of the highlights at this attraction is the transparent 83-metre (272ft) long acrylic tunnel with a moving walkway that leads under a huge tank containing some 2.8 million litres (615,000 gallons) of water and over 2,500 tropical sea creatures – from bright, luminous reef-dwellers to stingrays and sharks.

TIP

Cycling is a great way to explore Sentosa – hire a bicycle from rental kiosks at the Ferry Terminal or along the beach, pick up a Cycle Track Route Map (available at the kiosks) and just pedal away.

BELOW LEFT AND BELOW: Universal Studios.

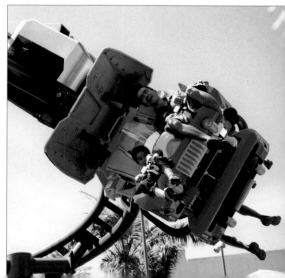

Nasty stone fish, sea urchins and moray eels lurk behind the rocks and amid colourful corals. At varying times daily, you can watch these denizens of the deep being hand-fed by divers.

The more adventurous can opt for a "Dive with the Sharks" and swim amongst these fearsome sea creatures, while intrepid scuba-certified divers can sign up for the "Extreme Bull Shark Encounter". There is also a "Dive with the Dugong" option for the shark-shy, and touch pools, where kids can have close encounters with starfish and baby sharks. Extra charges apply for these special encounters and advance reservations are essential.

Another interesting exhibit is the **Living Fossils** display at the Changing Exhibit Hall, where visitors learn about the importance of marine conservation. The exhibition highlights living fossils like the mangrove and coastal horseshoe crab, which have

managed to survive environmental upheavals. Also worth seeing is the **Dugong Cove**, where a dugong that was rescued from the seas off Pulau Ubin in 1998 and rehabilitated at Underwater World currently resides. The gentle sea creature, with its curiously shaped body and tail – long thought to have inspired sailors' tales of the mermaid – is named Gracie.

Note: your ticket to Underwater World includes admission to the Dolphin Lagoon (see page 187).

Fort Siloso

Address: www.fortsiloso.com
Opening Hrs: daily 10am–6pm
Entrance Fee: charge
Transport: Take the blue line bus from Beach Station

Also located at the western tip of the island and within walking distance of the Underwater World is **Fort Siloso** ❸, Singapore's only preserved coastal fort. The fort's tunnels and numerous guns pointing out to sea were built

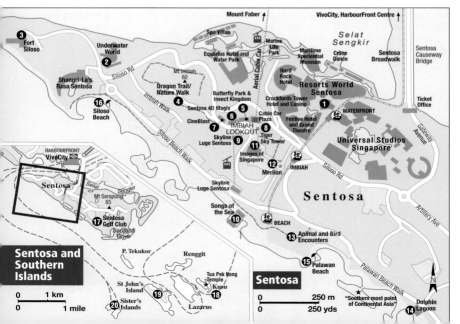

in the 1880s for the defence of Singapore by the British – albeit facing the wrong direction as the Japanese invaded from the north by land during World War II. This historic landmark, enhanced by lush greenery and landscaping, is another one of Sentosa's must-see sights.

Used as a prisoner-of-war camp during the Japanese Occupation (1942–5), the fort offers a one-stop overview of World War II history. A tram takes visitors from the foot of the hill through a series of films and exhibits detailing the fort's history, including its role during the war. Bunkers, tunnels and a six-inch gun that can "load and fire" add a fillip to this real-life vignette of Singapore's wartime past.

The displays at the adjoining **Surrender Chamber** take you through the years of World War II. Photographs, films, wartime mementoes and wax figures depict the surrender by the British in 1942, and that by the Japanese in 1945.

Dragon Trail/Nature Walk

If there is time to kill and you have small children with you, take them to the nearby **Nature Walk ❹**, a trail through 1.5km (1 mile) of secondary forest with the opportunity to observe tropical flora and fauna, including small animals like long-tailed macaques, squirrels, geckos and spotted doves.

You can also take a detour up to the summit of **Mount Imbiah**, a former gun battery, and be rewarded with views of the Western Anchorage and nearby Indonesian islands.

Around Imbiah Lookout

Cable-car passengers can alight at **Imbiah Lookout**, where a number of fairly interesting sights are clustered. First off is the **Butterfly Park & Insect Kingdom ❺** – a real treat for nature-lovers (daily 9.30am–7pm; charge). The first has some 1,500 live butterflies from more than 50 species that flit and flutter between lush tropical plants in a large enclosed garden, while the adjacent attraction has more than 3,000 mounted bugs, including some of the world's largest and rarest creepy crawlies.

Continue to the nearby **Sentosa 4D Magix ❻**, billed as the largest four-dimensional theatre in Southeast

ABOVE: Singapore's war history comes alive at Fort Siloso.
BELOW: an exotic bug – one of 3,000 – on display at Sentosa's Insect Kingdom Museum.

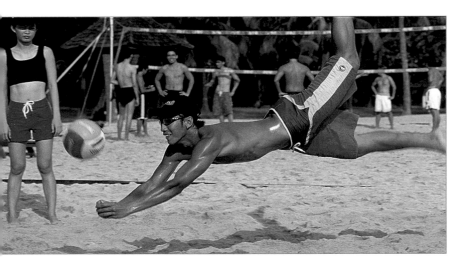

ABOVE: beach
volleyball action at
Palawan Beach.
BELOW: talking parrot
at the Animal and Bird
Encounters at Palawan
Beach.

Asia, and definitely worth experiencing. Enjoy an engaging multi-sensory experience complete with images leaping out at you and precisely timed environmental effects such as water sprays and blowing wind (tel: 6274-5355; www.sentosa4dmagix.com.sg; daily half-hourly shows 10am–9pm; charge). Nearby is another attraction for speed junkies. Take a cinema simulation ride at **Sentosa CineBlast ❼** (daily 10am–9pm; charge). With the aid of high-definition screens and a motion system, the experience of whitewater rafting or a stomach-turning plunge down a ravine is artfully simulated. To enjoy a panoramic view of Sentosa and its surrounding islands, ascend the disc-shaped **Tiger Sky Tower ❽** (www.skytower.com.sg; daily 9am–9pm; charge), which slowly spins up a central column to a height of almost 50 storeys or 110 metres (360ft). If you are looking for a little more heart-thumping action, proceed to the **Skyline Luge Sentosa ❾** (daily 10am–9.30pm; charge). Riders ascend a slope by chairlift and hurtle down in a luge that is part go-kart,

part-toboggan, at a speed that suits their fancy.

Songs of the Sea

In the evening, make your way to Beach Station to witness **Songs of the Sea ❿**, a night-time multimedia spectacle with a live cast and rousing music (daily, two shows at 7.40pm and 8.40pm; charge). The show combines shooting jets of water, bursts of fire, dazzling pyrotechnics and clever computer imaging.

Images of Singapore

South of the Cable Car Plaza is **Images of Singapore ⓫** (daily 9am–7pm; charge). The waxworks museum comprises three experiences – Warehouse of the Four Winds, Singapore Adventure and Singapore Celebrates. The exhibit promises to take visitors through Singapore's history and give them a sneak preview of the country's rich cultural diversity through multimedia shows and walk-through settings.

Merlion

For an experience in pure kitsch, take the lift up to the top of the gigantic

37-metre (120ft) high **Merlion** ⑫ – for views of the harbour and surroundings isles (daily 10am–8pm; charge). On a clear day, even the Riau Islands of Indonesia are visible.

Animal and Bird Encounters

Another attraction that the kids will enjoy is **Animal and Bird Encounters** ⑬ (daily noon–5.30pm) at the Palawan Amphitheatre on Palawan Beach. The family-friendly animal habitat promises encounters with talking parrots, cheeky primates and even a Burmese rock python, among other creatures (various shows throughout the day; free).

Dolphin Lagoon

Your ticket to Underwater World includes admission to the **Dolphin Lagoon** ⑭, along Palawan Beach (daily 11am–5.45pm), whose stars are the endangered Indo-Pacific humpbacked, or pink dolphins. "Meet the Dolphin" shows take place daily at 11am, 1.30pm, 3.30pm and 5.30pm. In addition, up to eight people can sign up to swim with the dolphins (advance booking required; tel: 6276-0030; www.underwaterworld.com. sg; Thur–Tue 9.45am).

Beaches and bars

Sentosa's other great appeal is recreation, especially watersports and golf. White sands stretch some 3km (2 miles) along the southern shore, interspersed by scenic saltwater lagoons and coconut groves. Each of the three beaches, Siloso, Palawan and Tanjong, has its own character, and they are probably Singapore's most pleasant stretches of sand – if you disregard the views of scores of container ships in the distance.

Watersports enthusiasts should head for either **Palawan Beach** ⑮ or **Siloso Beach** ⑯, where windsurfers, canoes and pedal boats can be hired. In addition, at Palawan Beach, you can traverse a suspension bridge to reach the southernmost point of Continental Asia. Beach volleyball has also gained popularity in recent years, attracting a lively crowd to the beaches. Getting from one beach to another is easy: a train plies all three beaches daily 9am–7pm. After the sun goes down, the action on Siloso Beach revs up, especially on Friday and Saturday nights, when a mix of fun-loving locals and expatriates descend on the beach bars. Siloso Beach is also host to **ZoukOut**, an annual dance fest that draws the best

TIP

Adrenalin junkies should head for Megazip Adventure Park on Mount Imbiah (tel: 6884-5602; www. megazip.com.sg), which boasts a dramatic zip wire that takes you from the top of the hill through the jungle canopy down to the beach at speeds of up to 50km/h (30mph). There's also an aerial rope course, a 16-metre (52ft) high climbing wall and a free-fall simulator.

BELOW: riding on the Sentosa Luge.

ABOVE: the *Cheng Ho* junk takes you to Kusu Island.

international DJs and thousands of young revellers. Tanjong Beach on the quieter eastern end also draws crowds to its nightspots.

Golf

The **Sentosa Golf Club** ⓱ (www.sentosagolfclub.com) near Tanjong Beach, one of Singapore's most challenging greens, sees avid golfers playing on its two 18-hole par-72 championship courses – Serapong and Tanjong. Serapong is the venue for the national golf tournament, the Barclays Singapore Open. Non-members who wish to play can fill in an application form and pay at the reception area. The sea and sunset views here are stunning and can be enjoyed at Il Lido Italian restaurant. The famous Nogawa Japanese restaurant is located in the club too.

SOUTHERN ISLANDS

Beyond Sentosa is an archipelago of tiny islands that lie within Singapore's territorial waters, ranging from uninhabited coral outcrops to popular weekend retreats like Kusu and St John's islands. Because thousands of ships ply the Straits of Malacca and Singapore harbour each year, the government has been especially vigi-lant in preventing water pollution and protecting the natural beauty of these islands.

Many islands are still enveloped in coral reefs, and Singapore's Nature Society has successfully completed a coral conservation project to trans-plant reefs that are threatened by land reclamation and industry. Two entire reefs have been moved thus far from the endangered waters around Pulau Ayer Chawan and Buran Darat to new homes off the south coast of Sentosa.

There is also an ongoing "reef ball" project by the Singapore Environmental Council and the Sentosa authorities in charge of developing the islands, which deploys reef balls that enable corals to anchor and grow. Meanwhile, the government is also drawing up plans to establish marine conservation areas to protect the reefs near Sudong, Hantu, Semakau and St John's Island.

Two of the offshore islands can be reached by regular ferry service from mainland Singapore; to reach the others, join a tour or hire a boat from Marina South Pier (*see box below*).

Getting to the Islands

Ferries to **Kusu Island** and **St John's Island** leave daily from the Marina South Pier in the Marina Bay area (Mon–Fri 10am and 2pm, Sat 9am, noon and 3pm, Sun and public holidays 9am, 11am, 1pm, 3pm and 5pm; tel: 6534-9339; www.islandcruise.com.sg).

Lazarus, **Sisters'** and **Hantu** islands are not served by regular ferries, so you have to hire water taxis at Marina South Pier if you want to visit. An alternative way to see the harbour and islands is on the *Cheng Ho*, a replica Chinese junk which cruises the southern islands with a half-hour stopover at Kusu (tel: 6533-9811; www.watertours.com.sg; daily 10.30am and 3pm; cruises last two and a half hours).

Kusu Island

Kusu Island , also called Turtle Island, is a place of both rest and worship. Legend has it that two shipwrecked sailors – one Chinese, one Malay – were saved from certain death when a giant turtle magically transformed itself into an island. Each man gave thanks according to his own belief, and so today the Taoist temple of Tua Pek Kong with its turtle pool and the Muslim *keramat* (shrine) on the hill are popular places of pilgrimage.

In the ninth month of the lunar calendar, usually straddling October and November, Taoists and Buddhists as well as Malays from Singapore flock to the island in droves. The Chinese arrive at the temple with offerings and pray for prosperity, good luck and fertility. The Malay pilgrims, on the other hand, climb the 152 steps to their shrine to offer their prayers to Allah.

Other islands

Conservationists in Singapore are overjoyed that the government has repeatedly shelved plans to develop the Southern Islands, although there is talk that Singapore's third casino resort could very well be established on **Lazarus Island**.

St John's Island was where Raffles anchored before meeting the Temenggong, or Malay chief, on the Singapore River in 1819. The island served as a quarantine centre for immigrants until the 1950s, when it was used as a holding centre for political detainees. In 1975, St John's was turned into a holiday haven, with lagoons, shady paths and picnic spots making it a popular weekend venue.

The two **Sisters' Islands**, made up of Pulau Subar Darat and Pulau Subar Laut, are also favourite spots for relaxation and diving, although the waters can sometimes be murky. Likewise, **Pulau Hantu**, or Ghost Island, to the northwest of Sentosa – said to be haunted by a Malay warrior – attracts mainly divers and fishermen to its waters.

If you're visiting the islands, be sure to bring your own picnic, as the islands do not offer food, drinks or facilities of any sort. ❑

ABOVE: turtles at Tua Pek Kong on Kusu Island.

RESTAURANTS AND BARS

Restaurants

Australian

Osia
Resorts World Sentosa, Crockfords Tower, Level 2. Tel: 6577-6560. www.rw sentosa.com Open: daily L & D. **$$$$**
Australian celebrity chef Scott Webster creates a menu inspired by fresh Aussie produce and Asian influences.

Chinese

Cassia
Capella Singapore, 1 The Knolls. Tel: 6591-5045. www.capellasingapore.com Open: daily L & D. **$$$$**
This fine modern Chinese restaurant is set in a beautiful 1880s colonial building. Feast on lobster with crispy garlic and Chilean sea bass in orange sauce.

Italian

il Lido
Sentosa Golf Club, 27 Bukit Manis Rd. Tel: 6866-977. www.il-lido.com Open: Sun–Thu 11am–midnight, Fri–Sat 11am–late. **$$$$**
Quality Italian regional fare, but the main selling point is the stunning views of the Singapore Straits, especially at sunset.

Seafood

The Cliff
The Sentosa Resort & Spa, 2 Bukit Manis Rd. Tel: 6275-0331. www.thesentosa. com Open: daily D. **$$$$**
Fabulous cliff-top views and contemporary seafood-inspired dishes

Bars

Siloso Beach's Wave

House™ Sentosa
36 Siloso Beach Walk, Sentosa. Tel: 6377-3113
After hanging up your wetsuit, have a margarita at this simulated surfing, dining and lifestyle venue.

Tanjong Beach Club
120 Tanjong Beach Walk. Tel: 6270-1355. www.tanjong beachclub.com
This gorgeous beach club is the latest trendy hotspot by the beach.

• • • • • • • • •
Prices for a three-course dinner per person without drinks and taxes. **$$$$** = *more than S$50,* **$$$** = *S$30–50,* **$$** = *$20–30,* **$** = *under $20.*

SOUTHERN AND WESTERN SINGAPORE

The south has some tranquil green oases worthy of a ramble. To the west is Jurong, where a number of family-friendly attractions are found amid the city's largest industrial zone

The west coast of Singapore has a split personality. At one end, it comprises industrial areas with docks, factories and refineries; at the other, it is a major recreation zone that embraces some of Singapore's top green spaces and theme parks. The Ayer Rajah Expressway (AYE) leads into the heart of the west, linking downtown Singapore with a bustling industrial suburb called Jurong. But a more pleasant way to explore the coast is by way of Telok Blangah and Pasir Panjang roads, which hug the coast.

Singapore's south and southwestern shorelines are dominated by the Port of Singapore, the world's busiest in terms of shipping tonnage and also Asia's main trans-shipment hub. The major port terminals stretch from Tanjong Pagar just outside the CBD to Jurong in the west.

SOUTHERN SINGAPORE

Southern Singapore is the gateway to Sentosa and has also gained cachet as a bona fide entertainment spot with the opening of several nightlife venues and the city's largest shopping mall, VivoCity.

Mount Faber

Start exploring the west coast from the south, at **Mount Faber ❶**, off Kampung Bahru Road. The name Mount Faber is rather a misnomer, as the hill is only 110 metres (360ft) high. Formerly called Telok Blangah Hill, it was renamed in 1845 after Captain C.E. Faber of the Madras Engineers, who constructed the narrow serpentine road leading to the summit in order to install a new signal station to replace the one on Pulau Blakang Mati (modern Sentosa).

LEFT: shoppers at VivoCity. The complex, next to the HarbourFront Centre, was built at a cost of S$280 million. **RIGHT:** Singapore's port is the busiest in the world.

TIP

Singapore's cable car was established more than three decades ago but has been given a new facelift. Now called the "Jewel Cable Car Ride", the cabins not only offer 360-degree bird's-eye views of the surrounding harbour and Sentosa, they are decked out in stylish metallic black and chrome design and have ambient lights. Look out for the world's first VIP jewelled cabin, whose interior and exterior are adorned with Austrian Swarovski crystals.

The sprawling rainforest-covered park which surrounds Mount Faber is one of the oldest in Singapore. Take a 10–15-minute walk up in the cool air of the early morning and stop at the various lookout points for panoramic views of the city and the port area. The **Jewel Box** on the summit is also worth a stopover. Wind down with fine food and drinks at its restaurants and bars while you take in fantastic vistas, especially at night. From here, you can also embark on a **cable-car** ride to Sentosa to enjoy a bird's-eye view of the harbour (tel: 6377-9688; www.mountfaber.com.sg; daily 8.30am–10pm; charge).

HarbourFront Precinct

The base of Mount Faber is home to the **HarbourFront Precinct**, a waterfront business and lifestyle hub. At 1 Maritime Square is the **HarbourFront Centre ❷**, where you will find a shopping mall and the HarbourFront MRT Station, a terminal for the northeast line. The adjacent Cable Car Tower is where the cable cars from Mount Faber stop to pick up passengers for the ride to Sentosa. Adjoining the HarbourFront Centre is the **Singapore Cruise Centre**, where passenger ships dock from all over the world.

VivoCity ❸, the mammoth 102,000-sq-metre (1.1 million-sq-ft) mall next to the HarbourFront Centre, was built at a cost of S$280 million and designed by the renowned Japanese architect Toyo Ito (www.vivocity.com.sg). Its architecture, a stunning blend of lunar and nautical themes, is something to behold. The mall has so many retail options that most visitors, on their first visit at least, never make it to the second floor. Other recreational highlights found here are the gigantic rooftop pool and Singapore's largest Cineplex. If you are on your way to Sentosa, board the Sentosa Express (*see page 182*), which stops at the

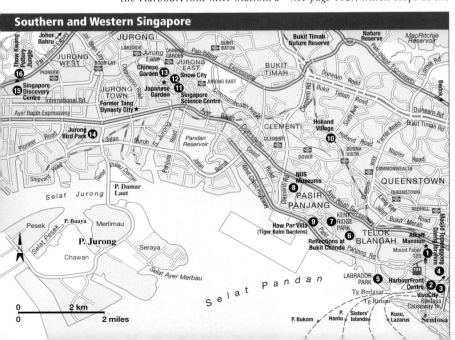

Southern and Western Singapore

third level. There are plenty of food choices here, including the massive Food Republic food court offering all manner of local fare.

An overhead bridge joins VivoCity to the redbrick **St James Power Station** at 3 Sentosa Gateway. This was Singapore's first coal-fired power station, now reinvented as a nightlife hub with nine party venues, including the hip dance club Powerhouse; Movida, which features world music; and the slick Bellini Room, which serves jazz and, of course, bellinis.

Mosques and mansions

Near the HarbourFront Centre and opposite the causeway to Sentosa is the **Masjid Temenggong Daeng Ibrahim** ❹ on Telok Blangah Road (tel: 6273-6043; daily 5.30am–9pm). Daeng Ibrahim was the son of Abdul Rahman, who was the Temenggong (chief) of Singapore when Raffles landed here in 1819. The Temenggong and his followers at that time lived around the south bank of the Singapore River, which Raffles had intended to develop. They were persuaded by Raffles to move to Telok Blangah. Soon others followed, including Arabs and Indonesian immigrants, turning the area into a Malay enclave. Adjacent to the mosque is the *makam* (tomb) of Temenggong Abdul Rahman.

Further up is **Telok Blangah Green**, which sits in the middle of tropical gardens with walkways and picnic areas. The opulent 1920s house, with its vast lawns near the crest of the green named Telok Blangah Hill Park, is **Alkaff Mansion**, built by the fabulously wealthy Alkaff trading family, who lived and entertained here. The house was converted into a restaurant in the 1990s and was closed for some years. It reopened in 2011 as an elegant Italian restaurant.

Keppel Bay

Further west is **Keppel Bay**, a passage that ships passed through as they sailed between the Straits of Melaka and the South China Sea in the old days. It is believed that the Chinese navigator Admiral Cheng Ho referred to this waterway in one of his exploration records. This was where Singapore burgeoned into the

ABOVE: table at the Jewel Box. **BELOW:** outside VivoCity.

Labrador's History Trail

Labrador Battery, where Labrador Park now sits, was part of the gun system that defended Singapore in World War II. Today, the park's History Walk traces the paths around the old defensive structures. Storyboards posted in the 17-hectare (42-acre) park explain the development of the battery and its fortification. The Bunker Path winds around underground chambers, gun emplacements, an 1892 ammunition storeroom, a six-pounder quick-fire gun and the remains of an old fort wall, among others. At the foot of the park is an opening in the Straits of Singapore – once known as Keppel Passageway and used by sailors and traders to sail into Singapore.

ABOVE: bronze sculptures at Bukit Chandu. **ABOVE RIGHT:** Labrador Park. **BELOW:** local sculptor Ng Eng Teng's "I See". His works can be seen at the NUS Museums in Kent Ridge.

world's busiest port. Today, the old Keppel Shipyard has moved out and the area has been transformed. Luxury apartments with full waterfront views are much sought after. There is also a private marina and a chichi restaurant called **Privé** on **Keppel Island**, which is linked to the mainland by a stunning bridge.

Labrador Park

The western end of Keppel Harbour is marked by a small cape called **Tanjong Berlayar**. British Army engineers built a powerful bastion here in 1892. They installed six-inch guns and christened their citadel the Labrador Battery. Now part of **Labrador Park ❺**, the World War II gun batteries, bunkers and other relics have been restored and trace a chapter of Singapore's war history (daily 7am–7pm). Guided tours of the **Labrador Park Secret Tunnel** are available (tel: 6339-6833; daily 10am–7pm).

An aerial staircase built into the edge of the secondary forest offers a panoramic view of the sea. The staircase also descends to the jetty and the shore. Labrador Park is also a gazetted nature reserve. There are forest trails *(see text box on page 193)* and a rich variety of flora and fauna, including exotic birds such as the white-crested laughing thrush, the yellow-vented bulbul and the white-bellied sea eagle. To get to the park, turn into Labrador Villa Road off Pasir Panjang Road, across PSA Building.

Bukit Chandu

Address: 31K Pepys Road (off Pasir Panjang Road); www.s1942.org.sg
Tel: 6375-2510
Opening Hrs: Tue–Sun 9am–5.30pm
Entrance Fee: charge

Further west is a World War II monument called **Reflections at Bukit Chandu ❻**. It is dedicated to the heroes of the 1st and 2nd battalions of the Malay Regiment, who along with the British, Australian and New Zealand forces, fought 13,000

Japanese soldiers at the Battle of Pasir Panjang in 1942.

The five galleries, showcasing artefacts and multimedia interactives, provide rich insight into the war, while the *Sounds of Battle* video in the theatre practically transports you onto the battlefield with realistic sound effects of machine-gun fire and human cries.

Kent Ridge area

Heading along Pasir Panjang Road, a right turn to South Buona Vista Road leads to the lush **Kent Ridge Park ❼** (daily 7am–7pm). From the bluff you can see dozens of ships anchored in the western harbour and the myriad southern islands of Singapore. The workout course here is popular with joggers from the nearby university and science park.

Along Kent Ridge Crescent is the **National University of Singapore** (NUS), which houses the first-rate **NUS Museums ❽** (tel: 6516-4617; www.nus.edu.sg/museums; Tue–Sat

10am–7.30pm, Sun 10am–6pm; free). Its three galleries are well curated and worth a detour. The impressive **Lee Kong Chian Art Museum**, named after the first Chancellor of the former University of Singapore, is noted for its collection of Chinese art, spanning some 7,000 years of civilisation and culture. There are close to 4,000 pieces of artwork, which include paintings and calligraphic works as well as ceramics, bronzes and sculptures.

The **South and Southeast Asian Gallery** mirrors classical traditions as well as modern trends, and comprises ceramics, textiles, sculpture and paintings. Be sure to stop at the **Ng Eng Teng Gallery**, which houses the works of the late Ng Eng Teng, Singapore's foremost sculptor and known for his whimsical renditions of the human form.

The **Raffles Museum of Biodiversity**, located at the university's Science Faculty, houses the collection started by Raffles in 1849 (tel: 6874-

ABOVE: display at NUS Museums.
BELOW: giant mask at the Haw Par Villa.

5082; http://rmbr.nus.edu.sg; Mon–Fri 9am–5pm; free). On display are exhibits from the oldest and largest collection of Southeast Asian plant, animal and fungi specimens. Some of these flora and fauna are extinct, such as the 19th-century leathery turtle from Siglap, the Changi dugong and the banded-leaf monkey, while others are still thriving in Singapore.

Haw Par Villa

Address: 262 Pasir Panjang Road
Tel: 6872-2003
Opening Hrs: daily 9am–7pm
Entrance Fee: free
Transport: Buona Vista MRT, then take SBS Bus 200

In vivid contrast to the museum exhibits at the NUS Museums are the somewhat bizarre displays at **Haw Par Villa ⑨**, which is also known as Tiger Balm Gardens. This collection of rather grotesque statues illustrates various Chinese mythological themes, and notorious crimes and vices from Singapore's history. These gaudy exhibits are the only remain-

ing collection of this genre in Asia, and for this reason are a must-see.

Haw Par Villa (Villa of the Tiger and the Leopard) was built by Aw Boon Haw (Gentle Tiger) for his brother Aw Boon Par (Gentle Leopard) in 1937. The Aw brothers were philanthropists who made their fortune with Tiger Balm, the cure-all that has now become world-famous. The gardens are actually a collection of bizarre tableaux depicting Chinese legends and folktales. The 1,000 statues and 150 tableaux may be too gory for some, but they were meant to be a lesson in morality, reflecting the brothers' beliefs in the values of filial piety. Be sure to walk through the **Ten Courts of Hell**; visitors often cringe at the kinds of torture meted out to wrongdoers, such as disembowelment or immersion in a wok of boiling oil.

Among the statues are brief glimpses of the brothers' lives. There are photographs of the old villa and their quirky collection of cars – one was even painted with tiger stripes and a tiger head fashioned out of metal mounted on the bonnet. The original villa was torn down by Boon Haw when Boon Par died in 1945. Boon Haw turned Haw Par Villa into public property as a way to preserve Chinese culture and to impart the values of the past to modern Chinese.

Holland Village

Holland Village ❿, once hailed by Senior Minister Goh Chok Tong as being "bohemian", is actually far from radical. It is really a charming village-like enclave well loved by expats, locals and students from surrounding tertiary institutions.

The village is a wedge bounded by Lorong Liput, Lorong Mambong and parts of Holland Road and Holland Avenue. No one knows exactly how the area got its name, but it's common speculation that it was perhaps the favourite place of residence for the Dutch in colonial times. When the British troops were still in Singapore, Holland Village and nearby **Chip Bee Gardens** across Holland Avenue were their preferred place of abode; long after they left (in 1968), the semi-detached bungalows and terrace houses in which they used to live are

still much sought after among new expat arrivals to Singapore. As if to relive its Dutch roots, **Holland V Shopping Mall**, at the junction of Lorong Liput and Lorong Mambong, sports a windmill atop its roof.

Holland Village has always had a reputation as a chill-out place to wine and dine. Casual chic restaurants and lively sidewalk cafés abound in the village and at Chip Bee Gardens, home to gourmet grocers, a cooking school, restaurants and art galleries.

Like the rest of Singapore, however, Holland Village inevitably favours the new over the old, the polished over the dilapidated, in line with the rest of clean and tidy Singapore. The old rattan and porcelain shops that used to be here have made way for newer but more humdrum stores, while the old and dank market and food centre have been transformed into bright and airy spaces. Even the artistic community that has burgeoned at Chip Bee Gardens is a coordinated effort by the powers that be.

THE WEST COAST

Anchoring the West Coast is **Jurong**, an industrial area where about

ABOVE: Holland Village Food Centre and Market. **BELOW:** eating out in Holland Village.

Housing the Masses

Singapore's public housing programme, which began in 1960, has been so successful that the majority of residents live in these flats

S ingapore has the second-highest population density in the world after Hong Kong, with 7,022 people per sq km. Even with ongoing reclamation, the land area cannot be increased much more, so it is essential to optimise its use.

Once out of the city centre, the predominant image is of high-rise, high-density public housing, for 85 percent of Singaporeans live in apartment blocks designed by the Housing and Development Board (HDB). Incredibly, more than 90 percent of these households own the apartments they live in, subsidised in part by the government.

Singapore's public housing programme began in 1960. Building homes was a priority, and by 2000, the HDB had designed and constructed over 800,000 units, most of which are located in self-contained New Towns. Singapore adopted the New Town

structure probably because of its close association with British planning practice in the 1950s and 1960s.

Each of the 26 New Towns is planned for about 250,000 to 300,000 residents, with essential facilities provided. These include commercial facilities such as cinemas, shopping malls and supermarkets; institutional facilities like libraries, schools and community clubs; and recreational facilities such as sports complexes and swimming pools. Each town is divided into neighbourhoods of about 24,000 residents, and each neighbourhood is further divided into precincts of between 2,000 and 3,000 residents. The larger facilities are sited at the town centre, which is also the transportation hub for bus and MRT stations. In the town centres are a range of eating places, malls and shops.

The earliest designs of apartment blocks were kept simple to facilitate speedy construction but, today, Singapore's younger generation are more demanding. The basic housing provision that satisfied their grandparents and even their parents is no longer sufficient. This has presented a challenge to the HDB, which, since 1992, has responded with better designs for new flats and a programme of upgrading existing public housing, starting with 30-year-old blocks of flats. Various means have been explored to achieve character: making buildings of different heights, and adding articulated roof forms and special architectural features. Natural elements like gardens and fountains are also incorporated to enhance the character of each new town.

Public housing has also become increasingly integrated with the private sector. Apart from waterfront living at Punggol 21 up north, the Pinnacle@Duxton in the city features 50-storey blocks with sky bridges and rooftop gardens.

Public housing in other parts of the world has generally received bad press, but in Singapore it has worked remarkably well. To many Westerners it looks monotonous, but urban planners study it with curiosity, astounded by its success. ❑

LEFT: typical public housing.

300,000, or 10 percent, of Singaporeans are employed. There are more than 2,600 factories in this part of the island. Nevertheless, it's not all work and no play, for Jurong has a number of parks, gardens and wildlife collections.

Singapore Science Centre

Address: 15 Science Centre Road;
www.science.edu.sg
Tel: 6425-2500
Opening Hrs: Tue–Sun 10am–6pm
Entrance Fee: charge
Transport: Jurong East MRT

Some 15km (9 miles) to the west of the HarbourFront Centre, about a 20-minute drive along the Ayer Rajah Expressway (AYE), is the family-friendly **Singapore Science Centre** ⑪. The principles of flight, the animal kingdom and the complex world of electronics and the human body are just some of the subjects embraced by the 1,000 exhibits in its 12 galleries.

These innovative and hands-on displays have never failed to enthrall adults and children since the centre opened in 1977. One highlight is the interactive **Mind's Eye** gallery,

where visitors experience optical illusions – watch how the body can miraculously "disappear". Another is the **Genome Exhibit**, where the basis of life and DNA structures and functions are explored through three-dimensional interactive exhibits. Kids will find the **Kinetic Garden**, an interactive garden with 35 sculptures, exhibits and water features, especially engaging.

The adjacent **Omni-Theatre** presents several wide-screen omnimax movies each day (starting at 10am with the last screening at 8pm; charge) on a five-storey-high hemispheric screen and sound from 72 amplifiers.

Snow City

Address: Snow City Building,
21 Jurong Town Hall Road,
www.snowcity.com.sg
Tel: 6560-2306
Opening Hrs: Tue–Sun 9.45am–5.15pm, public holidays 9.45am–6pm
Transport: Jurong East MRT

Next to the Omni-Theatre is **Snow City** ⑫, possibly the coolest attrac-

ABOVE: the Singapore Science Centre.
BELOW: Snow City.

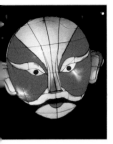

tion here, at least in terms of degrees Celsius. The arctic playground contains a 1,200-sq-metre (13,000-sq-ft) **Snow Chamber**, which allows tropical-bred locals a chance to snowboard, ski and snow tube down a three-storey high incline and dress up in full winter gear. Warning: you may not want to bother with this place if you've experienced the real thing.

Chinese/Japanese gardens

A short drive around Jurong Lake at Yuan Ching Road is the **Chinese Garden** (tel: 6261-3632; daily 6am–10.30pm, Bonsai Garden daily 9am–5pm; free). This is a collection of theme gardens in the style of Beijing's Summer Palace. The landscaping, inspired by the Sung dynasty, is a harmonious blend of natural elements. The lovely twin pagoda has pretty views of the lake.

Also worth seeing here is the **Garden of Beauty**, which is a Suzhou-style *penjing* (bonsai) garden with more than 1,000 specimens. This is one of the largest *penjing* collections outside China and includes many valuable plants, such as a pair of 200-year-old *Podocarpus* trees shaped like lions. In September/October each

year, the Chinese Garden becomes ablaze with pretty lighted lanterns during the annual Mid-Autumn Festival celebrations (*see pages 58 and 61*).

Now take the **Bridge of Double Beauty** to the adjacent **Japanese Garden** (tel: 6261-3632; daily 6am–7pm; free). With the accent on simplicity, the park exudes a sense of tranquillity with its Zen rock gardens, stone lanterns, ponds and shrubs.

Jurong Bird Park

Address: 2 Jurong Hill, www.birdpark.com.sg
Tel: 6265-0022
Opening Hrs: daily 8am–6pm
Entrance Fee: charge
Transport: Boon Lay MRT, then SBS Bus 194 or 251 from Boon Lay Bus Interchange

Just off the Ayer Rajah Expressway is **Jurong Bird Park** . Colourful macaws welcome visitors at the entrance to this 20-hectare (50-acre) park – home to 4,600 birds of 380 different species from all over the world. Acknowledged as the leading bird park in the region and known for its commitment to avian conservation,

ABOVE: in September or October each year, depending on the lunar calendar, the Chinese Garden is illuminated with thousands of lanterns. **BELOW:** Chinese Garden pavilions at sunset.

ABOVE: Jurong Bird Park.

the park attracts well over a million visitors every year.

There is much to see and do to occupy your time, including visiting the four walk-in free-flight aviaries. At the **African Waterfall Aviary**, visitors can immerse themselves in a Central African tropical rainforest. About 1,000 free-flying African birds can be found here, including white-faced tree duck, South African crown crane and Egyptian goose. More than 260 species of Southeast Asian birds fly almost free in the enormous **Southeast Asian Birds Aviary**, which enjoys a tropical thunderstorm experience at noon.

The **Lory Loft** is another free-flight aviary, the world's largest of its kind. It is built to simulate Australia's vast rural landscape, and visitors on boardwalks and bridges suspended in mid-air at a height of 12 metres (39ft) mingle with 1,000 free-flying lory birds at treetop level. The **Jungle Jewels Flight Aviary** is a re-creation of a South American rainforest.

Another highlight is the **Hornbill and Toucan Exhibit**, which has one of the world's largest collections of Asian hornbills and South American toucans. Also unique is the **World of Darkness**, a nocturnal bird house which uses a reversed lighting system so that during the day when there are visitors, it is night inside. Six aviaries feature night birds from different habitats around the world. They range from the snowy owl from the tundra to the buffy fish owl from the mangrove forest.

Aside from the aviaries, an interesting exhibition is Dinosaurs' Descendants, showcasing flightless birds in a simulated grassland habitat.

A relaxing way to explore the park is by the Panorail (daily 9am–5pm; charge), so named because of the panoramic vistas it affords.

Included in your ticket is admission to the entertaining bird shows. These are held throughout the day; most popular are the **Birds n' Buddies Show** with cockatoos, pelicans and hornbills at 11am and 3pm daily, and the **Birds of Prey** at 10am and 4pm daily. Those who can be at the park as early as 9am can aim for The Early Bird Breakfast Show, held at the Hawk Cafe Palm Plaza. Enjoy an American breakfast at this alfresco venue while watching the

Jurong Bird Park is the first in the world to breed the twelve-wired bird of paradise in captivity. The males of this species have 12 long, straggly, wire-like bristles protruding from their rump, which they rub against the female during an intriguing courtship ritual.

birds perform and "read your fortune".

Singapore Discovery Centre

Address: 510 Upper Jurong Road, www.sdc.com.sg
Tel: 6792-6188
Opening Hrs: Tue–Sun 9am–6pm; closed Mon except public holidays
Entrance Fee: charge
Transport: Joo Koon MRT

Just off the Pan Island Expressway (PIE) is the **Singapore Discovery Centre** ⓯. The centre is a one-stop complex for the whole family, which narrates the history of modern Singapore in nine main galleries that showcase the milestones and challenges Singapore has faced through images, shows and high-tech displays. Attractions include a Crisis Simulation Theatre and a Digital Dance Studio. Kids will love the many interactive and hands-on displays, such as the On Location Reporter exhibit that enables young visitors to step into the shoes of a broadcast journalist and report on various groundbreaking news. Also of interest are the simulated shooting range and the action-packed paintball games.

Thow Kwang Pottery Jungle

Tucked at the end of Jurong, near the Nanyang Technological University, is **Thow Kwang Pottery Jungle** ⓰, a sprawling 3,000-sq-metre (32,300-sq-ft) porcelain- and earthenware-filled space in the middle of a forest (tel: 6265-5808; daily 9am–5pm).

To get there, take a taxi from the Boon Lay MRT station to 85 Lorong Tawas, where the "dragon kiln" carries on the ancient 2,000-year tradition of firing pottery. Called a dragon kiln because of its 40-metre (132ft) length, it is filled with as many as 2,000 to 4,000 pieces of ceramics before being fired twice a year (in June and November). The dragon kiln has its origins in Shantou, China, and the one here was started by a migrant family from there.

Now run by the third generation Tan family, it is the only surviving dragon kiln in Singapore. Visitors can also see local potters honing their craft. A large variety of pottery pieces from all over Asia is on sale, including figurines, vases, jars and table lamps. Purchases can be shipped home if required. ❑

ABOVE: schoolkids outside Singapore Discovery Centre.
BELOW: potters at the dragon kiln.

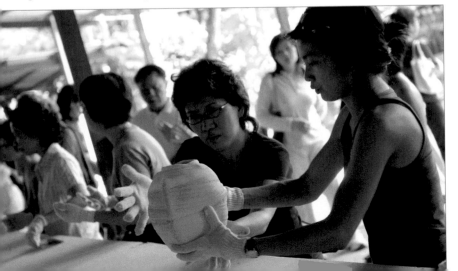

BEST RESTAURANTS AND BARS

Restaurants

Brazilian

Brazil Churrascaria
14–16 Sixth Ave. Tel: 6463-1923. Open: daily D. **$$$** (buffet only)
At this lively restaurant, *pasedors* come to your table and artfully shear slices of skewered meats onto your plate. There are 15 cuts of meat to choose from, and you can help yourself from the salad buffet.

Chinese

Crystal Jade Dining In
1 HarbourFront Walk, Vivo-City 01-112. Tel: 6278-5626. Open: daily L & D. **$$**
Choose Crystal Jade for satisfying Cantonese dishes and commend-able service. This family-style restaurant offers well-executed *dim sum* for lunch. It usually gets crowded during mealtimes, so get there early.

Min Jiang One North
5 Rochester Park. Tel: 6774-0122. Open: daily L & D. **$$$$**
Sichuan restaurant Min Jiang is located in a con-

served black-and-white colonial bungalow in Rochester Park. The rep-ertoire here extends beyond Sichuan fare to other regions of China, but the highlight is the Beijing duck with eight different condiments.

Tung Lok Signatures
1 HarbourFront Walk, Vivo-City 01-57. Tel: 6376-9555. www.tungloksignatures.com Open: daily L & D. **$$$**
This restaurant by the venerable Tung Lok Group faces the waters and Sentosa. The chefs whip up delicious signa-ture Chinese dishes such as fortifying double-boiled sakura chicken soup and grilled Kurubota pork.

International

The Jewel Box
109 Mount Faber Rd. Tel: 6377-9688. www.mount faber.com.sg Open: daily L & D. **$$$**
The Jewel Box has four elegant restaurants: Black Opal and Sapphire (both serving Western Continental fare), Empress Jade (Chinese cuisine and a lovely view) and Emerald Lodge (alfresco venue serving Italian food).

Italian

Da Paolo La Terazza
01-56 Chip Bee Gardens, Blk 44 Jalan Merah Saga. Tel: 6476-1332. www.da paolo.com.sg Open: Wed–

Bars

Wala Wala Café Bar
31 Lorong Mambong, Holland Village. Tel: 6462-4288.
This popular, decade-old neighbourhood bar hums with breezy vibes. It's a great place to munch on pizzas and down beer while listening to some live music in the Bar Above. Happy Hour is 4–9pm.

Mon L & D. **$$** (set lunch) **$$$$** (à la carte)
This well-known Italian restaurant manages to ooze sophistication yet remain laid-back. You won't go wrong with any of the pasta dishes on the menu.

Japanese

Shiro
24 Greenwood Ave. Tel: 6462-2774. Open: Mon–Sat L & D. **$$$** (set lunch) **$$$$** (à la carte)
Entry is by reservation only at this 30-seater in a sleepy neighbourhood. Inside, you will sample exquisite haute Japanese cuisine in minimalist but intimate surrounds. The nine-course *Kaiseki* meal is a sublime experience.

Mediterranean

Original Sin
01-62 Jalan Merah Saga, Blk 43, Chip Bee Gardens. Tel: 6475-5605. www.original sin.com.sg Open: Tue–Sun L

The Queen and Mangosteen
1 harbourFront Walk, VivoCity 01-106/107. Tel: 6376-9380.
This British gourmet pub has great outdoor seats facing the sparkling waters. order a Pimm's & lemon-ade or a craft brew and tuck into mini beef burgers, fish and chips, and other pub grub.

& D, Mon D. **$$** (set lunch) **$$$** (à la carte)
Whether you're on an ovo-lacto diet, a vegan or just plain health-conscious, chef-owner Marisa Bertocchi ensures there's something imagi-native for everyone. Her *meze* platter and *mous-saka* would convert any meat-lover.

Middle Eastern

Al Hamra
23 Lorong Mambong, Hol-land Village. Tel: 6464-8488. www.alhamra.com.sg Open: daily L & D. **$$$**
This Lebanese and Mid-dle Eastern restaurant has an authentic setting, with "flaming" lamps hanging from the ceiling and walls decked out with Middle Eastern antiques and artefacts. The real highlights are the authentic kebabs and *meze* platters cooked by native Lebanese chefs.

Prices for a three-course dinner per person without drinks and taxes:
$ = under S$20
$$ = S$20–30
$$$ = S$30–45
$$$$ = over S$45

THE EAST COAST

The palm-fringed East Coast offers visitors a taste of Malay culture in Geylang Serai, watersports at East Coast Park's beach, history in Changi, and the chance to unwind on rural Ubin Island

The East Coast is one of Singapore's most eclectic neighbourhoods and has a good mix of ethnic groups. Numerous churches, several mosques, and Chinese and Indian temples bear witness to this. The east is also a popular food hub, with many good restaurants and hawker fare – lots of it. Until the 1970s, when a huge chunk of the eastern shoreline was reclaimed, the sea was right at the doorstep of many of the bungalows that lined Tanjong Rhu, Fort Road and Meyer Road.

Today, instead of the sea lapping the shores of these houses, it's the expressway called the East Coast Parkway (ECP) stretching all the way from Tanjong Rhu to Changi Airport. Part of the reclaimed land has been transformed into a park, which has become a pleasant waterfront playground for the residents of the East Coast. Courting couples and families often come here to stroll in the evenings and enjoy the sea breezes. In place of rambling seaside bungalows, there are now towering highrise apartment blocks with sweeping views of the sea.

Kallang

Kallang – the part of the East Coast closest to downtown – is a massive sports and entertainment hub. Major sporting events were held at the **National Stadium**, which has now been demolished to make way for the new **Sports Hub**. Planned for completion in mid-2014, the iconic dome-shaped structure will cost a whopping S$1.2 billion to build. The 55,000-capacity sports stadium (which is what it mainly is in spite of its fancy moniker) will also house an Aquatic Centre, watersports facilities, a multi-purpose arena and retail space, as if Singapore needs

LEFT: yachting off the East Coast.

more of that. What is more interesting is the retractable roof that covers the main stadium, which can control the amount of natural light into the stadium during the day and allow spectators a view of the night sky and overhead visual displays. The new Stadium MRT Station on the Circle Line gives easy access to the Sports Hub. Next door is the wedge-shaped **Singapore Indoor Stadium**, designed by Kenzo Tange, which plays host to both sports and concerts.

On the fringes of the Indoor Stadium along the edge of the Kallang River is **Stadium Waterfront**, with riverfront bars and restaurants such as Vansh and Le Bistrot. Although it never really took off as a must-go dining enclave, it is particularly lovely spot in the evening if you can snag a table by the waterside.

Geylang

Colourful **Geylang** is further east, a short walk from the Paya Lebar MRT station. It is an area is full of contradictions: Buddhist temples coexist with brothels. Many visitors are sur-

prised to learn that prostitution is legal in Singapore. "Working" women are licensed, and brothels operate in designated red-light areas. On some streets in Geylang, women may draw unnecessary attention to themselves if they are unaccompanied.

Ironically, some of Geylang's best restaurants, like the **Geylang Famous Beef Kway Teow** *(see page 217)* at Lorong 9, for instance, are located around these seedy streets. Food-mad Singaporeans seem more concerned with finding a table than the area's ill repute. Geylang is a well-known hotspot for good Chinese hawker-style food and it really comes alive after midnight. This is also the place for durians, the pungent fruit that elicits a love-it-or-hate-it response. A string of streetside durian stalls are found along **Sims Avenue**, across Lorong 15.

Geylang Serai

Travelling further east, **Geylang Serai** lies at the end of **Geylang Road**. Although Geylang Serai is not one of the original districts established by Raffles, it has a strong ethnic flavour.

ABOVE: durians.
BELOW: eating in Geylang.

ABOVE: Geylang is the heart of Malay culture in Singapore.

More than Kampung Glam *(see page 170)*, this is the heart of Malay society and culture in Singapore, and home to many of the island's best Malay restaurants. The Malays had been living in a village built on stilts at the mouth of the Singapore River when Raffles arrived in 1819. When they were asked to move in 1840, they chose Geylang as their new home.

Originally coconut and rubber plantations and *serai* (lemongrass) fields, by the early 20th century Geylang had become urbanised, with rows of two-storey shophouses and terrace houses similar to those found in Chinatown and Kampung Glam. Indeed, some of the Chinese Baroque shophouses *(see pages 176–7)* here rank among the best preserved in Singapore. They are more flamboyant in the use of details such as tiles, motifs and bas-relief mouldings. The shophouses are tucked along the numerous *lorong* (lanes) between Geylang Road and Sims Avenue; perhaps the best examples can be seen in Lorong 35, Lorong 24A, Lorong 24, Lorong Bachok and Lorong 19.

Today, the heart of Geylang Serai is the section of Geylang Road between Jalan Eunos and Aljunied Road, lined with numerous restaurants and shops that are often open until late at night.

Geylang Serai Market

After a 40-month makeover costing S$18.2million, the 42-year-old **Geylang Serai Market ❶**, located on Jalan Turi, off Changi Road, now comprises a double-storey structure designed in the style of a traditional Malay *kampong* (village) house. This market is at its busiest during Ramadan, just before Hari Raya Puasa, when it's packed with housewives haggling for meat, vegetables, herbs and spices to prepare their festive meal. This is also the place to find the biggest range of halal food – there is a hawker centre with 365 stalls next to the market.

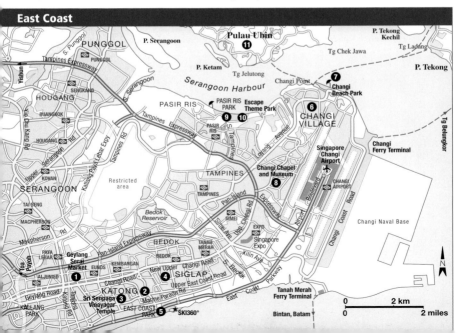

East Coast

Joo Chiat and Koon Seng

Near Geylang Serai Market is **Joo Chiat Complex** and the Joo Chiat area, which together with Katong *(see below)*, are strongholds of the Peranakan community – descendants of early Chinese immigrant men who married local Malay women *(see page 22)*. Joo Chiat Complex houses low-cost government-built flats on the upper floors and shops on the lower levels. It replaced the former Joo Chiat Market, where in the old days trishaws used to wait to ferry the sarong-clad Peranakan *bibik* (elderly ladies) and their laden baskets back to their homes after shopping. Today, Joo Chiat Complex is noted for its plethora of textile shops.

The Peranakan *bibik* have all but disappeared from Joo Chiat, but the area still has traces of its rich Straits Chinese heritage. **Kway Guan Huat** still produces by hand wafer-thin *poh piah* "skins" on griddles (95 Joo Chiat Road; tel: 6344-2875). The skins are used to wrap the myriad ingredients which make up *poh piah* or spring rolls, a delicious Peranakan dish that requires tedious preparation. The process of making the skins from dough can be seen from 9am to noon.

Perhaps the finest examples of Peranakan heritage are the beautifully restored Chinese Baroque shophouses *(see pages 176–7)* along **Joo Chiat Road** and **Koon Seng Road**, built in the 1930s. The richly decorated facades testify to the wealth of the original homeowners.

Katong

Joo Chiat Road connects with East Coast Road and an old suburb called **Katong ❷**. This area has long enjoyed a reputation for good food. Gentrified in appearance these days, the neighbourhood, with traces of its Eurasian and Peranakan past, is on the brink of losing its old-world charm. As with the now sanitised Chinatown, the newly refurbished pre-war shophouses are no longer affordable to old-timers who once plied their trade in the area. Recently, businesses in Katong have joined forces to keep the Peranakan culture alive and restore the area to its glorious old days.

Key among them is **Katong Antique House**, at 208 East Coast

TIP

Geylang is one of the best places to see how different cultures can coexist harmoniously. Along Geylang East Avenue 2, the ornate Sri Sivan Temple sits next to the Tang dynasty-style Foo Hai Ch'an Monastery.

BELOW: artist's impression of the new Sports Hub at Kailang.

Road, where a collection of age-old Peranakan artefacts are displayed by its Peranakan owner, Peter Wee (viewing by appointment only; tel: 6345-8544; charge to gallery). This century-old shophouse has been home to five generations of Straits Chinese families. The gallery on level two showcases Wee's private collection of porcelain, beaded shoes, *kebaya* (traditional embroidered blouses) and silver items among others. Typical spices used by the Peranakans in their cooking such as *belacan* (prawn paste) and curry powder are also on sale.

More traces of Peranakan culture can be seen further down the road. **Glory** (tel: 6344-1749) at 139 East Coast Road is best known for its pineapple tarts and traditional Peranakan confectionery, while **Kim Choo Kueh Chang** at No. 109/111 (tel: 6846-0375; Tue–Sun 9.30am–6.30pm) sells delicious rice dumplings wrapped in fragrant pandan leaves. Nonya dumpling wrapping demonstrations are offered daily – call for appointment. The little store adjacent to the restaurant also sells

jars of *sambal*, *kaya* and plenty of colourful Nonya cakes.

Two doors away at No. 113 is **Rumah Bebe**, a treasure trove of Peranakan artefacts in a 1928 Peranakan-style shophouse (tel: 6247-8781; www.rumahbebe.com). A tour around its premises allows a peek into a traditional Peranakan house setting – check out the lovely bridal chamber on level two. Look out also for intricate *kasut manik manik*, dainty slippers made of fine beadwork. The owner, Bebe Seet, is regarded as an expert in the art of beading, a craft that is fast disappearing in urban Singapore. She can customise beaded shoes (beadwork classes are also available) and *kebaya* outfits for visitors.

Peranakan culinary classes are offered at Rumah Bebe. Peranakan fare is in fact Singapore's very own fusion cuisine, blending Chinese and Malay cooking styles and ingredients with flair. A number of restaurants in the area offer authentic Peranakan fare – like **Guan Hoe Soon** (*see page 217*), a family-run business that has dished up great Nonya food for decades.

ABOVE: Katong Antique House at 208 East Coast Road is a treasure trove of Peranakan artefacts. **BELOW:** Chinese shophouses on Koon Seng Road.

Sri Senpaga Vinayagar Temple

Address: 19 Ceylon Road, off East Coast Road; www.senpaga.org.sg
Tel: 6345-8176
Opening Hrs: daily 5.30am – 12.30pm, 5.30 – 11pm
Transport: Paya Lebar MRT, then taxi or Bus 14

The **Sri Senpaga Vinayagar Temple** ❸, rebuilt in 2003, features an ornate five-tier, 21-metre (68ft) *rajagopuram* (royal entrance tower), sculptured according to Indian Chola traditions. Unique features abound at this Hindu temple: the granite footstone at the temple's entrance is a feature found in ancient Chola temples; *dwarapalakas* (gatekeepers) at the base tier of the tower entrance are apparently not found anywhere else in Asia; and its *vimanam* (temple dome) is covered in gold.

The temple's history dates back to the 1850s, when Ceylonese Tamil Ethirnayagam Pillai built a thatch-roof temple under a *senpaga* tree on the banks of a pond where a statue of Lord Vinayagar was believed to be found. It moved to its present site in the early 1900s. A bomb dam-aged the temple during World War II, though the main shrine remained intact. Today, the temple remains an important place of worship for the Hindu community on the East Coast.

Not far from the temple, at the junction of Ceylon and Fowlie roads, is the quaint 1934 St Hilda's Anglican Church (42 Ceylon Road; tel: 6344-3463; daily 9am–6pm). Designed after an English parish church, it features beautiful stained glass and a Victorian-style conical tower.

Siglap

Further up is Upper East Coast Road and another suburb, **Siglap** ❹, made up of a number of private housing estates of bungalows and terrace houses like Frankel (built by a Jewish developer) and Opera Estate (with street names like Tosca Terrace and Aida Avenue), and styl-ish condos. Rows of newly built ter-races with shops, alfresco wine bars, smart cafés and restaurants on the ground floor and apartments on the upper floor have proliferated here. Weekends often see the most crowds, and parking is sometimes a problem.

ABOVE LEFT: handmade beaded Peranakan slippers.
ABOVE: roof detail from the Sri Senpaga Vinayagar Temple.

EAT

One of Katong's stalwarts must surely be the Chin Mee Chin Confectionery, where two generations of Katongites have snacked on the famous toasted bread with *kaya* (coconut jam) and old-school cakes (204 East Coast Road; tel: 6345-0419).

East Coast Park

The visitor's first encounter with Singapore starts with the lush East Coast while travelling into town from Changi Airport. The area could be aptly described as Singapore's riviera, with coconut groves and sandy beaches on one side of the coastal highway and expensive condos on the other. The East Coast is packed at weekends as Singaporeans escape for a day at the beach, but during the week the beaches and picnic areas are blissfully quiet.

East Coast Park ❺ stretches for more than 10km (6 miles) along the coast between Changi Airport and Marina Bay. Fringed with casuarinas and coconut palms, the park affords superb views of ships anchored in the Straits of Singapore. The sea breeze blows gently, and it's often peaceful enough for birds to flock to special tall-grass sanctuaries found along the coastline.

The park is the playground for residents living in the eastern part of the island. T'ai chi practitioners can be seen exercising in the park as early as 6am, together with joggers and cyclists. Picnic tables and barbecue pits are set up under the trees, and at weekends campers pitch their colourful tents.

The beach gets very crowded at the weekends, especially around car park C3 where **Marine Cove** and McDonald's are, but there's always plenty of space for a picnic in the coconut groves and wooded areas behind the shore. Swimming is pleasant here; the water may not be crystal clear, but at least it and the beach are clean.

There is plenty here to keep you occupied. For watersports with a difference, head to **SKI360°** which offers cable-skiing (1206A East Coast Parkway; tel: 6442-7318; www.ski360degree.com). Water-skiers and wakeboarders are pulled by an overhead cable instead of a boat. Bicycles and roller blades can be hired from several kiosks in the park for use along the 12km (7-mile) bike path which follows the coast. Other recreational facilities include a watersports centre, bowling alleys, in-line skating, tennis courts and a new Xtreme SkatePark.

East Coast dining

Many people come to the East Coast just to eat, especially at the popular **East Coast Seafood Centre**, housing several restaurants near the swimming lagoon. The specialities here range from steamed *grouper* in ginger and soy sauce, to chilli or pepper crabs and grilled butter prawns. A stone's throw away is the popular **East Coast Lagoon Food Village**, where some stalls are in such demand that it is not uncommon to find queues 10 people deep.

A few kilometres further on (towards the city) is **Marine Cove**, another restaurant and recreation hub. (It's been reported that this popular area will be redeveloped towards the end of 2011). A number of good restaurants are found here (**Tung Lok Seafood Gallery** and **the Mango Tree**, among others), and there are also pubs where you can sit out in the open air to enjoy the fresh sea breezes. **Bernie's BFD** (ask them what the acronym stands for) is noted for its huge margaritas *(see page 216)*.

Another exciting food hub is **Playground @ Big Splash**, previously a water theme park, which opened in 2008 after a major revamp. Among its offerings are the **Seafood International Market and Restaurant, 1 TwentySix**, a chic yet laid-back gastrobar, **Claypot Fun**, a family-style restaurant, and a huge **Carl's Junior** drive-in burger restaurant.

Changi Village

Before Changi Airport was opened in the early 1980s, the rustic and laid-back **Changi Village ❻** was the only reason to venture to the far eastern shore of Singapore. This sleepy corner of the island is a charming slice of Old Singapore and is home to a splendid variety of old trees (the magnificent Shorea Gibbosa tree with a cauliflower-like crown at the junction of Netheravon Road and Turnhouse Road is believed to be one of the last two left standing in Singapore). The stretch of sea here is a favourite rowing area for kayakers. The horizon is often dotted with the sails of dinghies and keelboats manned by weekend sailors from the nearby sailing clubs.

Once considered the boondocks, the seafood restaurants and pubs flanking Netheravon Road in Changi Village have revived the bustling atmosphere the place enjoyed when

ABOVE: café at East Coast Park. **BELOW:** boats at Changi Village.

ABOVE AND BELOW:
eating at Changi Village
Food Centre. **ABOVE
RIGHT:** Changi Point.

the British troops were stationed here.
Changi Village Hotel (1 Netheravon
Road; tel: 6379-7111, www.stayvillage.
com) offers the only hotel accommodation in the area. Take time to
wander along the village's sleepy
streets. **Salvation Army Thrift Shop**
has interesting merchandise (01-2082,
Block 4; tel: 6545-5722).

Changi Village Food Centre
behind offers some of the island's
best local fare – and not surprisingly
gets very crowded at weekends.

A short walk away is the **Changi
Point Jetty**, which offers a ferry service to Pulau Ubin (*see pages 214–15*)
and to Tanjong Pengelih, the jump-
off point for mountain biking trips
to **Penggarang**, at the southeastern
tip of Johor in Malaysia.

Changi Beach Park

The footbridge nearby leads to
Changi Beach Park ❼, a short but
pleasant stretch with views across the
water to Malaysia and Pulau Tekong
island, which is a Singapore military
training area. It isn't as popular as the
East Coast Park, and is therefore far
less crowded. The beach is a craggy
stretch and high tides can conceal

sharp rocks, so be careful if you want
to wade in the water. Look out for the
Changi Beach Massacre Site nearby,
marked by a storyboard, where 66
male Chinese civilians were killed by
a Japanese firing squad on 20 February 1942. The same spot is a campsite
and popular picnic spot.

Changi Chapel/Museum

Address: 1000 Upper Changi Road
North; www.changimuseum.com
Tel: 6214-2451
Opening Hrs: daily 9.30am–5pm
Entrance Fee: free
Transport: Tanah Merah MRT, then
SBS Bus 2

The Japanese Imperial Army turned
barracks built by the British into a
POW camp at Changi after they captured Singapore in early 1942. This
camp became a notorious hellhole
where both military and civilian prisoners were interned by the thousand.
Many of the POWs were sent to work
at the Thailand–Burma railroad,
including the infamous Bridge of the
River Kwai, but those who remained
at Changi weren't much better off.
They had to endure appalling conditions, described in a number of
poignant books, including *King Rat*
by James Clavell – who was a POW at
Changi himself.

Changi Prison still exists today, but it's now a place for criminals. The historic **Changi Chapel and Museum ❽**, formerly located next door to Changi Prison, moved to its new site in nearby Upper Changi Road North in 2001. The museum focuses on the memories and lives of both POWs and civilian internees who survived the horrific Japanese Occupation (1942–5) with a collection of wartime memorabilia, including drawings by W.R.M. Haxworth and photographs by George Aspinall (taken and developed in great danger when he was interned by the Japanese). Life as a POW is depicted in searing clarity here.

Particularly compelling are the **Changi Murals**. Painted by British POW Stanley Warren, the five murals, each depicting the life of Christ, are replicas of the restored originals at Changi Camp. The Changi Chapel, a symbolic replica of the one at Changi Prison, is housed in the open-air courtyard (visitors are welcome to join the Sunday service, which takes place from 9.30am to 11.30am). There are also video screenings and rare books depicting life during the war years.

Johore Battery

Further up off Upper Changi Road North, along Cosford Road, lies the **Johore Battery** (tel: 6546-9897; daily 9am–5pm; free), a former gun emplacement with a labyrinth of underground tunnels built by the British in 1939. The battery displays a replica of the 15-inch "monster guns" – the largest to be installed outside Britain during World War II and capable of firing at battleships over 32km (20 miles) away.

Pasir Ris Park

Pasir Ris, at the northeast coast of Singapore and the end of the eastern MRT line, is home to the idyllic **Pasir Ris Park ❾**, another pleasant stretch of beach that overlooks Pulau Ubin just across the waters. Part of the park, near car park C (entry via Pasir Ris Green Road), encloses a reserve which protects a 6-hectare (15-acre) mangrove swamp, where many migrating shore birds feed and build their nests.

A wooden boardwalk leads across the mud flats and brackish ponds, with signboards that provide descriptions of the flora and fauna. Nature

ABOVE: poignant notes left behind in remembrance of war heroes at the Changi Chapel.

TIP

The Changi Point Coastal Walk stretches 2.6km (1½ miles) from Changi Village to Changi Beach Club (originally the Royal Air Force Officers' Club), along six sections of boardwalk. It's especially scenic at dusk. As you meander along, look out for the many heritage trees along the way and stop to enjoy the sunset at one of the viewing platforms.

lovers will also enjoy **Sungei Api Api** nearby (*sungei* is "river" in Malay and *api api* is a mangrove variety). A bridge spanning the river connects car parks C and D. This river is one of the few remaining natural rivers in Singapore, and about 26 species of mangrove have been documented at this mangrove swamp. If flora and fauna do not interest you, spend a lazy afternoon relaxing or swimming at this undulating stretch of sand. A string of beach pubs, cafés and restaurants are also located along this side of the beach, and this area is much quieter than East Coast beach.

Twin theme parks

With the opening of Universal Studios, the **Escape Theme Park ⑩** at 1 Pasir Ris Close has probably lost much of its fan base. It's still an ideal playground for families with restless children, however (tel: 6581-9112; www.escapethemepark.com.sg; Sat–Sun and public and school holidays 10am–8pm; charge). The gravity-defying rides and speed races will especially appeal to thrill-seekers. The adjacent **Wild Wild Wet** water theme

park promises more thrills and spills of the watery kind, with rides like the Tsunami and snake-like Ular-lah (www.wildwildwet.com; Mon, Wed–Fri 1–7pm, Sat–Sun and public and school holidays 10am–7pm; charge).

Both parks are part of a larger development called **Downtown East**, a leisure, food and shopping hub that also provides comfortable chalet-style accommodation at reasonable rates (tel: 6582-3322; www.ntucclub.com.sg).

Pulau Ubin

Just off the northeastern tip of Singapore is the island of **Pulau Ubin ⑪**, which basks in the Johor Straits, a stone's throw from the Malaysian coast. A 15-minute boat ride from **Changi Point Jetty** (*see page 212*) is all it takes to reach Ubin, measuring just 8km (5 miles) across and 1.5km (1 mile) wide. Left behind by developments on the main island, Ubin was for a long time the last stronghold of Old Singapore. Despite scars caused by quarrying, its pastoral charm remains intact, a tapestry of sandy roads, prawn farms, abandoned rub-

ber plantations and coconut groves. An information kiosk run by the National Parks (tel: 6542-4108; daily 8.30am–5pm) has a map and leaflets detailing the flora and fauna of Ubin and things to do on the island.

Ubin's main "town centre" boasts a handful of grocery stores that have taken on a lucrative sideline renting mountain bikes, and a couple of eateries; one of them is Ubin First Stop Restaurant, serving seafood. These services cater to the ever-increasing crowds from the mainland, especially during weekends and holidays. Most visitors walk around Ubin, although mountain biking is also popular. Taxis can also be hired near the ferry pier, but agree on the fare before hopping in.

Pulau Ubin is one of Singapore's last great nature areas, with vast tracts of secondary jungle and mangrove swamp that sustain a wide variety of animals such as the flying fox, long-tailed macaque and monitor lizard, and birds like the ruby-cheeked sunbird, kingfishers, brahminy kite, white-bellied fish eagle, buffy fish owls and various types of egrets and herons.

A walk in the swamps or forest may reveal unexpected surprises such as sightings of an oriental whip snake curled up on a tree or fruit bats rustling in the trees in the evenings. There are wild orchids and flowers to be found and, if one is lucky, carnivorous pitcher plants with insects trapped in their huge pitcher cups.

Fish and prawn farming are a source of income for the island's inhabitants. The island has a population of about 100 people, most of whom live in wooden houses surrounded by fruit orchards. Apart from birdwatching, visitors to Ubin can go fishing or crabbing in the mangrove swamps. The best angling spots are near the Ketam Channel (between Ubin and its sister island, Pulau Ketam), and along waterways near the coast during high tide.

There are three beaches on the island – **Jelutong**, **Noordin** and **Mamam** – where visitors can pitch tents. In recent years, plans to develop Ubin have been shelved after the public voiced its concerns, preferring to leave the island as the last bastion of rural Singapore.   ❑

ABOVE: starfish at Chek Jawa. **BELOW:** trail riding at Pulau Ubin.

Chek Jawa

Call it nature's outdoor classroom if you wish. Thanks to passionate nature-lovers, Chek Jawa, on Pulau Ubin's southeast coast, has been saved from reclamation. The vast expanse of sand and mud flats is so fertile it has created an astonishing marine biological diversity and a coastal ecosystem found nowhere else in Singapore. There is a boardwalk and viewing tower to help visitors better appreciate this wetland reserve. To get there, hire a van, cycle or take a 40-minute walk. You can take a two-hour guided tour during low tide, but you must book in advance and tours get booked up quickly (tel: 6542-4108; www.nparks.gov.sg; daily 8.30am–6pm; charge for large groups).

BEST RESTAURANTS

American

Bernie's BFD
East Coast Recreation Ctr, 1000 East Coast Parkway. Tel: 6244-4434. Open: Mon–Thur 4pm–2am, Fri 4pm–3am, Sat noon–3am, Sun noon–2am. **$$$**
With an energetic band, tanned women in tight outfits, oversized burgers and steaks, intoxicating margaritas and a beach-front location, no wonder Bernie's is such a hit.

European

Le Bistrot
01-03 Singapore Indoor Stadium, 2 Stadium Walk. Tel: 6447-0018. www.lebistrot.com.sg Open: Mon–Wed D, Thur–Fri L & D, Sat–Sun brunch 10.30am–2.30pm, D. **$$$**

You can expect classic bistro staples such as steak frites, gratinated onion soup and duck leg confit. The menu is prix fixe – pay S$50 for a two-course meal (either entrée and main, or main and dessert) or $60 for a three-course meal. Now who'd have thought you could find solid provincial French cooking in the suburbs of Singapore?

1 Twenty Six
902 East Coast Parkway, #01-26 Playground @ Big Splash. Tel: 6348-2126. www.1-twentysix.com Open: Mon–Sat D, Sun brunch 10am–3pm, D. **$$$**
The East Coast welcomed its first chic venue when the dynamic One Rochester Group launched 1 Twenty Six. With its floor-to-ceiling glass windows and curvilinear bar, you can soak in sea views while sipping cocktails and tucking into oysters and modern European dishes with distinct Asian touches.

Indian

Chat Masala
158 Upper East Coast Rd. Tel: 6876-0570. Open: Mon D, Tue–Sun L & D. **$$**
With its quirky tagline – "North Indian, South Indian and Not So Indian" – the family-run eatery has a menu that is both authentic and creative. The eggplant strips, *bindi masala* (spicy okra), *briyani*, naan, Keralan curries and butter chicken are incredibly good.

The Mango Tree
1000 East Coast Parkway, B23. Tel: 6442-8655. www.themangotree.com.sg Open: Mon–Fri L & D, Sat–Sun 11.30am–11pm. **$$$**
This is one of those beach-side places where you'll want to linger over your meal, while watching cyclists whizzing past the tree-lined path outdoors. The hospitable staff, the decor – modern with Indian accents – and the menu, featuring the best of India's coastal regions, all lend a sophisticated but relaxed air.

LEFT: Jumbo at the East Coast Seafood Centre.

Vansh
01-04 Singapore Indoor Stadium, 2 Stadium Walk. Tel: 6345-4466. www.vansh.com.sg Open: daily L & D. **$$** (set lunch) **$$$$**
The setting for this modern Indian restaurant is ultra-trendy. You may just want to sip the Kamasutra cocktail horizontally – reclining on the low lounge chairs around the open tandoor kitchen. Modern Indian cuisine means everything is individually plated and creatively presented.

Italian

Al Forno
400 East Coast Rd. Tel: 6348-8781. Open: daily L & D. **$$$**
Al Forno means "In the Oven", and the restaurant has certainly won many hearts (and stomachs) with its lip-smacking pizzas and calzones. That's because they are lovingly crafted by Italian chefs before they go into the large wood-fired oven.

Local

Changi Village Food Centre
Blk 2, Changi Village Rd. Open: daily B–late. **$**
It's most famous for *nasi lemak*, a coconut-based rice dish. Just S$2 gets you rice with fried chicken, *ikan bilis* (whitebait) and egg. Many Malay stalls offer this dish, but the longest queues are at

stall 57. Also check out Charlie's Corner at stall 8 for fish and chips and more than 50 varieties of beer.

Claypot Fun
902 East Coast Parkway Block B, #01-11 Playground @ Big Splash. Tel: 6440-7975. www.claypotfun.com.sg Open: daily L & D. **$$**
A range of Cantonese-style claypot rice items is available in this small but popular restaurant. Take your pick from Chinese sausages, marinated beef with egg, or chicken with mushroom, and mix them with the piping-hot rice and enjoy. The setting is adorned with old-school memorabilia, bringing diners back to Singapore's good ol' days of the 1960s and 70s.

East Coast Lagoon Food Village
1220 East Coast Parkway, next to car park E2. Open: daily B–late. **$**
Where else can you have some of the best local food in a lovely Indonesian-style structure and just within a stone's throw of the sea? Make a beeline for the barbecue chicken wings, vermicelli with *satay* sauce and barbecue pork noodles. There are

at several *satay* stalls, but No. 55 (Haron's) is the best. Best visited at night when all the stalls are open.

Geylang Famous Beef Kway Teow
237 Geylang, Lorong 9. Open: Mon 5pm–3am, Tue–Sun 11–3am. **$**
It's indeed famous. Just look at the number of cars risking parking fines just for a plate of beef noodles. Industrious chef-owner Leong Wan Hui serves up to 700 plates of it on a Saturday night. It's the super-tender beef slices and thick gravy of black beans and chilli that make this dish stand above others.

Marine Parade Laksa
Nan Sin Food Ctr, 57/59 East Coast Rd. Open: daily 10am–6pm, closed alternate Tue. **$**
Laksa is noodles with a curry-like, coconut-based soup. This particular stall is said to have pioneered Katong *laksa*, the now famous variety that has even warranted a story in *The New York Times*. You can ask for clams (or without), and you eat the short noodles with your spoon – no chopsticks required.

Prices for a three-course dinner per person without drinks and taxes:
$ = under S$20
$$ = S$20–30
$$$ = S$30–50
$$$$ = over S$50

Peranakan

Baba Inn
01-103 Frankel Ave. Tel: 6445-2404. Open daily L & D. **$$**
Located in the sleepy Siglap neighbourhood, this no-frills restaurant may have a functional

setting, but the menu features delicious home-style Peranakan dishes such as *assam sotong* (fried squid with tamarind sauce) and spicy prawn and pineapple soup.

Guan Hoe Soon
214 Joo Chiat Rd. Tel: 6344-2761. www.guanhoe soon.com Open: Wed–Mon L & D. **$$**
Singapore's oldest Peranakan restaurant was a mere coffee shop when it was founded in 1953 by an enterprising Hainanese man. You can't go wrong with traditional Straits Chinese dishes such as *satay babi* (pork satay curry), *ngo hiang* sausage and *ayam tempra* (chicken stew).

Kim Choo
109–111 East Coast Rd. Tel: 6741-2125. www.kim choo.com Open: daily 8am–9pm. **$$**
This two-storey restaurant is known for its simple home-cooked Peranakan food and delicious rice dumplings. Try authentic fare such as *bakwan kepiting* (soup with crabmeat and minced pork balls) and *babi pongteh* (stewed pork with fermented beans). The upper floor doubles up as a gallery of Peranankan artefacts, including porcelain and beadwork.

Seafood

East Coast Seafood Centre
1110 East Coast Parkway, Car Park E1. **$$$**

A collection of informal, family-type seafood restaurants that fill up at weekends. A good seaside place to gorge on seafood prepared Singapore-style. Prices are reasonable unless you order Sri Lankan crabs. Good bets include Red House (tel: 6442-3112; www.redhouse seafood.com), Jumbo (tel: 6442-3435; www. jumboseafood.com.sg) and Long Beach (tel: 6448-3636; www.long beachseafood.com.sg).

Hua Yu Wee
462 Upper East Coast Rd. Tel: 6241-1709. Open: daily D. **$$$**
Located in an old Chinese mansion, families living in the east flock in droves to this nondescript restaurant for its satisfying Singapore-style seafood dishes. Its chilli and pepper crabs, butter prawns and seafood rolls are highly recommended.

Tung Lok Seafood Gallery
2/F, Building B, East Coast Recreation Ctr, 1000 East Coast Parkway. Tel: 6246-0555. www.tunglok.com Open: daily L & D. **$$$–$$$$**
Who says you can't negotiate crab claws and business deals at the same time? The elegant dining room, vigilant waiting staff, beautifully presented dishes and creative menu (including deep-fried fish with spicy sauce and the signature prawns with *wasabi* mayo) are all geared towards impressing your VIP guests.

CENTRAL AND NORTHERN SINGAPORE

A verdant oasis of green marks the centre of the island, where Singapore's remaining natural habitats are found. But it's not all flora and fauna, as the area also hosts some age-old Chinese temples

Central and Northern Singapore are a paradox. The two areas house some of the island's most heavily populated districts yet contain, at the same time, most of its pockets of nature. In fact, these parts of the island offer such large tracts of tropical forest, mangrove and swamp that getting close to nature here is as much a part of Singapore life as eating and shopping.

Lian Shan Shuang Lin

Some 5km (3 miles) north of Orchard Road is **Lian Shan Shuang Lin Monastery ❶** (tel: 6259-6924; daily 8.30am–5pm). Better known as Siong Lim Temple, it is located in Toa Payoh, one of Singapore's oldest Housing and Development Board (HDB) estates.

Its full name, Lian Shan Shuang Lin Shi, means "Twin Grove of the Lotus Mountain Temple". Completed in 1912, the temple was modelled after Xi Chan Si, a well-known *cong lin* temple in Fuzhou. *Cong lin* means "layers of forest", and Xi Chan Si is a monastery that was built according to an established layout which allows monks to move around to a set pattern to perform rituals. This enables them to find their way about in any *cong lin* temple they might be in, whatever its size.

Siong Lim Temple was the result of one man's dream, Low Kim Pong (1838–1908), a Buddhist who was a successful trader, landowner and a leader of the local Fujian community.

The story goes that one day in 1898, Low had a dream in which he saw a golden light shining from the west. He found out, the next day, that his son had the same dream. Taking it as an omen, father and son went to the harbour and waited. At sunset, a boat sailed in from the west, carrying

LEFT: Lian Shan Shuang Lin Monastery.

a family of 12 Buddhist monks and nuns who were on their way back to China after six years of pilgrimage in India, Sri Lanka and Burma. It was Low's dream come true. Inspired, he persuaded the group to stay and promised to build a Buddhist monastery for their use.

It was a massive exercise that took over 10 years to finish. The work was done in stages and with substantial funds donated by Low. Though he did not live to see the completion, his name has always been associated with it. In fact, it was often referred to as Low Kim Pong's temple.

Over the years, the Siong Lim Temple deteriorated and in 1991, it underwent major restorations. Four of its structures were restored – the impressive **Entrance Hall**, topped by a granite wall panel depicting scenes of Chinese culture and history; the **Drum Tower** and **Bell Tower** flanking the main courtyard; and the **Main Hall**, housing the key altar.

The Main Hall is the hub of the monastery and is noted for the beauty of its decorative panels, wood carvings and sculptures of deities. Other secondary buildings of no architectural value that were added over the years were replaced with new ones built in traditional style. Then in June 2002, a huge seven-storey granite **Dragon Light Pagoda** – topped with a golden spire – was completed by craftsmen from China, culminating an 11-year restoration programme that had cost over S$40 million.

Although the farms and villages that used to surround Siong Lim Temple have been replaced with high-rise apartment blocks and the Pan-Island Expressway, the traditions of the temple continue to endure.

Memories at Old Ford Factory

Address: 351 Upper Bukit Timah Road; www.s1942.org.sg/s1942/moff/visit1.htm

Tel: 6332-7973
Opening Hrs: Mon–Sat 9am–5.30pm, Sun 1–5.30pm
Entrance Fee: charge
Transport: SMRT Bus 67, 75, 171, 173 to Upper Bukit Timah

Established in 1941, the Ford Motor Factory was the first Ford vehicle assembly plant in Southeast Asia, but it is most notable as the venue for the formal surrender of Malaya by the British to the Japanese in 1942. This marked the start of the Japanese Occupation in Singapore during World War II. The Japanese took over the facility and used it to assemble military trucks and other vehicles for their army. After the war, the factory was reopened and remained operational until 1980. It has since been gazetted as a national monument and has a well-thought-out gallery filled with memories of the war, including interactive displays. Look out for the small paintings and sketches, now turned into colourful window displays, depicting the harsh living conditions in the POW camps, as well as archival records and first-hand historical accounts.

ABOVE: buddhas at Lian Shan Shuang Lin.
BELOW: enjoying the Treetop Walk at MacRitchie Resevoir.

ABOVE: bundles of "hell money", which the Chinese burn as offerings to the deceased.

Sun Yat Sen Nanyang Memorial Hall

Address: 12 Tai Gin Road; www.s1942.org.sg/s1942/moff/visit1.htm
Tel: 6256-7377
Opening Hrs: Tue–Sun 9am–5pm, closed for renovation until October 2011
Entrance Fee: charge

A national monument, **Sun Yat Sen Nanyang Memorial Hall ❷** is a lovely two-storey, Victorian-style bungalow, built in 1900 at Balestier. To find it, look out for the seated statue of Sun Yat Sen, the leader of China's nationalist movement, just in front of the building in the garden.

In 1906, when Dr Sun Yat Sen arrived in Singapore to drum up support for his nationalist cause among the overseas Chinese in *Nanyang* (meaning "southern seas" in Chinese and referring to Southeast Asia), he was given the villa for his use. It was here that he plotted the overthrow of the Qing dynasty in China. It was also at the villa that the Tong Meng Hui Nanyang Branch was founded and the villa made its Southeast Asian quarters. Soon after, the bungalow became known as the Sun Yat Sen Villa.

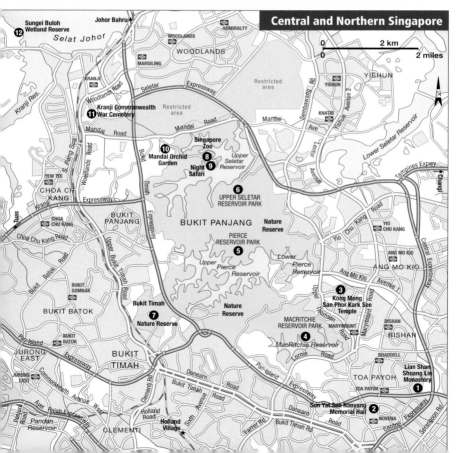

Central and Northern Singapore

After the successful revolution in China in 1911, the villa fell into disrepair. In 1938, a group of philanthropists, who were members of the Tong Meng Hui society, bought the building with the purpose of preserving it.

In 1942, during World War II, the Japanese used the villa as a communications centre, and then after the invaders departed in 1945 it became the headquarters of the Singapore Branch of the Kuomintang. In 1949, the villa was handed over to the Singapore Chinese Chamber of Commerce and Industry to manage. It was restored in 1965 and turned into a library and museum. In 1966, on the centenary of Dr Sun's birthday, the villa opened to the public.

In 1997, the villa was closed for major refurbishments, before reopening four years later on the 135th anniversary of the famed revolutionary's birth. Among the cvarious exhibits, the Father of Modern China's revolutionary exploits in Southeast Asia are also told through the collection of some 400 black and white photographs.

Kong Meng San Temple

Five kilometres (3 miles) north of the villa is the **Kong Meng San Phor Kark See Temple** ❸, located at Bright Hill Drive (tel: 6849-5300; www.kmspks.org; daily 6am–9.30pm). Built in 1980, it is Singapore's largest Buddhist temple and one of the largest temple complexes found in Southeast Asia.

Spread over 12 hectares (29 acres) of land, its gilded roofs are visible from afar. It's easy to get lost among the many halls of prayer and meditation. The **Hall of Great Compassion** houses a 9-metre (30ft) high Goddess of Mercy, Kuan Yin, carved in marble. This Bodhisattva image is crafted in the Indian tradition and has 1,000 arms and eyes. Look out also for one of Southeast Asia's largest images of the Medicine Buddha, which sits beneath a golden stupa in the **Pagoda of 10,000 Buddhas**.

Also on the grounds is a Bodhi Tree (the Buddha gained enlightenment under such a tree), a home for the aged, a crematorium and a columbarium. There is also a pond housing turtles and an enclosure where doves

ABOVE: Sun Yat Sen travelled to many parts of the world, including Singapore, to drum up overseas Chinese support to overthrow China's Qing dynasty.
BELOW: Sun Yat Sen Nan-yang Memorial Hall.

are released every year as a merit-making gesture on Vesak Day, which celebrates Buddha's birth, death and attainment of nirvana.

In May, Vesak Day celebrations are held here on a grand scale, sometimes stretching over three weeks, and visitors are welcome.

Central Catchment Reserve

West of the temple is a lush green expanse known as **MacRitchie Reservoir Park** ❹ which, together with the **Pierce Reservoir Park** ❺ further north (comprising the Upper Pierce and Lower Pierce parks) and **Upper Seletar Reservoir Park** ❻, form what is collectively known as the **Central Catchment Nature Reserve**, one of four gazetted nature reserves in Singapore (www.nparks.gov.sg; all daily 6.30am–7.30pm; free). The other protected green areas on the island are Bukit Timah Nature Reserve, Sungei Buloh Wetland Reserve and Labrador Nature Reserve. Together, they comprise some 3,347 hectares (8,271 acres) – which is no mean feat in land-scarce Singapore.

ABOVE: don't be tempted to feed the animals at the reservoir parks. The monkeys have been known to behave viciously.
BELOW: ceremony at Kong Meng San.

The Central Catchment Nature Reserve consists of a rich mixture of secondary and primary forests, and contain a surprising array of species, including the lesser mouse deer, pangolin and flying lemur. The reservoirs – MacRitchie, Upper and Lower Pierce and Upper Seletar – trap rain-water caught and filtered by the natural vegetation. The Central Catchment Nature Reserve also contains the only patch of freshwater swamp remaining in Singapore.

The reservoirs are surrounded by landscaped parks that are popular with joggers and mountain bikers. **MacRitchie Reservoir** particularly, with its boardwalks bordering the water's edge and well-posted signboards, make for scenic tramps (*see panel, below*). Picnickers are a common sight at weekends.

MacRitchie can be accessed via Lornie Road, Upper and Lower Pierce reservoirs via Upper Thomson Road. A map of the Central Catchment Nature Reserve can be obtained from Bukit Timah Nature Reserve Visitor Centre, or downloaded from www.nparks.gov.sg.

Into the Woods

MacRitchie Reservoir Park's easiest trails are the six boardwalks along the forest fringes. The trails – ranging in length from 450 metres (¼ mile) to 2.2km (1½ miles) – are named after native trees. Four of these – Prunus, Petai, Chemperai and Jering – skirt the edge of the reservoir and are readily accessible from MacRitchie's only car park at Lornie Road. The truly indefatigable can also undertake the 11km (7-mile) Treetop Walk. This brings you across a suspension bridge 27 metres (88ft) high and 250 metres (820ft) long, which rewards hikers with a bird's-eye view of the lush forest canopy. For more information, visit the park's website www.nparks.gov.sg.

Bukit Timah Nature Reserve

To the west of MacRitchie is **Bukit Timah Nature Reserve** ❼ (www.nparks.gov.sg; daily 8.30am–6.30pm; free). This reserve is in the geographic centre of Singapore, 12km (7 miles) from the city, and most easily reached by taxi. After the taxi turns into Hindhede Drive from busy Upper Bukit Timah Road, the reserve's moist and dark-green quietness, overlaid by the uninterrupted buzzing of cicadas, will seem almost unreal, an isolated patch of land showing how the region would look if man had not intervened.

The reserve's car park is surrounded by new private housing estates. At the **Visitor Centre** (tel: 1800 468-5736; daily 8.30am–6pm) is an exhibition of Bukit Timah's history, including its role in the war years and Singapore's flora and fauna. A collection of old photographs includes one of the last tigers that was shot in Singapore, in 1924.

The reserve includes Singapore's highest hill, **Bukit Timah**, at a mere 164 metres (538ft), and protects 163 hectares (403 acres) of the nation's only virgin lowland rainforest.

Much of Singapore's forest was intensively logged right up to the middle of the 19th century. In 1884, in response to research on climatic changes arising from deforestation, Bukit Timah was declared a nature reserve. Over the past 100 years, boundary changes have reduced the size of the reserve, and poaching of timber and animals have reduced its ecological diversity. Today, most large mammals, including tiger, leopard and deer, are extinct in Singapore, as are ecologically sensitive birds such as hornbills, trogons and broadbills.

To explore the reserve, follow the asphalted road from the car park to the hilltop. Many trees along this road are labelled in English and

ABOVE: MacRitchie Resevoir.

with scientific names, and give the newcomer to the tropics a feeling for the enormous diversity of plant species in Southeast Asia. In fact, noted conservationist Dr David Bellamy has pointed out that the number of plant species in the reserve exceeds that found in the whole of North America. Although few mammal species have survived, the frequently heard hissing identifies slender squirrels and plantain squirrels. Another squirrel-like mammal with a long pointed nose is the unrelated common tree shrew.

Bukit Timah Hill is a popular training spot for mountaineers. Understandably, it gets crowded at weekends – if you're planning a trek, weekdays are your best bets. There are five trails, all clearly marked and with varying levels of difficulty, taking from 45 minutes to two hours to complete. There is a also a challenging 6km (4-mile) mountain bike trail for enthusiasts. Free brochures and trail maps are available from the Visitor Centre.

TIP

Fit and feeling adventurous? Head to Bukit Timah Nature Reserve. Past the three caves along Cave Path, up Tuip Tuip Path through Dairy Farm Loop, you'll cross a stream, scramble up a steep slope then walk some distance before coming to Seraya Hut – where you will be rewarded with a view of picturesque Singapore Quarry.

Though the view from the hilltop is unspectacular, it is a good place to wait for white-bellied sea eagles or brahminy kites, and the besotted birdwatcher can meet the challenge of identifying at least nine species of swifts and swallows. The view over the protected forest of several water reservoirs makes visitors forget that they are in one of the world's most densely populated cities.

Singapore Zoo

Address: Mandai Lake Road;
www.zoo.com.sg
Tel: 6269-3411
Opening Hrs: daily 8.30am–6pm
Entrance Fee: charge
Transport: Ang Mo Kio MRT, then SBS
bus 138, or Choa Chu Kan MRT, then
SMRT bus 927

About 15km (9 miles) northeast of the reserve at Mandai Lake Road is **Singapore Zoo ❽**. Occupying 28 hectares (69 acres) of greenery just beside the Upper Seletar Reservoir, the zoo stands out in nearly every category by which animal collections are judged: variety of wildlife (about 2,500 animals from 315 species, 29 percent of which are threatened), open-air enclosures that present animals in their natural environment, captive breeding of endangered species and attractive landscaping. But where the zoo really excels is melding education and entertainment into a delightful combination that reaches out to both adults and children.

It would be hard to find a zoo elsewhere in the world with a more creative approach to wildlife display. Modern glass enclosures offer visitors an underwater view of crocodiles and pygmy hippos in their riverine environment, while polar bears swim in deep-blue waters. Gibbons leap through the trees, as rhinos share space with antelopes in a stunning re-creation of the African plains. The home for the **Elephants of Asia** – one of its exhibits – is reminiscent of the logging areas in the hill tracts of

Arakan in Burma. The zoo also has the world's largest captive orang-utan colony. From 2012 visitors can see a pair of giant pandas on loan from China.

A popular attraction is the **Fragile Forest** – an ecological wonder highlighting the interplay between animals and plants living in the rainforest, and man. The first zoo exhibit to display invertebrates and vertebrates under one roof, the Fragile Forest features a walk-through flight area and four centres showing various ecosystems. Venture into the flight enclosure and look out for tamarins, marmosets, lemurs, sloth, parakeets and butterflies.

Animal shows are performed several times each day at the zoo's open-air amphitheatre. One features coastal wildlife (pelicans, penguins and sea lions), while others feature elephants and assorted reptiles. Feeding times of the various animals are posted near the park entrance; the most spectacular feasts are at the polar bear and lion habitats.

Night Safari

Address: 80 Mandai Lake Road; www.nightsafari.com.sg

Tel: 6269-3411
Opening Hrs: daily 7.30pm – midnight
Entrance Fee: charge
Transport: Ang Mo Kio MRT, then SBS bus 138, or Choa Chu Kan MRT, then SMRT bus 927

The world's first night wildlife park, the **Night Safari** ⑨, is next door to the zoo. It has 1,000 nocturnal animals from 115 species housed in eight geographical zones. Visitors will find habitats such as the Nepalese river valley, Indian subcontinent, Himalayan foothills and African plains.

The Night Safari features afterhours hunters such as tigers and lions, as well as lesser-known creatures like the Himalayan tahr mountain goat, babirusa pig, one-horned rhino and barasingha swamp deer. It may not be a real safari, but it's probably the closest you can get to feeling you're in the wilderness. With clever, unobstrusive lighting and realistic habitat re-creations, visitors do feel they are in the middle of a thick tropical jungle on a moonlit night. Free-ranging deer and other small animals wander to the tram, which makes a 45-minute journey around the park. Even tigers

TIP

If you plan to visit Singapore Zoo, Night Safari and Jurong Bird Park (see page 200), save money by purchasing a Park Hoppers ticket. The discounted package includes a single admission to all three parks and is valid for a month. Call 6269-3411 for more information.

BELOW AND BELOW LEFT: a pair of hippos and an albino python at the Singapore Zoo.

Little ones will be enthralled with the Rainforest Kidzworld at the zoo, which fuses ecological and conservation themes with fun interactive features. There are animal rides, a water playground and an animal show for them to look forward to.

and lions appear to be roaming freely in their natural enclosures, oblivious to observers just a stone's throw away. Walking trails are clearly marked and there are rangers to guide you along the way – there is no danger of stepping on a lion's tail! Just remember that flash photography is prohibited.

Not to be missed is the interactive **Creatures of the Night** show (daily 7.30, 8.30 and 9.30pm) featuring 19 species of night animals including the puma, leopard cat and spotted hyena.

Mandai Orchid Garden

Address: 200 Mandai Lake Road; www.mandai.com.sg
Tel: 6269-1036
Opening Hrs: Mon 8am–6pm, Tue–Sun 8am–7pm
Entrance fee: charge
Transport: Ang Mo Kio MRT, then SBS bus 138, or Choa Chu Kan MRT, then SMRT bus 927

West of the zoo is the **Mandai Orchid Garden** ⑩, on a hillside covered with a riot of glorious colour. This lush garden has one of the world's finest displays of orchids in

all shapes, shades and sizes. Growing in a mixture of charcoal and brick chips, orchids clamber up poles in vivid profusion, while others hang in delicate sprays from suspended pots.

The brilliant orchids are exported all over the world from here. Visitors can make their selections to take away, boxed for the flight. In cool climes, the blooms can last several weeks if the stems are regularly trimmed and the water changed.

Kranji War Cemetery

Further west along Woodlands Road is **Kranji Commonwealth War Cemetery** ⑪ (tel: 6269-6158; daily 7am–6pm; free). Some 4,000 Allied soldiers who died in World War II and two of Singapore's past presidents lie buried in this state cemetery. In the middle of the cemetery is the **War Memorial**. Over 24,000 names of soldiers who died in various battles in the Asia Pacific but whose bodies were never recovered are inscribed on the 12 columns. The design of the memorial is symbolic, representing the three arms of the service – army, air force and navy.

BELOW: an anteater with baby on the Night Safari.

Sungei Buloh Reserve

Address: Neo Tiew Crescent; www.sbwr.org.sg
Tel: 6794-1401
Opening Hrs: Mon–Fri 7.30am–7pm; Sat–Sun and public holidays 7am–7pm
Entrance Fee: free, except at weekends
Transport: Kranji MRT, then SMRT Bus 925. Alight at Kranji Reservoir car park and take a 15-min walk to the reserve

On the extreme northwestern coast of Singapore is the **Sungei Buloh Wetland Reserve ⑫**, about 15km (9 miles) west of the Kranji War Memorial. This reserve is remarkable for its abundant and diverse bird life (over 212 species). It is also one of the few spots in Singapore where endangered heron species nest and breed.

A boardwalk guides visitors through part of the park, with hides at regular intervals from which birds can be observed and platforms that jut out at vantage points. There are three trails, which last from one to five hours, including one through a mangrove.

The old freshwater ponds still remain, supporting flora like water lilies and lotuses, and surrounded by mangroves. Some of the fish still thrive, and with the farmers long gone, birds have a heyday. Collared as well as white-throated kingfishers sit on the low stakes by the bunds, waiting to swoop while cinnamon and yellow bitterns stalk the reedy edges. But it is the migrating waders, of which more than 20 species have been sighted feeding on exposed mud beds, that are the stars of the reserve. From September to April, large flocks of plovers, sandpipers, stints, curlews, godwits and egrets gather to feed on the mud exposed by the ebbing tide.

With the reclamation of other coastal areas in Singapore, this sanctuary now stands out as its last sizeable feeding ground for migrating wading birds. The ornithological importance of the site is underlined by the fact that Singapore is the last stopover in the migration path down the Malaysian peninsula before the thrust to regions further south. ❑

ABOVE: a crimson sunbird – one of several migratory birds sometimes spotted at Sungei Buloh Wetland Reserve.

RESTAURANTS

Bukit Timah
Italian

Ristorante Da Valentino's
11 Jalan Binka (off Rifle Range Rd). Tel: 6462-0555. Open: Tue–Sun L & D. **$$$$**
This charming trattoria is incredibly popular, even though it is somewhat off the beaten track. The Milanese chef's parents and brother help out at the restaurant, while his sister whips up Italian cakes and tarts at their

pastry shop next door. Must-tries include the squid ink and crabmeat pasta, and parma ham and rocket pizza.

Peranakan

Ivins
19/21 Binjai Park, Bukit Timah. Tel: 6468-3060. www.ivins.com.sg Open: Fri–Wed L & D. **$** (set lunch); **$$** (à la carte)
Droves of people come here for delicious Peranakan fare at down-to-earth prices. A lavish meal of chilli prawns, spring rolls,

honey pork and stewed chicken with Indonesian black nuts can be had for a song.

MacRitchie
Local

The Roti Prata House
246M Upper Thomson Rd. Tel: 6459-5260. Open: daily 7am–1am. **$**
Enjoy *roti prata* bread stuffed with cheese or with chicken, mutton, sardine or veggies. Then work off the calories at MacRitchie Reservoir Park – only 15 minutes' walk away.

Mandai
Ulu Ulu

Night Safari, 80 Mandai Rd. Tel: 6360-8560. Open: daily 6pm–midnight. **$$**
Fuel your stomach before or after your Night Safari tour at the zoo's main eatery. Serves an array of local and international favourites. The charcoal-grilled *satay* and *mee goreng* (fried noodles) are particularly good.

- - - - - - - -
Prices for a three-course dinner per person without drinks and taxes. **$$$$** *= more than S$45,* **$$$** *= S$30–45,* **$$** *= $20–30,* **$** *= under $20.*

INSIGHT GUIDES TRAVEL TIPS
SINGAPORE

TRANSPORT

GETTING THERE AND GETTING AROUND

GETTING THERE

By Air

More than 90 airlines operate about 5,000 flights a week from 200 cities to **Changi Airport**'s four terminals, **Terminal 1** (T1), **Terminal 2** (T2), **Terminal 3** (T3) and the **Budget Terminal** (BT), which is aimed at low-cost travellers. Terminals 1, 2 and 3 are linked to each other by the free, fully automated Skytrain and a free shuttle bus service. Passengers can transfer between the Budget Terminal and Terminal 2 via a free, 24-hour shuttle bus service.

Changi is easily one of the best airports in the world, having accumulated over 250 awards over the years. For instance, readers of UK's *Business Traveller* magazine have voted Changi Airport as the world's best for 23 consecutive years (since 1988). With the opening of the impressive Terminal 3 in 2008, the airport now has a handling capacity of 70 million passengers a year.

The airport levies a passenger service charge of S$21 per traveller. This should be incorporated into the price of the air ticket; if not, you may have to pay during check-in when you leave. Some airlines may absorb this airport tax.

Airport Facilities

Changi Airport has been conceived for maximum comfort and convenience, and has a superb range of services: a post office, foreign currency exchange outlets, free wireless internet, TV lounges and cinema, clinic, supermarket, games arcade, gym and an airport hotel, among others. The latest to be launched is a new airport lounge concept called the Green Market – a relaxing space with a "natural" ambience and a great Japanese dining experience.

The stand-alone luxury terminal, JetQuay, offers VIP services, such as a meet-and-greet service and a five-star lounge. Disabled travellers are well catered for, with specially designed toilets, ramps and elevators.

This being Singapore, food and shopping options are plentiful. There are shops selling everything from cosmetics to candies, tobacco to toys, liquors to lingerie – all at prices that are no higher than what you get downtown. For the hungry traveller, more than 100 food and beverage establishments cater to different palates.

Transit passengers who have at least five hours to spare before their connecting flight can book a two-hour free city tour. Approach the Singapore Visitors Centre in the Transit Halls of T1, T2 and T3 to find out more about this and the other transit services available.

AIRLINES

Air New Zealand
Tel: 6734-5595
www.airnewzealand.com.sg
British Airways
Tel: 6622-1747
www.britishairways.com
Emirates
Tel: 6622-1770
www.emirates.com
Lufthansa
Tel: 6245-5600
www.lufthansa.com.sg

Qantas Airways
Tel: 6415-7373
www.qantas.com
SilkAir
Tel: 6223-8888
www.silkair.com
Singapore Airlines
Tel: 6223-8888
www.singaporeair.com
United Airlines
Tel: 6873-3533
www.unitedairlines.com.sg

Free maps and guides to the city are available, including copies of the free airport magazine, *Changi Express*, which details all the airport services. If you need help, look out for the Information and Customer Service counters scattered in the terminals or the 24-hour help phones. These phones will link you to the appropriate customer service officers.

For more information on airport services contact **Changi Airport Customer Service** (tel: 6541-2267; www.changiairport.com.sg). For information on flight arrival and departure times, tel: 1800 542-4422.

Flying from UK and US

The national carrier, Singapore Airlines (SIA), is based at Changi Airport and flies to some 93 destinations in 38 countries. Its sister carrier, SilkAir, serves 33 Asian destinations.

There are regular daily flights out of London and major European cities direct to Singapore. Flying time is between 12 and 13 hours. Many UK and European travellers heading to Australia and New Zealand use Singapore as a transit point to break the long journey. From Singapore it is

another 4½ hours to Perth, between 7 and 8 hours to Sydney and Melbourne, and 10 hours to Auckland.

Flying from the US takes longer: a flight from Los Angeles or San Francisco which crosses the Pacific Ocean takes about 16 to 18 hours with a stop in Seoul, Taipei or Tokyo along the way. From New York, flight time is about 20 hours, excluding transit time.

Singapore Airlines offers non-stop all-business-class flights from Los Angeles and New York to Singapore. These flights typically shave two to four hours off flying time.

Singapore is also an excellent base for travel to other Southeast Asian destinations like Bali, Phuket, Bangkok, Penang and Langkawi among others, many of which are served by SilkAir as well as regional budget carriers like Air Asia, Jetstar Asia and Tiger Airways. Many of these budget airlines are expanding their networks to places further afield, like Perth, Melbourne, Macau, Taipei and Bangalore.

As a major hub in Southeast Asia, Singapore is an excellent place to purchase air tickets to the region and beyond.

BELOW: Chinatown.

REGIONAL TRAVEL

Singapore is a perfect place from which to explore the region. When looking for good deals, it's best to check out the travel agents' section of the classified advertisements in *The Straits Times*. Destinations in peninsular Malaysia can be easily accessed by road, rail, sea and by air, while the islands of Batam and Bintan in Indonesia are connected by ferries. Other destinations of interest in the region are a short flight away.

Another option is to take a leisurely cruise to ports in Malaysia, Thailand, Vietnam and Hong Kong. Contact **Star Cruises** (tel: 6226-1168; www.starcruises.com).

By Sea

Arriving slowly by sea is a pleasant experience. Most visitors arrive at the **Singapore Cruise Centre** (tel: 6513-2200; www.singaporecruise.com) located at the HarbourFront Centre. The facility is also used by several regional cruise operators, such as Star Cruises, and by many large cruise liners stopping over on their long voyages from around the world.

Tanah Merah Ferry Terminal (tel: 6545-2048), located near Changi Airport, handles boat traffic to the resorts on Indonesia's Bintan Island as well as Tanjung Pinang, its capital, and to Nongsa, on neighbouring Batam Island. Ferries to Malaysia's Sebana Cove also depart from here.

Changi Ferry Terminal (tel: 6214-8031), also near Changi Airport, handles regular ferry services to Tanjung Belungkor, on Malaysia's east coast.

By Train

Travelling by train through Malaysia and across the Causeway at Woodlands in the north of Singapore is a leisurely way to arrive.

EXCURSIONS FROM SINGAPORE

Pulau Tioman

Berjaya Air flies (40 minutes) to Tioman from Singapore once daily (tel: 6481-6302; www. berjaya-air.com). A cheaper but longer option is a coach ride (4 hours) to Mersing on the Malaysian mainland, followed by a ferry (1½ hours) to Tioman. The most convenient option is to book a holiday package with Discovery Tours (tel: 6733-4333; www.discoverytours.com.sg).

Melaka

The cheapest option is the 4½-hour, air-conditioned Malacca–Singapore Express bus service departing Lavender bus station hourly (tel: 6292-2436; daily 8am–7pm). Alternatively, book a package tour with hotel and sightseeing included. Contact Grassland Express (5001 Beach Road, 01-26 Golden Mile Complex; tel: 6293-1166; www.grassland.com.sg).

Pulau Bintan

Bintan Resort Ferries has regular ferry services (45 minutes, up to 7 times daily) from Tanah Merah Ferry Terminal to Bandar Bentan Telani (tel: 6542-4369; www.brf.com.sg). Penguin Ferry Services has ferries (2 hours) serving Tanjung Pinang up to 5 times daily.

Malaysia's **Keretapi Tanah Melayu** (KTM) has two lines: one links Singapore to Kuala Lumpur, Butterworth, Alor Setar and north across the Thai border into Bangkok, and the other branches off at Gemas and connects to Tumpat, near Kota Bahru along Malaysia's east coast.

Both Malaysian and Singapore immigration facilities are located at Woodlands. Following the closure of **Tanjong Pagar Railway Station** at Keppel Road in July 2011, KTM will relocate to Woodlands Train Checkpoint. The historic railway building is being conserved and is set to be redeveloped.

If money is no object, plump for the **E&O Express** (tel: 6392-3500; www.orient-express.com), the ultimate re-creation of a bygone age of romantic Asian rail travel. Decked out in the E&O livery of cream and racing green, it carries a maximum of 132 passengers on the three-night trip from Bangkok through southern Thailand and Malaysia, via Butterworth and Kuala Lumpur, to Singapore.

By Bus/Coach

There are good roads down the west and east coasts of peninsu-lar Malaysia crossing either the Causeway at Woodlands or the Second Link in Tuas into Singapore. The Second Link is far less prone to the frequent congestion that the Woodlands checkpoint experiences.

Private air-conditioned buses run from Hatyai in Thailand and many towns in Malaysia to Singapore. Call **Grassland Express** (tel: 6293-1166; www.grassland.com. sg) for bus tickets to Hatyai.

A number of bus companies, like First Coach (tel: 6822-2111; www.firstcoach.com.my) and Konsortium Express (tel: 6392-3922; www.konsortium.com.sg) operate a variety of buses that connect Singapore to key Malaysian cities like Kuala Lumpur, Penang and Melaka.

Also recommended are coach operators such as **Aeroline** (tel: 6341-9338; www.aeroline.com.sg) and **Transtar** (tel: 6299-9009; www.transtar.com.sg), which offer luxury buses that link Singapore with Kuala Lumpur and other major Malaysian cities. The comfortable seats have ample leg room, and light meals and refreshments are served on board. Travel time between KL and Singapore is about five hours.

GETTING AROUND

From the Airport

The airport authority aims to get arriving passengers on their way to their hotels within 30 minutes of landing. The formalities are brief and luggage arrives in no time.

Changi Airport is linked to the city centre by the East Coast Parkway (ECP) and to the other parts of Singapore by the Pan Island (PIE) and Tampines (TPE) expressways. There are five types of transport from the airport – taxi, car, bus, airport shuttle and MRT.

By Taxi

At all four airport terminals, the taxi stands are situated on the same level as the arrival halls. A surcharge of S$3 (or S$5 Fri–Sun 5pm–midnight) applies in addition to the fare shown on the taxi meter. There are two other surcharges that are added to the fare where applicable: for rides between midnight to 6am and ERP (Electronic Road Pricing) tolls (see page 235). The taxi fare to the city centre will cost around S$20, excluding the surcharges. Travel time to the city centre is about 20 to 30 minutes, depending on traffic conditions.

By Limousine Taxi

For a flat price of S$45, luxury limousine taxis will take you to any destination in Singapore. The limousine taxi counter is located at the arrival hall of the terminals. A surcharge of S$10 applies to passengers who board between midnight and 6am.

By Private/Rented Car

If being picked up by a private car at Terminal 1, take the inclined travelator in the arrival hall to the ground level, which leads to the Passenger Crescent, where a private car pick-up point is located. At Terminals 2 and 3, the car pick-up point is on the same level as the arrival hall. Car rental companies such as Avis and Hertz are located at the Arrivals level of the terminals.

By Public Bus

In the basements of Terminals 1, 2 and 3 are public bus depots. Buses depart between 6am and midnight daily, and information on bus routes is available at the bus stands. Service No. 36 gets you direct into the city for less than S$2. You'll need the exact fare as no change is given on board. Bus stops closest to the Budget Terminal are a 15-minute walk away on Airport Boulevard. It's easier to take the BT Shuttle Service to Terminal 2 to transfer to the MRT service or to transfer to the main terminals for the bus service to the city.

By Airport Shuttle

The comfortable airport shuttle operates between the airport and most hotels in Singapore. Tickets – S$9 for adults and S$6 for children – are available at the Ground Transport Desk in the Arrivals halls.

By Mass Rapid Transit

The MRT station in Changi Airport is located on the basement levels of Terminals 2 and 3. A ride to the city takes about 30 minutes and the fare costs from S$1.61,

ABOVE: the MRT, Singapore's efficient subway system.

depending on the mode of payment. Note: trains do not go direct to the city, so you have to switch to the city-bound line at Tanah Merah MRT station.

Orientation

Singapore lies 137km (85 miles) north of the equator and is separated from peninsular Malaysia in the north by the Straits of Johor. To its east, west and south, it is surrounded by the sprawling Indonesian archipelago.

Singapore consists of the main island, 699 sq km (267 sq miles) in area, and some 63 other small islands, making up a total land area of 714 sq km (275 sq miles). North to south it stretches for about 23km (14 miles); east to west, the distance is roughly 42km (26 miles). This land mass is constantly growing, however, as a result of land reclamation.

Singapore is an easy city to get around. The hardy walker can cover most areas of interest such as the Singapore River area, Chinatown, Civic District, Arab Street, Little India and the

PUBLIC TRANSPORT FOR TOURISTS

An excellent deal for tourists is the **Singapore Tourist Pass**. (www.thesingaporetouristpass.com). For just S$8 a day (and a S$10 refundable deposit), you get unlimited rides on the public transport system. There are also 2-day (S$16) and 3-day (S$24) cards available. The cards can be purchased at TransitLink offices in selected MRT stations, and used on the MRT, LRT and buses.

To use the card, either flash or tap it on the electronic readers mounted at bus entrances and entry turnstiles of MRT stations. When you arrive at your destina-

tion, flash the card at the exit reader as you leave the bus or train station.

If you're planning to be in Singapore for a longer period, buy an **ez-link Card** (www.ezlink.com.sg) instead, which costs S$15. This gives you rides up to the value of S$7, and can be topped up at ticket offices when the value runs low. When the card is returned at the end of your trip, S$3 is refunded. The remaining S$5 is a non-refundable administration charge, but the convenience of using this card far outweighs the expense.

A helpful source for information on the use of public transport is the **"Travel with Ease" Public Transport Guide for Tourists**, available at Singapore Visitors Centres and MRT stations. This guide gives travel directions to major tourist spots. Or contact:
- **TransitLink:** tel: 1800 225-5663; www.transitlink.com.sg
- **SMRT Corporation:** tel: 1800 336-8900; www.smrt.com.sg
- **SBS Transit:** tel: 1800 287-2727; www.sbstransit.com.sg
- **SMRT Buses:** tel: 6482-3888; www.smrtbuses.com.sg

Orchard Road area on foot. These and all the outlying attractions can be reached easily using the city's excellent public transport (MRT and buses), or by taxi.

There are no great distances to cover: from the Central Business District, it takes you no more than 20 to 30 minutes to Changi Airport, about 30 minutes to the western tip (Jurong) and a little more than 35 minutes all the way to the Woodlands Causeway.

The East Coast area has some of Singapore's more traditional neighbourhoods (Katong and Geylang, for example) and two major beach parks (East Coast and Pasir Ris) with cycle paths, and picnic and camping grounds. The central and northern areas of the island still have some forest reserves while the west, although largely industrialised, has a few key tourist attractions.

Public Transport

Singapore's public transport system is comprehensive, efficient and cheap. If you prefer to take a guided tour, see the **Sightseeing Tours** section *(pages 251–3)*.

Mass Rapid Transit (MRT)

The MRT system (see map on back flap) started in 1987 and has now grown to 131 air-conditioned trains serving 64 stations along the **East–West Line**, the **North–South Line**, the **Northeast Line** and the **Circle Line**.

TAXI NUMBERS

Booking taxis in advance is recommended; try one of the following companies:
CityCab/Comfort Taxi: 6552-1111; www.cdgtaxi.com.sg
Premier Taxis: 6363-6888; www.premiertaxi.com
Prime Taxi: 6778-0808
SMART Cabs: 6485-7777
SMRT Taxis: 6555-8888; www.smrttaxis.com.sg
TransCab: 6555-3333

In addition, a Light Rapid Transit (LRT) system services the towns of Bukit Panjang, Sengkang and Punggol.

During any one day the MRT system transports close to two million passengers in comfort and with clockwork precision. The six-car trains, each of which can accommodate 1,800 persons, travel at 45kmh (30mph) and arrive at each of the 78 stations every few minutes. Depending on the station, the first train rolls out at about 5.15am; last trains run until around 12.49am.

The system is easy to use, fares are easy to figure out and collection is automatic: magnetically coded cards cost between 90 cents and S$1.90 for single trips, plus a S$1 deposit. You can purchase tickets at any MRT station from the general ticket machines. Flash your ticket at the electronic card reader on the entry turnstile and walk through when the green indicator comes on. When you arrive at your destination, flash your ticket at the reader on the exit turnstile to pass through. At the end of the trip, make sure you insert your card into the general ticket machine to get back your S$1 deposit.

For added convenience, buy a **Singapore Tourist Pass** or stored-value **TransitLink ez-link Card**. These cards *(see text box on page 233)* give users the advantage of a small discount when connecting from buses to MRT and vice versa.

Buses

Around 3,500 buses operated by **Singapore Bus Service** (SBS) and **SMRT Buses** ply over 200 routes, covering practically every corner of the island. Buses (single- and double-deckers with or without air conditioning) run from around 6am to midnight, with an extension of about half an hour for both starting and ending times at weekends and public holidays.

Fares are cheap (minimum 90 cents on non-air-conditioned buses; maximum S$1.80 on air-

conditioned buses) depending on the number of sectors travelled. Have loose change ready; bus drivers are generally helpful and will tell you the exact fare on boarding. Tickets are issued by automatic dispensers on board.

For convenience, buy a stored-value ez-link Card, which can be used on both buses and MRT and LRT trains *(see text box on page 233)*.

In addition, there are various specialised bus services covering tourist areas such as Orchard Road, Chinatown, East Coast Park and Mount Faber Park.

Taxis

Taxis are a popular mode of transport, and more than 23,000 taxis ply the roads; but be warned that during morning and evening rush hours, and when it rains, it is almost impossible to get one if you haven't booked ahead.

Singapore's taxis are clean and generally in good condition. Most drivers speak or understand some English. Still, make sure the driver knows exactly where you want to go before starting out. Tipping is not necessary.

There are several taxi companies in Singapore – CityCab, Comfort Taxi, SMRT Taxis, Premier Taxis, SMART Cabs, Prime Taxi and TransCab. All taxis, regardless of company, have either SH or SHA on their licence plates. Each taxi may carry a maximum of four adult passengers. All taxis are metered with a flagfall of S$2.80, S$3 or S$3.20 (depending on type of car) for the first kilometre, and 20 cents for every 385 metres travelled up to 10km, or every 330 metres travelled after 10km, and every 45 seconds of waiting time.

Most taxi stands are found just outside shopping centres, hotels and other public buildings. Within the CBD (including Orchard Road) taxis can only be boarded and alighted at taxi stands and along side roads; elsewhere in Singapore, simply flag one down along the road. However, thanks – or actually no thanks – to a very efficient computerised booking system, it has become increasingly difficult to flag down cruising taxis during peak hours.

A long list of extra charges in addition to the fare shown on the meter are applicable:
• S$3 (or S$5 Fri–Sun 5pm–midnight) for trips originating from Changi and Seletar airports;
• surcharge of 50 percent for trips between midnight and 5.59am;
• 35 percent peak period surcharge for trips between 7am and 9.30am and 5pm and 8pm from Monday to Saturday;
• S$3 for trips leaving the CBD (Central Business District) between 5pm and midnight from Monday to Saturday;
• S$3 for trips originating from Marina Bay Sands and Resorts World Sentosa;
• S$1 public holiday surcharge from 6pm on the eve of a public holiday to midnight the next day;
• A 10 percent charge for credit card payment;
• booking fee of S$3.50 for peak-hour current bookings, S$2.50 for off-peak current bookings and S$5.20 when booking at least half an hour in advance. Fancier limousine cabs cost S$8 for current bookings and S$16 when booked at least half an hour in advance;
• finally, under the ERP (Electronic Road Pricing) system, additional charges apply when the taxi passes ERP gantry points along the ECP (East Coast Parkway), CTE (Central Expressway), PIE (Pan Island Expressway) and Nicoll Highway during morning peak hours, and from 7.30am to 7pm in the CBD area where ERP gantry points are located.

Trishaws

The quaint trishaw, a bicycle with a sidecar, has virtually disappeared from Singapore's streets. Today, it exists only for tourists who want to experience something of the old days.

For more information on trishaw tours, ask your hotel concierge or tour desk. Otherwise,

ABOVE: the city is well served by numerous bus routes.

just turn up at the trishaw station behind Bugis Village next to Fu Lu Shou Complex and find a driver, usually between 5 and 11pm. Or contact the licensed trishaw operators directly, such as Singapore Explorer (tel: 6339-6833), Trishaw Tours (tel: 6545-6311) or Pedicab Tours (tel: 6336-0500).

A tour around town including Chinatown and Little India for around 30 to 45 minutes is priced from S$25. For safety, it's best to wait until heavy traffic has dispersed after 8pm.

A word of caution: be sure you agree upon a fare before getting on. Licensed riders are distinguished by their coloured badges.

Driving

Thanks to an efficient public transport system, it is highly unlikely that the average visitor is going to drive. But if you do, Singapore has great roads and driving is relatively painless – compared to the rest of Asia. Keep a lookout, though, for drivers who routinely don't switch on indicator lights to signal their intention, and annoying tailgaters and lane drifters.

Rental companies will ask to see a valid international driver's licence. Self-drive cars are not cheap and cost from S$175 for a 1.3-litre car to S$295 for a 2-litre car per day including mileage but not insurance. These rates are only applicable for driving in Singapore; taking the car to Malaysia will cost you extra.

Before you head out, stock up on parking coupons and make sure you have a complete understanding of the Electronic Road Pricing system (see page 112).

A valid driver's licence from your country of residence or an international driver's licence is required for driving in Singapore. Driving is on the left. Wearing seat belts and using special child seats for children under eight is compulsory. Speed limits are 60–70km/h (37–43mph) in residential areas and 80–90km/h (50 to 56mph) on expressways.

International car rental companies include **Avis**, tel: 6737 1668; www.avis.com.sg; and **Hertz**, tel: 1800 734-4646; www.hertz.com.sg.

Smaller companies, however, listed in the Yellow Pages under "Car Rental", offer lower rates and are more open to negotiation.

A CCOMMODATION

SOME THINGS TO CONSIDER BEFORE YOU BOOK THE ROOM

Choosing a Hotel

In terms of accommodation, amenities and service standards, Singapore's top-end hotels easily compare with the best in the world. De luxe, first-class and business-oriented hotels all have conference and business facilities, in-room computer ports, cable TV, IDD phones and high-speed internet access.

There are price categories to suit all pockets. No question, accommodation in Singapore is pricier than in some Southeast Asian cities, but keep an eye out for promotional rates offered by top hotels – these can go as low as 50 percent off the published rates.

If you intend to stay longer, you might want to consider checking in to a serviced apartment. Singapore's serviced apartments generally offer all the amenities of 4- to 5-star hotels, but come with the added facilities of a fully equipped kitchen and dining area. The savings really add up when you take a long-term lease.

In recent years, a number of backpacker hostels have proliferated, a few in the city centre, but mainly on the outskirts of the city. These are generally well run and tend to attract a younger and more rowdy crowd, eager to meet and socialise with fellow travellers. You might be better off in a good budget hotel if you're more interested in a good night's rest than in expanding your social network.

Hotel Areas

Most visitors stay in the city centre, especially around the Civic District and Orchard Road areas. The former is where you'll find attractions like the Singapore Art Museum and Esplanade – Theatres on the Bay as well as a thriving nightlife scene in places such as Clarke Quay and Boat Quay, while Orchard Road is the city's shopping hub.

For those who want to avoid the crowds (which can get quite chaotic at weekends) and stiff prices, head for the atmospheric charm of Chinatown or Little India. Here you will find budget accommodation in small hotels occupying old-style shophouses. The East Coast area is also worth considering for its laid-back appeal, range of local food options, proximity to the beach, and generally lower rates. Even closer to sun, sand and sea is Sentosa. Hotels on this holiday island are mainly luxury resorts, so be prepared for their higher-than-mainland rates. Singapore's efficient transport system, however, makes getting around a breeze, so even if you're staying in the suburbs, the city is still within easy reach.

The new "integrated resorts" in Sentosa and Marina Bay have also sprouted a whole range of luxury hotels, with many leisure activities on offer.

Prices and Bookings

Hotel rates have risen quite dramatically in recent years, mainly because of Singapore's rise in popularity as a tourist and business destination and a corresponding shortage in rooms, mainly in the city centre.

Hotels are listed by price range. Rates are subject to 10 percent service charge and 7 percent GST (Goods and Service Tax).

If you arrive without prior reservations, the Hotel Reservations counters (managed by the **Singapore Hotel Association**) at Singapore Changi Airport's Terminals 1, 2, 3 and Budget Terminal arrival halls can help you with bookings. Payment of the first night's room charge (by cash or credit card) is required at the point of reservation. Alternatively, you may book online at the SHA's website: www. stayinsingapore.com. Peak seasons include the local school holidays in June and December, when occupancy levels rise. But unless there is a big convention in town or a regional crisis, you should have no problem being accommodated at the last minute.

ACCOMMODATION LISTINGS

THE CIVIC DISTRICT

Luxury

Conrad Centennial Singapore
2 Temasek Boulevard
Tel: 6334-8888
www.conradhotels.com
❶ p270, C3
Stylishly modern business hotel adjacent to the Suntec Convention Centre and Mall, Marina Square and Millenia Walk, making it a great location for both business and shopping. Excellent Chinese restaurant and popular 24-hour café. Only a five-minute walk from Promenade MRT station.

The Fullerton
1 Fullerton Square
Tel: 6733-8388
www.fullertonhotel.com
❷ p273, D1
The city's former General Post Office, this restored historical landmark stands on the Singapore River and is only a five-minute walk from Raffles Place MRT station. Business travellers will appreciate its proximity to the financial district. Fine-dining Chinese restaurant and trendy bar on site.

Raffles Hotel
1 Beach Road
Tel: 6337-1886
www.singapore.raffles.com
❸ p270, B3
The city's most famous (and most expensive) luxury hotel, beautifully restored to its former grandeur. Expect old-world atmosphere and charm. Part of the hotel

is an upmarket shopping annexe where guests can do their last-minute shopping. Across the road is the City Hall MRT station.

The Ritz-Carlton Millenia
7 Raffles Avenue
Tel: 6337-8888
www.ritzcarlton.com
❹ p271, C4
A plush contemporary hotel, with Singapore's largest guest rooms (and stunning bathrooms with views to match). Located beside the Suntec Conference Centre and less than a five-minute walk away from the Promenade MRT station. The bar, with a riveting glass sculpture as its talking point, is perfect for after-dinner drinks.

Expensive

Fairmont Singapore
80 Bras Basah Road
Tel: 6339-7777
www.fairmont.com/singapore
❺ p270, B3
Plush hotel next to the much taller Swissôtel The Stamford, with very easy access to the City Hall MRT station. Comfortable guestrooms with private balcony and contemporary furnishings. Top-of-the-line facilities include a pampering spa and a stylish Japanese restaurant.

Hotel Fort Canning
11 Canning Walk
Tel: 6559-6770
www.hfcsingapore.com
❻ p269, E3

This colonial building was the British Far East Command headquarters during World War II. Rooms are individually styled, and there's also a gym, pool and Thailand's renowned Thann Spa. Complimentary internet for all guests.

Mandarin Oriental
5 Raffles Avenue
Tel: 6338-0066
www.mandarinoriental.com
❼ p270, C4
Thoroughly modern hotel, with rooms on the high floors offering excellent views of the surrounding Marina Bay, and just a five-minute walk from Promenade MRT station. Restaurants comprise an all-day café, an American-style steakhouse, a Chinese restaurant, and a Mediterranean-style eatery by the poolside.

Marina Mandarin
6 Raffles Boulevard Marina Square
Tel: 6845-1000
www.meritushotels.com
❽ p270, C4
Another five-star hotel conveniently located near Marina Square, Suntec City and the Esplanade. Rooms have private balconies with views of Marina Bay, wireless broadband internet, and large flat-screen TVs. It has fine Cantonese and Italian restaurants.

Naumi Hotel
41 Seah Street
Tel: 6403-6000

www.naumihotel.com
❾ p270, B3
Naumi is conveniently located between the City Hall and Bugis MRT stations. Among its luxury facilities are a 24-hour yoga room, a rooftop infinity pool with views of the bustling city and a dedicated ladies' floor with enhanced security. The suites come with kitchenettes – perfect for longer stays.

Pan Pacific Singapore
7 Raffles Boulevard
Tel: 6336-8111
www.panpacific.com
❿ p270, C4
John Portman-designed five-star hotel with a lofty 35-storey atrium and comfortable good-sized rooms, five minutes' walk from Promenade MRT station. It has a Cantonese restaurant with grand views (from 37th floor), traditional-style Japanese restaurant with garden,

PRICE CATEGORIES
Price categories are for a double room without breakfast and taxes:
Luxury: over S$500
Expensive: S$350–500
Moderate: S$150–350
Budget: under S$150

ABOVE: The Stamford at night.

and an award-winning North Indian restaurant.

Swissôtel The Stamford
2 Stamford Road
Tel: 6338-8585
www.swissotel.com
⑪ p270, B3
This hotel, above the City Hall MRT station and next to both the CBD and colonial Civic District, is practically part of a large shopping complex. A huge number of restaurants and bars, plus a luxurious spa and a well-equipped fitness centre add to its attractions.

Moderate

Carlton
76 Bras Basah Road
Tel: 6338-8333
www.carlton.com.sg
⑫ p270, B3
In the heart of the museum district, this business-class hotel has a great location. Premier rooms in the Annexe Wing offer marble bathrooms and flat-screen TVs. The hotel also has an award-winning Cantonese restaurant and a 24-hour international

café. A five-minute walk to City Hall MRT station.

Grand Plaza Park Hotel City Hall
10 Coleman Street
Tel: 6336-3456
www.parkhotelgroup.com
⑬ p270, A3/4
This business hotel near City Hall MRT station is located near popular sights like the Armenian Church and Fort Canning Park. Dining options include a Chinese restaurant, brasserie and alfresco grill. Also known for its marine-themed spa.

Hotel Rendezvous
9 Bras Basah Road
Tel: 6336-0220
www.rendezvoushotels.com
⑭ p270, A2
Right next door to the Singapore Art Museum and close to the Civic District. Its Straits Café@Rendezvous is known for its famous spicy *nasi padang* (Indonesian-style rice and curries). Less than five minutes from Bras Basah MRT station.

Budget

Hangout@Mt.Emily
10A Upper Wilkie Road
Tel: 6438-5588
www.hangouthotels.com
⑮ p270, A1
You sleep in Zonk Out rooms, meet fellow

travellers in the Veg Out lounge, surf the web at the Log Out room, eat at the Pig Out café, do your laundry at the Wash Out room and exercise at the Work Out room. A 10-minute walk to Dhoby Ghaut MRT station.

Ibis Hotel
170 Bencoolen Street
Tel: 6593-2888
www.ibishotel.com
⑯ p270, B1
An international economy hotel that has an excellent location, close to museums, shopping centres and the buzzing Bugis Street. Bugis MRT station is a five-minute walk away. Hotel restaurant serves Asian tapas.

Strand
25 Bencoolen Street
Tel: 6338-1866
www.strandhotel.com.sg
⑰ p270, A2
Clean and comfortable, this is one of the better budget options. Close to the museum district, within walking distance of the top end of Orchard Road and less than five minutes from Bras Basah MRT station. Its Blabbers Café on the ground level is great for coffee and sandwiches.

CHINATOWN, THE CBD AND MARINA BAY

Luxury

Marina Bay Sands
10 Bayfront Avenue
Tel: 6688-8888
www.marinabaysands.com
⑱ p273, E2
Located in the stunning "integrated resort" of the

same name, this hotel overlooks the city centre. Pick from 18 types of room, such as Atrium rooms or Horizon rooms. Then enjoy the facilities in the complex, including casino, shops and trendy bars and clubs.

Expensive

The Fullerton Bay Hotel
80 Collyer Quay
Tel: 6333-8388
www.fullertonbayhotel.com
⑲ p273, D2
An elegant hotel in a historic location that boasts

stunning views of the Singapore skyline and bay. Exquisite touches include double-glazed floor-to-ceiling windows and Nespresso machines in all rooms. Rooftop bar Lantern is a must-visit. A short walk to Raffles Place MRT.

New Majestic
31–37 Bukit Pasoh Road
Tel: 6511-4700
www.newmajestichotel.com
⓴ p272, B3
This hip boutique hotel occupies a vintage Art Deco building. Expect themed rooms, each painted with murals by local artists. The small swimming pool with portholes at the bottom that look down into the Cantonese Majestic restaurant is a much-talked-about feature. A two-minute walk to Outram MRT station.

Moderate

Amara
165 Tanjong Pagar Road
Tel: 6879-2555
www.amarahotels.com
⓴ p272, B4

Contemporary hotel located within the Central Business District. Has a spa, fitness centre, swimming pool and tennis courts. Dining options include award-winning Thai restaurant Thanying, and a Chinese restaurant and coffee shop. Short walk to Tanjong Pagar MRT station.

Berjaya Hotel
83 Duxton Road
Tel: 6227-7678
www.berjayaresorts.com
⓴ p272, B3
A boutique hotel occupying a row of restored shophouses in the heart of Chinatown's conservation area. Rooms are smallish, but the Garden suites have a little courtyard. Ten-minute walk to Tanjong Pagar MRT station.

The Club Hotel
28 Ann Siang Road
Tel: 6808-2188
www.theclub.com.sg
⓴ p272, C3
A trendy new boutique hotel housed in a heritage building. Many design features littered around the hotel. Ying

Yang rooftop bar is an ideal spot to while away the nights. Tanjong Pagar MRT is less than 10 minutes away.

Furama City Centre
60 Eu Tong Sen Street
Tel: 6533-3888
www.furama.com
⓴ p272, C1
After a S$22-million renovation to woo business travellers, its rooms are now comfortable and cosy. Good location for shopping and nightlife as it's near Boat Quay, Clarke Quay and Chinatown. Restaurants serve local, Western and Chinese food, plus a bar. Ten-minute walk to Chinatown MRT station.

Grand Copthorne Waterfront
392 Havelock Road
Tel: 6733-0880
www.millenniumhotels.com.sg
⓴ p269, C4
A modern business hotel by the Singapore River and just next to Zouk nightclub. Guestrooms are all equipped with broadband internet access. Piano bar with alfresco dining options,

and a good Italian restaurant.

Hotel 1929
50 Keong Saik Road
Tel: 6347-1929
www.hotel1929.com
⓴ p272, B2/3
Ultra-chic boutique hotel in the heart of Chinatown that has made the headlines in various design magazines. Highlights here include a rooftop jacuzzi, a well-known contemporary European restaurant, and retro vintage furniture in the rooms.

Klapsons
15 Hoe Chiang Road Tower Fifteen
Tel: 6521-9030
www.klapsons.com
⓴ p272, B4
For the chic and design-conscious, this boutique hotel is conveniently located in the CBD and a short walk away from Tanjong Pagar MRT. Relax in the lobby and admire the art on display, before heading up to bed and the comfort of goose-down pillows and Egyptian cotton sheets.

M Hotel Singapore
81 Anson Road
Tel: 6224-1133
www.mhotel.com.sg
⓴ p272, C4
Excellent location in the financial district for business travellers and only a five-minute walk from Tanjong Pagar MRT station. It offers wireless internet access and top-notch business facilities.

BELOW: de luxe bathroom at the New Majestic.

PRICE CATEGORIES

Price categories are for a double room without breakfast and taxes:
Luxury: over S$500
Expensive: S$350–500
Moderate: S$150–350
Budget: under S$150

All rooms have harbour or city views.

Scarlet
33 Erskine Road
Tel: 6511-3333
www.thescarlethotel.com
㉙ p272, C2/3
A sexy, Baroque-inspired boutique hotel with a rooftop bar. The rooms are small (so plump for the premium or executive rooms), and there's a tiny jacuzzi and gym.

Wangz Hotel
231 Outram Road
Tel: 6595-1388
www.wangzhotel.com
㉚ p272, A2
Hip meets classic in this new boutique hotel

located five minutes from Outram Park MRT. The stylish bathrooms have rain showers and view of the city, while the rooftop lounge offers a panoramic view of the Singapore skyline. Nectar serves modern cuisine with an Asian touch.

Budget

Chinatown
12–16 Teck Lim Road
Tel: 6225-5166
www.chinatownhotel.com
㉛ p272, B3
No-frills budget business hotel with friendly and efficient service in the

heart of Chinatown. Rooms are tiny but modern, clean and comfortable. Five-minute walk to Outram Park MRT station.

The Inn at Temple Street
36 Temple Street
Tel: 6221-5333
www.theinn.com.sg
㉜ p272, B2
Five restored Chinatown shophouses reflecting the Peranakan heritage make up the Inn. It's a mix of years of tradition with some modern luxury. Has a business centre, café and bar. Three-minute walk to Chinatown MRT station.

Apartments

Ascott Raffles Place
2 Finlayson Green
Tel: 6272-7272
www.the-ascott.com
㉝ p273, D2
The Ascott Group's latest offering sits on a prime spot within the financial district and overlooks the new Marina Bay development. Set in a restored 1950s Art Deco building, luxury apartments come in studio, one- or two-bedroom options. Raffles Place MRT station is a short walk away.

ORCHARD ROAD AND SURROUNDS

Luxury

Four Seasons
190 Orchard Boulevard
Tel: 6734-1110
www.fourseasons.com/singapore
㉞ p268, B4
Luxurious interiors, large plush rooms and expen-

sive artworks belie its rather plain facade. Restaurants serving contemporary fare and refined Cantonese cuisine, plus a cosy alfresco bar with views of Orchard Road. The air-conditioned tennis

courts are a dream in humid, sticky Singapore. Five-minute walk to Orchard MRT station.

Grand Hyatt
10 Scotts Road
Tel: 6235-4111
www.singapore.grand.hyatt.com
㉟ p268, B4

BELOW: bedroom in the Valley Wing of the Shangri-La.

A stone's throw from Orchard Road and its MRT station. Minimalist, almost stark decor, comfortable rooms and excellent service are its defining hallmarks. Italian restaurant, stylish mezza9 restaurant with elegant Martini bar, and a café.The Hyatt's free-form pool with lush gardens is a haven in this busy neck of the woods.

St Regis
29 Tanglin Road
Tel: 6506-6888
www.stregis.com
㊱ p268, A4
St Regis brings its trademark style to a prime spot on Orchard Road, with a stupendous range

of facilities: six dining outlets serving everything from Mediterranean to Cantonese fare, spa, swimming pool, business centre, private butlers for every room, and a fleet of Bentleys to chauffeur guests around.

Shangri-La
22 Orange Grove Road
Tel: 6737-3644
www.shangri-la.com
③⑦ p268, A3
A lush green haven just outside the city area. Its luxurious Valley Wing is where visiting heads of state and other VIPs stay. Superb Cantonese and classy Californian eateries, excellent Japanese restaurant and a 24-hour coffee shop. A good 15-minute walk to Orchard MRT station.

Expensive

Goodwood Park
22 Scotts Road
Tel: 6737-7411
www.goodwoodparkhotel.com
③⑧ p268, B4
Charming historical building dating back to 1900, near the heart of Orchard Road and Orchard MRT station. This luxury hotel has suites that open out to the swimming pool. Five eateries including a grill, Chinese restaurant and coffee lounge for local high tea.

Hilton International
581 Orchard Road
Tel: 6737-2233
www.singapore.hilton.com
③⑨ p268, B4
The city's longest operating 5-star hotel, with a shopping arcade housing international fashion boutiques. Also conveniently located near shopping malls and 10

minutes' walk from Orchard MRT station. Fine-dining Western restaurant, as well as a bakery and café.

Marriott
320 Orchard Road
Tel: 6735-5800
www.marriott.com
④⓪ p268, B4
The pagoda-roofed hotel at the corner of Scotts and Orchard roads is a well-known landmark and just opposite Orchard MRT station. Popular café with outdoor seating, Chinese restaurant serving *dim sum* and a poolside café. The famous Tangs department store is just next door.

Meritus Mandarin Singapore
333 Orchard Road
Tel: 6737-4411
www.mandarin-singapore.com
④① p269, C1
Serious shoppers should stay here, as all the major malls and boutiques (and two MRT stations) are within walking distance. It has its own shopping arcade called Mandarin Gallery, filled with independent shops and great eateries. The hotel's 24-hour Chatterbox coffee house is noted for its speciality of Hainanese chicken rice.

The Regent
1 Cuscaden Road
Tel: 6733-8888
www.regenthotels.com
④② p268, A4
Another chic hotel, in keeping with the Regent brand name. Expect well-appointed rooms and excellent service. It has an excellent Italian restaurant by the pool and Cantonese gourmet restaurant serving *dim sum*. Orchard MRT sta-

tion is a good 10- to 12-minute walk away.

Royal Plaza On Scotts
25 Scotts Road
Tel: 6737-7966
www.royalplaza.com.sg
④③ p268, B4
Owned by the Sultan of Brunei, this business hotel has an excellent location for shopping. Perks include complimentary minibar in all rooms, and special discounts at the adjacent DFS Galleria mall. The poolside café serves Italian fare, while the restaurant is popular for its high-tea buffet.

Sheraton Towers
39 Scotts Road
Tel: 6737-6888
www.starwood.com/sheraton
④④ off p268, B4
Swanky and well-run hotel close to Newton MRT station, and a short walk from the start of Orchard Road. Executive tower rooms come with butler service. Speciality restaurants serving Chinese and Italian fare, and a café with local and Western food (which also serves an excellent brunch on Sunday).

Moderate

Concorde Hotel Singapore
100 Orchard Road
Tel: 6733-8855
www.concordehotel.com.sg
④⑤ p269, E2
After taking over the former Le Meridien and undergoing a refurbishment, Concorde unveiled its revamped rooms, including the tastefully appointed Premier rooms and Premier Lounge. Its Spices Cafe serves food all day, with a focus on Peranakan

flavours for lunch and seafood for dinner.

Grand Park Orchard
270 Orchard Road
Tel: 6603-8888
www.parkhotelgroup.com
④⑥ p269, C1
Smack in the middle of Orchard Road and surrounded by shopping malls. The exterior glass facade is stunning, and rooms are filled with modern comforts. And Knightsbridge is a four-storey retail podium. Conveniently located between Somerset and Orchard MRT stations.

Orchard Hotel
442 Orchard Road
Tel: 6734-7766
www.orchardhotel.com.sg
④⑦ p268, A/B4
Conveniently located along the main Orchard stretch, the hotel's de luxe rooms in Claymore and Orchard wings have been refurbished. The lobby coffee shop serves decent buffet, and the Cantonese restaurant is one of the best in town and is popular for *dim sum*.

Quincy
22 Mount Elizabeth
Tel: 6738-5888
www.quincy.com.sg
④⑧ off p269, C1
Just a five-minute walk from Orchard MRT lies this smoke-free boutique hotel. It's hard to miss this unique building, with its bold facade of anodised steel and

PRICE CATEGORIES

Price categories are for a double room without breakfast and taxes:
Luxury: over S$500
Expensive: S$350–500
Moderate: S$150–350
Budget: under S$150

individually custom-
designed windows.
There's free internet
access throughout the
hotel.
York
21 Mount Elizabeth
Tel: 6737-0511
www.yorkhotel.com.sg
🔞 off p269, C1
A small hotel with a
quiet location behind
Scotts Road, but close
to Orchard Road shop-
ping, nightlife and MRT
station. The rooms have
been renovated and are
now more contemporary
in decor. Good café serv-
ing Western and local
cuisines, and a bar.

Budget

**RELC International
Hotel**
30 Orange Grove Road
Tel: 6885-7888
www.relcih.com.sg
🔞 p268, A3
Humble neighbour to
the upscale Shangri-La
Hotel but manages to
impress nevertheless
with its much, much
lower rates. Rooms are
spacious with balconies,
and business travellers
will appreciate its well-
equipped conference
rooms. Good Chinese
restaurant. The hotel
has a free shuttle serv-

ice to Orchard Road.
**YMCA International
House**
1 Orchard Road
Tel: 6336-6000
www.ymcaih.com.sg
🔞 p269, E2
Situated at the top end
of Orchard Road, border-
ing the colonial Civic
District and a stone's
throw from Dhoby Ghaut
MRT station. It has con-
ference facilities, a café,
rooftop swimming pool,
fitness centre, snooker
room and cybercafé.
Choose from guest-
rooms with attached
bathrooms or four-
person dormitories.

Apartments

Orchard Parksuites
11 Orchard Turn
Tel: 6839-1233
www.fareastsvcapts.com.sg
🔞 p268, C1
Luxurious apartments in
the heart of Orchard
Road just next to the
Orchard MRT station. In
the opulent lobby sits a
baby grand piano, and
the swimming pool has
piped-in underwater
music. Floor plans vary
from one-bedroom lofts
to four-bedroom suites;
minimum one-week
lease. Daily maid service
on weekdays.

LITTLE INDIA AND KAMPUNG GLAM

ABOVE: the exterior of the Inter-Continental.

Expensive

Inter-Continental
80 Middle Road
Tel: 6338-7600
www.singapore.intercontinental.com
🔞 p270, B2
Stylish hotel with some
rooms built in the shop-
house style. Located
near museums and
beside Bugis MRT
station. Casual
Mediterranean-style

restaurant, elegant
Chinese restaurant
serving *dim sum* and
creative Cantonese
dishes, Japanese
restaurant and jazz bar.
The Asian artworks
scattered throughout the
hotel are a nice touch.

Moderate

Albert Court
180 Albert Street

Tel: 6339-3939
www.albertcourt.com.sg
🔞 p270, A1
Boutique hotel just adja-
cent to the Little India
district. The interior
decor is nostalgically
charming, with carved
Peranakan teak furnish-
ings and old brass elec-
trical switches, but the
comforts are thoroughly
modern. Continental
café and bar. No pool.
Five minutes' walk from
Little India MRT station.

**Landmark Village
Hotel**
390 Victoria Street
Tel: 6297-2828
www.stayvillage.com
🔞 p270, C1
Located adjacent to
Kampung Glam, this
modern high-rise offers
good-value, comfortable
accommodation in this
neighbourhood. There
are lots of good local
eateries around the
hotel. Three minutes'
walk from Bugis MRT
station.
Moon @ 23 Dickson
23 Dickson Road
Tel: 6827-666
www.moon.com.sg
🔞 p267, C/D4
A cosy hotel just an

eight-minute walk from Bugis MRT, in a bustling location that will give you a taste of traditional Singapore, while still being near museums, shopping and the financial district and bay area.

Parkroyal on Beach Road
7500 Beach Road
Tel: 6505-5666
www.parkroyalhotels.com
❺❼ p271, C2
This modern hotel is located minutes from the gentrified Arab quarter of Kampung Glam, with well-appointed rooms and an executive club wing. Its lauded Chinese restaurant serves

an exquisite menu of Sichuan, Cantonese and Hunan dishes. Six minutes' walk from Bugis MRT station.

Parkroyal on Kitchener Road
181 Kitchener Road
Tel: 6428-000
www.parkroyalhotels.com
❺❽ p267, D3
Located near the bottom end of Serangoon Road close to the 24-hour Mustafa Centre (great for shopping) and next to Farrer Park MRT station. Rooms are spacious and feature the usual comforts. It has a café serving Asian and Western cuisines, and a

Cantonese restaurant. Conference facilities, fitness centre and swimming pool.

Wanderlust Hotel
2 Dickson Road
Tel: 6396-3322
www.wanderlusthotel.com
❺❾ p267, D4
An exciting experimental boutique hotel housed in an old school built in the 1920s, a 10-minute walk from Little India MRT. The rooms on the four levels were designed by award-winning Singapore design agencies. Go for a monochrome room – all fuchsia or yellow, say – pop art, or

one of the whimsical themed loft rooms. Restaurant serves rustic French cuisine.

Budget

Perak Hotel
12 Perak Road
Tel: 6299-7733
www.peraklodge.net
❻⓿ p270, B1
Occupies a restored shophouse in colourful Little India. But like most budget-priced hotels in this area, the rooms are small, and it's best to scale down your expectations. Only five minutes' walk from Little India MRT station.

SENTOSA

Luxury

Capella
1 The Knolls
Tel: 6377-8888
www.capellasingapore.com
Besides its rooms, suites and villas, Capella has two

restored colonial manors constructed in the 1880s. Former homes of British officers, these stand-alone double-storey houses have three bedrooms, living and dining rooms, kitchen and a mini-pool.

The historic Tanah Merah building, once used by the British for their gala parties, has also been restored by architect Lord Norman Foster and now houses the lobby and library.

Expensive

Amara Sanctuary Sentosa Resort
1 Larkhill Road
Tel: 6825-3888
www.amarasanctuary.com
A resort nestled on a hillside and surrounded by acres of sprawling gardens and natural tropical rainforest. Design-wise it is an exotic blend of colonial architecture and modern minimalism. The guestrooms, suites and villas provide plush comfort and state-of-the-art facilities.

Resorts World Sentosa
39 Artillery Avenue, Sentosa

Tel: 6577-8899
www.rwsentosa.com
Only three of five hotels are open so far, plus the by-invitation-only Crockfords Tower, which houses the casino. Hotel Michael is a tribute to one of America's greatest contemporary architects, Michael Graves, Hard Rock

PRICE CATEGORIES

Price categories are for a double room without breakfast and taxes:
Luxury: over S$500
Expensive: S$350–500
Moderate: S$150–350
Budget: under S$150

BELOW: room at the Wanderlust Hotel.

Hotel has a rock and roll theme and Festive Hotel is the perfect family hotel.

The Sentosa
2 Bukit Manis Road
Tel: 6275-0331
www.thesentosa.com

This sprawling resort hotel features both hotel-style rooms and suites as well as villas with private pools. It is linked by a path directly to the beach. Its stunning restaurant, the Cliff, offers a contemporary menu with a focus on seafood (see page 189). There is also a sea-facing bar that's perfect for sunset cocktails. Book a massage at Spa Botanica, set in lush gardens.

Moderate

Siloso Beach Resort
51 Imbiah Walk
Tel: 6722-3333
www.silosobeachresort.com

The rooms at the Siloso are comfortable and offer splendid sunset views, while the more expensive suites each come with a private rooftop garden where you can soak and rejuvenate in the jacuzzi. Kids will enjoy splashing about in the pool, which has water slides and an 18-metre-high (60ft) waterfall.

THE EAST COAST

Moderate

Changi Village
1 Netheravon Road
Tel: 6379-7111
www.changivillage.com.sg

A S$45-million renovation has completely transformed this former transit hotel into a modern resort. Convenient location for Changi Airport and Singapore Expo. Free shuttle to both the airport and the city. Both Changi Beach and Changi Village nearby are great places to chill out.

Grand Mercure Roxy Hotel
50 East Coast Road
Tel: 6344-8000
www.grandmercureroxy.com.sg

Value-for-money 4-star hotel with Parkway Shopping Centre just opposite and a short walk from the East Coast beach. It has modern design with spacious rooms, and a good fusion Chinese restaurant. There is no MRT station nearby, but there are public buses across the street that service the city.

Budget

Betel Box Hostel
200 Joo Chiat Road
Tel: 6247-7340
www.betelbox.com

One of the best backpacker hostels in this neck of the woods. Owned by seasoned backpackers who know what the budget

traveller wants. Clean, air-conditioned dormitory-style rooms in a quaint shophouse setting complete with attractive Asian furniture. Paya Lebar MRT station is a 15-minute walk away.

BELOW: the pool at the Resorts World Sentosa.

ACTIVITIES

THE ARTS, NIGHTLIFE, SPORTS, CHILDREN'S ACTIVITIES AND SIGHTSEEING TOURS

THE ARTS

Singapore is trying to make a name for itself as Asia's centre of the arts and entertainment by staging regular theatre, dance, music and opera events and also by encouraging home-grown productions. The Singapore Arts Festival (www.singaporeartsfest.com) in June is an annual three-week-long celebration of the arts, with international acts from all over the world showcasing their talents.

Art Galleries

Commercial art galleries offer a whole gamut of choices – from rare European masterpieces to modern abstracts by young, up-and-coming local artists.

Art-2 Gallery
01-03 MICA Building, 140 Hill Street
Tel: 6338-8713
www.art2.com.sg
Collection includes sculptures, ceramics, paintings and prints from around the region.

Artfolio
02-25 Raffles Hotel Arcade, 328 North Bridge Road
Tel: 6334-4677
www.artfolio.com.sg
Contemporary Asian art, including works by prominent Malaysian-born artist Eng Tay.

Art Forum
82 Cairnhill Road
Tel: 6737-3448
www.artforum.com.sg
Well-established gallery with a focus on contemporary Asian art.

Art Seasons Gallery
02-12 Block 7, Eunos Techlink, Kaki Bukit Road 1
Tel: 6741-6366
www.artseasonsgallery.com
International contemporary art pieces are housed in this attractive three-storey gallery above a wine bar.

Opera Gallery
03-05 ION Orchard, 2 Orchard Turn
Tel: 6735-2618
www.operagallery.com
Showcases paintings and sculptures of renowned contemporary artists and 19th-century masters.

Singapore Tyler Print Institute
41 Robertson Quay
Tel: 6336-3663
www.stpi.com.sg
Gallery and teaching facility for artists housed in a restored 19th-century warehouse.

Soobin
Uni Techpark 10, 10 Ubi Crescent
Tel: 6837-2777
www.soobinart.com.sg
Specialising in Southeast Asian and Chinese art.

Chinese Opera

Outdoor performances are staged in suburban neighbourhoods during the seventh month of the Chinese lunar year (August/September). Taoists believe that during this time the gates of hell are thrown open, allowing the spirits of the deceased to wander the earth. To appease them, Chinese operas and pop concerts (getai) are staged along with offerings and sumptuous banquets. For year-round performances, contact **Chinese Opera Teahouse** at Smith Street in Chinatown. Performances every Friday and Saturday at 7pm, tel: 6323-4862; www.ctcopera.com.sg.

Cinema

There are more than 50 cinemas in Singapore, showing everything from Hollywood blockbusters to art movies and Chinese and Indian dramas. Details are published daily in the Life! section of The Straits Times. Censorship – while recently relaxed – keeps out films dealing with themes which are too sexually explicit or on subjects deemed undesirable. R21 films are for those over 21 years old, M18 or Mature 18 is for 18 years and above, NC-16 stands for No Children Under the Age of 16, G is for general viewing and

PG indicates that parental guidance is advisable.

Cineplexes offer a choice of several movies in smaller theatres. The main ones are at Great World City, Orchard CineLeisure (24-hour screenings on Fri, Sat and eve of public holidays), Plaza Singapura, Marina Square, The Cathay and VivoCity.

A number of venues offer arthouse films – Cinema Europa (www.gv.com.sg), Cinematheque (www.nationalmuseum.sg) at the National Museum, and The Picturehouse (www.thepicturehouse.com.sg). Local films can be viewed at Sinema Old School (www.sinema.sg) at Mount Emily.

The annual **Singapore International Film Festival** offers a chance to view critically acclaimed films that are normally subjected to limited distribution. The well-received cinefest usually takes place in April – check www.filmfest.org.sg for updates. In addition, the **Singapore Film Society** holds weekly screenings of non-mainstream films for its members (tel: 9017-0160; www.sfs.org.sg).

Music and Dance

Singapore Chinese Orchestra
7 Shenton Way
Tel: 6440-3839

www.sco.com.sg
Known for its versatile ability to fuse Western and Chinese musical styles, this much-lauded orchestra holds regular concerts.
Singapore Dance Theatre
Fort Canning Centre, 2nd Storey, Cox Terrace
Tel: 6338-0611
www.singaporedancetheatre.com
Critically acclaimed home-grown ballet company with a busy performance schedule.
Singapore Symphony Orchestra
4 Battery Road
20-01 Bank of China Building
Tel: 6602-4200
www.sso.org.sg
Gives regular concerts at the Esplanade, often with eminent guest conductors and famous soloists from all over the world.

Performing Arts Venues

The Arts House
1 Old Parliament Lane
Tel: 6332-6900
www.theartshouse.com.sg
This arts centre is housed in the Old Parliament House.
Drama Centre
3/F, National Library, 100 Victoria Street
Tel: 6837-8400
A mid-sized venue with a 615-seat theatre and a 120-seat

black box.
Esplanade – Theatres on the Bay
1 Esplanade Drive
Tel: 6828-8377
www.esplanade.com
Sprawling performing arts centre with a world-class concert hall and theatres.
Jubilee Hall
Raffles Hotel
1 Beach Road
Tel: 6412-1335
A theatre playhouse designed in late Victorian style featuring plays, musicals and concerts.
Singapore Indoor Stadium
2 Stadium Walk
Tel: 6344-2660
www.sis.gov.sg
Asian and international concerts are held in this large sports and entertainment centre.
The Substation
45 Armenian Street
Tel: 6337-7535
www.substation.org
Multimedia arts centre and venue for cutting-edge works.
Victoria Concert Hall
11 Empress Place
Tel: 6338-4401
www.vch.org.sg
Singapore Symphony Orchestra holds occasional concerts here.
Victoria Theatre
9 Empress Place
Tel: 6338-8283
Venue for international and local theatre and musicals.

Theatre

For a complete listing on local theatre companies and updates on arts performances, check www.singaporetheatre.com. Several main players are listed below.
Action Theatre
42 Waterloo Street
Tel: 6837-0842
www.action.org.sg
Notable theatre group that stages mainly contemporary plays on topical issues, and big musicals.
The Necessary Stage
B1-02 Marine Parade Community Building, 278 Marine Parade Road

BELOW: performance by the Singapore Repertory Theatre.

Tel: 6440-8115
www.necessary.org
A major theatre company in Singapore with a strong emphasis on youth theatre.
Sands Theater
10 Bayfront Avenue, Galleria Level
Tel: 6348-5555
www.marinabaysands.com
Marina Bay Sands' The Sands Theater is home to famed Broadway musical *The Lion King*. The Grand Theater stages an array of major performing arts events.
Singapore Repertory Theatre
DBS Arts Centre, 20 Merbau Road
Tel: 6221-5585
www.srt.com.sg
Leading theatre group that focuses on performances with a strong Asian theme. Its productions are consistent winners.
TheatreWorks
72-13 Mohamed Sultan Road
Tel: 6737-7213
www.theatreworks.org.sg
A leading local avant-garde theatre company; stages works at its own premises.
Wild Rice
3A Kerbau Road
Tel: 6292-2695
www.wildrice.com.sg
Creates acclaimed "glocal" works inspired by Singapore society and universal issues.

BUYING TICKETS

Tickets for events can either be obtained directly at the ticket offices of performance venues or at the outlets of SISTIC and Tickets.com.
   SISTIC city outlets: Bugis Junction, DBS Arts Centre, Esplanade – Theatres on the Bay, Millenia Walk, Plaza Singapura, Raffles City Shopping Centre, Singapore Indoor Stadium, Victoria Concert Hall, Wisma Atria, ION Orchard and VivoCity. Hotline: 6348-5555, www.sistic.com.sg.
   Tickets.com outlets: Great World City and Tanglin Mall. Hotline: 6296-2929; www.tdc.sg.

ABOVE: live music at Bar None.

NIGHTLIFE

The city's nightlife scene is alive and booming. A law introduced in 2003 has allowed dancers to get on top of bars and do their thing, and some nightspots, away from residential areas, can remain open throughout the night.
   Whether you plan to rip it up on the dance floor, unwind with a glass of premium wine, down a frothy pint or join a snaking queue of trendy young things at the newest, hottest nightspot, there are enough choices to satisfy party animals of all inclinations (and budgets).
   The best time to enjoy your favourite bar is during happy hour, usually between 5 and 8 or 9pm, when prices are more affordable. At clubs, a cover charge of between S$15–30 will give you admission on Friday and Saturday nights and a drink.

Gay and Lesbian Venues

Singapore's unofficial gay hangout is Tanjong Pagar, where most of the gay bars are located. Velvet Underground at Zouk attracts a mixed straight and gay crowd.

Play
01-02, 21 Tanjong Pagar Road
Tel: 6227-7400
www.playclub.com.sg
With a tagline that says "It's time to play", the dance floor gets a mean workout. Lots of youthful and buff boys who party into the wee hours.
Taboo
65/67 Neil Road
Tel: 6225-6256
www.taboo97.com
A perennial favourite among local and foreign gay men, Taboo's new location boasts three levels of partying. Expect long queues on Friday and Saturday nights.

Live Music Venues

Bar None
Singapore Marriott Hotel,
320 Orchard Road
Tel: 6270-7676
www.barnoneasia.com
This basement club is a hotspot for live music fans and those who want to dance the night away to rock and pop classics. It's a winning formula that has lasted many years.
Blu Jaz Cafe
11 Bali Lane
Tel: 6292-3800
www.blujaz.net
This relaxed spot near Haji Lane

and Arab Street has a café and lounge that offers great live jazz by different artistes.

Crazy Elephant
01-03/04 Clarke Quay, 3E River Valley Road
Tel: 6337-7859
www.crazyelephant.com
This small, smoky den is always full of people jamming to the great house band playing passionate jazz and heartfelt blues. The outdoor tables are usually busy, but they're the nicest spots to sample the pub's pizzas and pastas.

TAB
02-29 Orchard Hotel, 442 Orchard Road
Tel: 6493-6952
www.tab.com.sg
A live music venue that provides the "total concert experience". Three levels showcase the talents of local and international artists.

Timbre@The Substation
45 Armenian Street
Tel: 6338-8030
www.timbregroup.asia
An alfresco venue that offers live music nightly.

Nightclubs

Clarke Quay

After an extensive makeover,

Clarke Quay has been drawing the crowds that used to frequent Boat Quay. The nearest train station is Clarke Quay MRT.

Attica/Attica Too
01-03 Clarke Quay, 3A River Valley Road
Tel: 6333-9973
www.attica.com.sg
An open courtyard setting with lush greenery and a fountain is the perfect setting to unwind to Latin, jazz and funk. Upstairs is Attica Too, a stylish dance pad.

The Clinic
01-03 Clarke Quay, 3C River Valley Road
Tel: 6887-3733
www.theclinic.sg
Not for the faint-hearted, cocktails at the Clinic are served in test tubes and syringes, while customers sit on wheelchairs with intravenous drips attached.

The Pump Room
01-09/10 Clarke Quay, 3B River Valley Road
Tel: 6334-2628
www.pumproomasia.com
An excellent place to unwind or dance the night away. Pop hits, rock and jazz tunes are performed by resident band Jive Talkin' from Tue to Sun. This microbrewery also serves scrumptious Aussie fare.

BELOW: Timbre@The Substation.

LOCAL LISTINGS

Visitors can obtain information on the arts, nightlife, shopping and eating out through several publications available free at hotels, shopping centre information counters and STB visitor centres. *Changi Express* and *WHERE Singapore* magazines are full of useful information, especially for listings of hot bars and clubs. *I-S* magazine is a free, mostly listings publication available at restaurants and bars.

The *Straits Times*' What's On section, *Time Out Singapore* and *8 Days* magazine provide useful information as well, but they are not free.

Civic District

The watering holes in this area are strewn over quite a large area, from the **Raffles City** and **Suntec City** areas to historical **Chijmes** – a convent school whose church is now a performance hall and whose classrooms are shops, bars and restaurants.

The Butter Factory
02-02/03/04 One Fullerton, 1 Fullerton Road
Tel: 6423-9804
www.thebutterfactory.com
A swimming pool complete with life buoys and ladders is the dance floor (what this has to do with butter is anyone's guess). Expect to see celebs, models and other beautiful people among the more plebeian jeans-and-tees clubbers.

Dbl-O
01-01/02, 222 Queen Street
Tel: 6735-2008
www.dblo.com.sg
Pronounced "Double-O", this club is high on the glamour quotient and an excellent place to people-watch. Plays a mix of house, disco, garage and retro.

Equinox
2 Stamford Road, Swissôtel The Stamford
Tel: 6837-3322
www.equinoxcomplex.com

This exclusive dining complex on the 68th to 72nd floors houses five restaurants and bars offering a huge selection of cocktails and wines and *the* best views of the city skyline. Dancing takes place at its 71st-floor **New Asia Bar** after 10pm on Fridays and Saturdays, while **City Space** on the 70th floor is a classy bar with the best seats in the house to see the eye-popping skyline.

Insomnia Bar & Restaurant
01-21 Chijmes, 30 Victoria Street
Tel: 6334-4693
Good food and retro music by live bands in a stylish setup.

Mohamed Sultan Road/ Robertson Quay
This hotspot area also includes **Robertson Walk** and **Robertson Quay**, where there is a sprinkling of classy whisky bars.

Zouk
17 Jiak Kim Street
Tel: 6738-2988
www.zoukclub.com.sg
Singapore's hippest club in a converted warehouse is a must-go for serious clubbers – all the international magazines have raved about this place. The bustling **Wine Bar** plays acid jazz as a prelude to the cutting-edge dance music that rules on the main dance floor. The smaller **Phuture** caters to a hip-hop crowd, while **Velvet Underground** is where an older and more beautiful crowd converges.

Marina Bay

Ku De Ta
Marina Bay Sands North Tower,
1 Bayfront Avenue
Tel: 6688-7688
www.kudeta.com.sg
Ku De Ta's Club Lounge appeals to the trendy set, with its sleek bar and intimate dance floor.

Orchard Road/Tanglin Village

Singapore's most popular shopping belt is also home to some buzzing nightspots. Also jumping is **Tanglin Village**, near the Botanic Gardens, abandoned military barracks that have morphed

into a hip wining and dining enclave.

Brix
Grand Hyatt, 10 Scotts Road
Tel: 6732-1234
Offers a sophisticated environment for after-work gatherings and live music. The bar is divided into the quiet Whisky Bar, the relaxing Wine Bar and the livelier Music Bar.

Sentosa Island

After the sun sets, party animals are unleashed and the island turns into party central.

Azzura Beach Club Sentosa
46 Siloso Beach Walk
www.azzura.sg
This entertainment, dining and hydrosports complex has a nightclub called The Harem on the second level. Look out for the line-up of international DJs.

Café del Mar
40 Siloso Beach Walk
Tel: 6235-1296
www.cafedelmar.com.sg
Romp in the jacuzzi, sunken pools and cabanas, or shimmy on the tiny dance floor at this Ibizan-style hotspot. Also serves food all day long.

Coastes
50 Siloso Beach Walk
Tel: 6274-9668
www.coastes.com
All-day beach-side bar with ice-cold beers, exotic cocktails and basic food like pizzas, burgers and barbecued ribs. Evenings see more when the dance music and DJs take over.

Wave House™ Sentosa
36 Siloso Beach Walk
Tel: 6377-3113
www.wavehousesentosa.com
A simulated surfing, dining and lifestyle venue where partygoers can enjoy live music and late night parties at the two beach bars. Enjoy music by top DJs, as well as local and international acts.

HarbourFront Precinct

The latest lifestyle hub in Singapore, the HarbourFront Precinct has some of the city's coolest

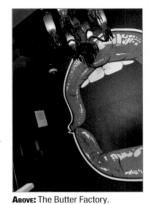

ABOVE: The Butter Factory.

nightlife spots.

St James Power Station
3 Sentosa Gateway
Tel: 6270-7676
www.stjamespowerstation.com
Three restaurants and nine entertainment spots vie for your attention here. Pick one that suits your fancy – choices include a dance club, chill-out lounge, world music bar and more.

SPORTS

Participant Sports

There are a number of sporting events that take place throughout the year. These typically draw a sizeable crowd of local and international participants.

Singapore Biathlon: Feb/Mar. www.safra.sg/singaporebiathlon.
Aviva Ironman Triathlon: Mar. www.ironman703singapore.com.
OSIM Singapore International Triathlon: July. www.triathlon.sg.
Standard Chartered Singapore Marathon: first Sun in Dec. www.marathonsingapore.com.

Bowling

There are several bowling alleys spread across the island, many of them in the suburbs and some, like Superbowl (www.superbowl.com.sg), are open until the early hours of the morning. Shoes are available for hire and charges are reasonable. Remember to book a lane before you go, especially at weekends. Expect to pay between S$3 and S$5 per game.

Kallang Bowl
5 Stadium Walk, Leisure Park
Tel: 6345-0545
www.leisurepark.com.sg

Superbowl
03-200 Marina Square
Tel: 6334-1000
www.superbowl.com.sg

Cable Skiing

SKI360°
1206A East Coast Parkway
Tel: 6442-7318
www.ski360degree.com
The first cable-ski park in Singapore has a 650-metre (2,130ft) cableway along the East Coast Parkway, along which skiers are pulled. Ski passes are available on an hourly basis or on a "rounds" basis.

Golf

Singapore is said to have more golf courses per capita than any other place on earth. Many of these are designed by leading course architects. Many of the clubs welcome non-members. Green fees range from as little as S$70 on weekdays to as much as S$240 at weekends, when nearly every course in Singapore is crowded. Caddies cost S$15–30.

Keppel Club
Bukit Chermin Road
Tel: 6375-1818
www.keppelclub.com.sg
An 18-hole, par-71 course. The front nine is over rolling hills, while the back nine cuts across wooded flatlands. From S$144.

Raffles Country Club
450 Jalan Ahmad Ibrahim
Tel: 6861-7655
www.rcc.org.sg
Two 18-hole courses, the tree-shaded Palm Course and the picturesque Lake Course, priced from S$128.40.

Sentosa Golf Club
27 Bukit Manis Road
Tel: 6275-0022

www.sentosagolf.com.sg
Visitors are welcome on both 18-hole courses, the Serapong and the Tanjong, priced from S$280.

Racquet Sports

Many hotels have tennis courts. Otherwise, the island offers a number of courts for hire.

Kallang Tennis Centre
52 Stadium Boulevard Road
Tel: 6348-1291
Charges are S$9.50 for weekend and primetime play (6–10pm) and S$3.50 at other times for tennis. Hourly fees for squash are S$5 and S$10 (for weekends and from 6pm onwards).

Reverse Bungy

G-Max Reverse Bungy
Clarke Quay, River Valley Road
Tel: 6338-1766
www.gmax.com.sg
For a thrilling adrenalin rush, try Singapore's first G-Max Reverse Bungy at Clarke Quay. You're seated in an open-air capsule and hurled into the air 60 metres (197ft) from the ground at a speed of 200km/h (124mph). Also worth a shot is the GX-5 Extreme Swing, which will send you swinging back and forth as you take in the sights of Clarke Quay. Each ride costs S$45 (or S$60 for both).

Trail Sports

Singapore is great for hikers, bikers and runners. The island is quite flat – perfect for beginners. At the same time, there is enough rugged topography for those who crave challenges. The island's longest jogging and biking paths run through **East Coast Park**, a total length of 10km (6 miles) between Fort Road and Sungei Bedok. The route winds along the sea's edge, through coconut palms and bird sanctuaries. Bikes and roller blades can be rented from several places in East Coast Park for around S$6–10 an hour.

The best areas for off-road running and bike riding – and also one of the best places for a walk in the jungle – is the **Central**

Catchment Nature Reserve, which comprises the MacRitchie, Pierce and Upper Seletar reservoir parks. The parks are especially popular with mountain bikers and birdwatchers.

Trails and unpaved roads lead through secondary rainforest, swampland and around the edge of scenic lakes. Monkeys frolic in the jungle, and you can spot many different types of tropical birds.

An alternative off-road venue is **Pulau Ubin**, a maze of country roads winding through old rubber and fruit plantations.

Other popular walking and running spots include the **Botanic Gardens**, with an entrance at the corner of Holland and Cluny roads; **Labrador Park**, at the foot of Alexandra Road; **Kent Ridge Park**, near the National University of Singapore; **Bukit Batok Park**, near the town of the same name; and **Bukit Timah Nature Reserve** (see the respective Places chapters for more information on the above).

Watersports

Sentosa Island and **East Coast Park** are the most obvious choices to partake in watersports because of easy access and their variety of activities.

Extreme Sports
Kallang Riverside Park
Tel: 6344-8813
www.extreme.com.sg
Learn to water-ski or wakeboard, with beginner lessons (four sessions) at S$150. Or brush up your skills from S$25 per person.

Ponggol Sea Sports Accessories
600 Punggol Seventeen Avenue
Tel: 6386-3891
www.pssa.com.sg
Offers waterskiing and wakeboarding; a boat with driver and gear costs from S$98 per hour.

Spectator Sports

Cricket

Singapore Cricket Club
Connaught Drive
Tel: 6338-9271

www.scc.org.sg
Holds regular weekend matches from March to October. Access to the club is restricted to members, but visitors can watch games at the Padang on most weekends from 10am for free.

Formula One

SingTel Singapore Grand Prix
Tel: 6738-6738
www.singaporegp.sg
This premier racing event is held annually in September, but may possibly cease after 2012. The world's best drivers will gather for an exhilarating street race that passes through key landmarks in the Civic District. The first night race in F1 history (and Asia's first street race) gives spectators at strategically located grandstands a multi-sensory experience as the cars zoom by.

Horse Racing

Singapore Turf Club
1 Turf Club Avenue, Kranji
Tel: 6879-000
www.turfclub.com.sg
The four-level grandstand accommodates 30,000 race-goers. The club incorporates all the best features from race courses the world over. Races are run 32 weekends each year. Check the Turf Club website for exact dates.

The race track is easily accessible by MRT (Kranji station), public buses and taxis. Admission is S$3 (cashless payment) or S$4 (cash payment) in the non-air-conditioned stands and S$7 (cashless payment) and S$8 (cash payment) for the air-conditioned stands; S$20 gives you access to a special club area. Dress code applies: no shorts or slippers for public grandstands; no jeans, shorts or collarless shirts for members' areas.

Rugby

SCC International Rugby Sevens
Connaught Drive
Tel: 6338-9271
www.sccrugbysevens.com
The annual International Rugby

ABOVE: the Singapore Grand Prix.

Sevens tournament is held at the Padang. Teams from around the world come to compete in this action-packed sporting event. Check website for exact dates.

Soccer

Football Association of Singapore
01-02 Jalan Besar Stadium, 100 Tyrwhitt Road
Tel: 6348-3477
www.sleague.com
Singapore has its very own professional football league, the S-League. Check its website for details of matches and venues.

CHILDREN'S ACTIVITIES

The **Singapore Zoological Gardens** is one of the best zoos in the world. Enjoy breakfast with wildlife, watch various animal shows or visit Rainforest KidzWorld. The **Night Safari**, next door to the zoo, is not to be missed either. Walking trails and trams provide exciting adventures at this wildlife park.

Children will also be enthralled by various bird shows at the **Jurong Bird Park**.

Sentosa is full of fun things to do. **Underwater World** offers a touch pool of marine creatures

and **Universal Studios** Singapore is guaranteed to entertain everyone with its thrilling rides.

Escape Theme Park at Pasir Ris offers go-karts and fun rides from choo-choo trains to pirate ships and Ferris wheels. Just next door is **Wild Wild Wet**, a water theme park with exciting rides and lagoons to laze in.

East Coast Park is a pleasant stretch of beach where bicycles, roller blades, windsurfers and barbecue pits are available for hire. Thickly forested **Bukit Timah Nature Reserve** is great for jungle walks.

The **Singapore Science Centre** has hundreds of hands-on exhibits that will delight children. And don't forget the **Singapore Discovery Centre**: its five galleries offer interactive multimedia games and presentations which give an insight into the development of modern Singapore.

(See the Places section for more details of the above sights.)

SIGHTSEEING TOURS

Brewery Tours

Tours can also be arranged at the **Tiger Brewery** (tel: 6860-3007;

ABOVE: Hippo Tour bus in Little India.

www.apb.com.sg), which brews Singapore's favourite beer. The brewery is open to visitors from Monday to Friday and tours cost S$10.70.

Customised Tours

A personal guide can come up with an excursion to suit your specific needs and interests and provide you with snippets of gossip and inside information. Call the **Society of Tourist Guides** (Singapore), tel: 6338-8659; www.societyoftouristguides.org.sg. Walking tours start from S$18.

DIY Walking Tours

Singapore's streets are safe, and although it's generally hot and humid, the covered walkways lining many streets can make walking pleasant and also protect you from the sun and the occasional downpour.

A permanent **Heritage Trail** has been set up at the **Civic District**, **Chinatown** and **Little India**. Strategic markers placed along the trail in these areas will guide you along a walking route and provide nuggets of information on the area's historical sights. You can also obtain Heritage Trail

maps of the Civic District, Little India and Chinatown from STB's visitor centres.

DUCKtours & HiPPOtours

A half-boat, half-truck amphibious vehicle is your mode of transport in the zany **DUCKtours**. The "duckhicle" starts with a scenic cruise on the Singapore River and then goes ashore, waddling through the historical Civic District. Tickets for the 60-minute tour (S$33 adults,

S$17 children) can be bought at Suntec City Mall and next to the STB Visitors Centre at the corner of Orchard and Cairnhill roads. Tours operate from 10am to 6pm daily (tel: 6338-6877; www.ducktours.com.sg).

Also available are open-top double-decker buses called **HiPPOtours**. You can hop on or off at designated stops during the tour. The daytime tour operates from 10am to 6.30pm but can be uncomfortably hot in Singapore's weather. Much better is the

COOKING CLASSES

At-Sunrice GlobalChef Academy
Fort Canning Centre,
Fort Canning Park
Tel: 6336-3307
www.at-sunrice.com
Offers guided tours of the nearby Spice Garden followed by a variety of cooking classes, from half-day to two weeks. There is a strong emphasis on the cuisines of Southeast Asia.

Coriander Leaf
3A Merchant Court, 02-03 River Valley Road, Clarke Quay
Tel: 6732-3354
www.corianderleaf.com

Chef-owner Samia Ahad conducts classes at her cooking studio for groups of 10. The four-hour classes (covering Italian, Mediterranean, Indian and Middle Eastern fare) tend to be informal and chatty affairs.

Shermay's Cooking School
01-76 Chip Bee Gardens, 43 Jalan Merah Saga
Tel: 6479-8442
www.shermay.com
Some of Singapore's best chefs guest-star as instructors. A fine place to pick up Peranakan cooking too.

evening tour from 6 to 9.30pm (S$23 adults, S$13 children).

Guided Walking Tours

Original Singapore Walks promises to "bring people into places most other tours don't". Hosted by personable and energetic guides who inject humour and insider knowledge into the walks, itineraries include the red-light district of Chinatown, the hidden charms of Little India, and Singapore's (supposedly) haunted grounds in search of spirits. No pre-booking is necessary. All you need to do is show up at the designated meeting place (usually at an MRT station) at the tour time and pay on the spot. Tours cost S$28 for adults and S$15 for children. Contact **Journeys**, tel: 6325-1631; www.journeys.com.sg.

River and Harbour Cruises

Board the hardy "bumboat", which used to be the traditional way of travelling on the Singapore River in days gone by. Operated by **Singapore River Cruises** (tel: 6336-6111; www.rivercruise.com.sg), the boats ply two routes: tickets for the 30-minute route cost S$15, while the 45-minute route costs S$20.

The *Cheng Ho*, a replica 15th-century Chinese junk, has cruises three times daily (S$27 for adults and S$14 for children). It also has high tea at 3pm (S$32 for adults, S$16 for children) and dinner cruises at 6.30pm (S$55 for adults, S$29 for children). Contact **WaterTours** at tel: 6533-9811 or www.watertours.com.sg for bookings.

SIA Hop-On

This tourist bus service plys the major landmarks and attractions around the city area, from Bugis through Chinatown and Clarke Quay to Sentosa. As its name implies, you hop on (and off) as you wish along various desig-

nated stops. One-day tickets are S$6 for Singapore Airlines and SilkAir passengers visiting Singapore, free for SH Tours' customers and S$12 (adult), S$6 (child) for other passengers. SIA Hop-On is operated by **SH Tours** – for more information call 6734-9923; www.asiatours.com.sg.

Special Interest Tours

If pressed for time, take the standard three-hour **City Tour** (from S$32) offered by a number of tour agencies. This coach tour normally includes a drive along Orchard Road to the colonial heart of Singapore, with a stop along the Singapore River. Tours continue to the financial district, and then to Chinatown, Mount Faber with its panoramic views, Botanic Gardens and end at Little India.

More novel are the special-interest tours that the STB has devised with several tour agencies. The **Flavours of Singapore** (S$29) tour begins at the Spice Garden (Fort Canning Park) and continues on to sample local cuisines with visits to Little India, Geylang Serai, Katong and China-

town. **Heartlands of Singapore** tour (from S$30) is for those interested in the everyday life in Singapore's suburban housing estates. There is also a Peranakan Tour in the Katong and Joo Chiat area featuring beadwork demonstrations and food tastings.

STB's visitors centres (*see page 263*) and its website, www.yoursingapore.com, have full details of the tours available. Otherwise, contact any of the tour operators listed here or your hotel concierge.
Holiday Tours & Travel/Tour East; tel: 6735-1221; www.toureast.net.
RMG Tours; tel: 6220-8722; www.rmgtours.com.
Faber Tours; tel: 6270-8855; www.fabertours.com.sg.
SH Tours; tel: 6734-9923; www.asiatours.com.sg.

Taxi Tourist Guides

The **Taxi Tourist Guide** organised by the STB and the Singapore Taxi Academy allows visitors to explore Singapore at their own pace with a trained taxi driver who doubles up as a tourist guide. Call the STB (tel: 1800 736-2000) for more information.

BELOW: Singapore River Cruise.

A – Z

AN ALPHABETICAL SUMMARY OF PRACTICAL INFORMATION

A ddresses

Singapore is easy to navigate, with a logical street layout and well-posted signs. The number preceding the road name in an address indicates the building or block number on that road, and in the case of high-rise buildings, the number of the floor precedes the shop's unit number. For example, 02-11 Centrepoint, 176 Orchard Road means the shop is unit number 11 on the 2nd floor of the Centrepoint building at 176 Orchard Road.

Admission Charges

Admission to the various muse-
ums in Singapore ranges from S$5 to S$10 for an adult. The Asian Civilisations Museum has discounted admission every Friday, from 7 to 9pm. Singapore Art Museum is free to enter on major public holidays, on week-days between noon and 2pm and on Fridays from 6 to 9pm.

The Park Hopper ticket offers reduced-price admission for the Singapore Zoo, Night Safari and Jurong Bird Park. It can be pur-chased at those venues, in either a 2-in-1 or 3-in-1 variation.

B udgeting for Your Trip

Accommodation can cost any-where from S$20 for a bed in a
dormitory with shared facilities to S$80 a room in a budget hotel to more than S$400 per night in a top-end luxury hotel.

Food is cheap – you can eat very well at a hawker centre for S$5 – and so is public transport (S$0.90 to S$1.90 per trip on the bus or MRT). Taxi rides in Singa-pore are reasonably priced as well; short journeys around the city centre will cost about S$8.

If you live frugally, it's possible to survive on a budget of S$50 a day. If, however, you intend to live it up by eating out at good restaurants and checking out the city's night-spots, be prepared to budget about S$30 for a two- to three-course meal (without drinks), and a similar amount for entry into the clubs (inclusive of one drink). Drinks at bars are cheaper than at clubs, but the best deals are during happy hours, from about 5 to 8pm, when prices are reduced by between 20 and 50 percent on average. At other times, beer is priced from S$12 a pint and a glass of house wine from around S$14.

Business Travellers

As a country aggressively promoting free trade and foreign investment, Singapore is a good place for businesspeople. International-class hotels have business centres with all the requisite services. Other support services, such as office rental, staff hiring and translation and interpretation services, are all easily available.

Singapore's modern and efficient airport, telecommunications and superb infrastructure have all helped to make it one of the leading convention cities in the world. There are several world-class venues for large conventions and exhibitions. For details on conventions, contact the **Singapore Tourism Board** (see page 263). For information on starting a business in Singapore, contact the **Singapore Economic Development Board**, tel: 6832-6832; www.edb.gov.sg.

C hildren

Singapore is relatively child-friendly in terms of attractions and activities. There are plenty of attractions for kids, as long as they are able to take the hot weather. Most attractions have reduced-price admission for children under 12 and even free admission for children under a certain age, usually three. Most restaurants and cafés also have kids' menus, while many hotels offer babysitting services, so call before booking to find out.

Climate

Singapore lies very close to the equator and has a tropical climate

ABOVE: kids at Siloso Beach.

with very little variation in temperature through the year. Average daytime temperature is 31°C (88°F), dropping to around 25°C (77°F) at night. Most of the rain falls during the northeast monsoon (Dec–early Mar) and to a lesser degree during the southwest monsoon (June–Sept). Thunderstorms, though, can occur throughout the year. Generally the weather is hot with high humidity levels, averaging 84 percent daily.

What to Wear

Light summer clothes that are easy to move around in, and preferably in porous cotton, are the right choice for a full day out in town.

CLIMATE CHART

°C | J F M A M J J A S O N D | mm
40 — 400
35 — 350
30 — 300
25 — 250
20 — 200
15 — 150
10 — 100
5 — 50
0 — 0

▢ Maximum temperature
▢ Minimum temperature
— Rainfall

Wear a white or light-coloured shirt and tie if you have business meetings. Jackets are usually out of place except for very formal functions.

Most hotels and restaurants don't impose a strict dress code. While slippers and shorts are taboo at clubs, casually dressed – but not sloppy – diners are generally welcomed at most restaurants, and increasingly so as many upmarket dining hubs have alfresco seating. To be sure, call in advance to check on an establishment's dress code.

If visiting temples and mosques, avoid wearing brief shorts and scanty tops (see also "Etiquette", page 257).

When to Visit

Singapore is a year-round destination: as temperatures hardly vary from month to month, any time is a good time to visit. May and June are slightly hotter and more humid than other months of the year, while December is the wettest month, with several heavy rain spells.

Crime and Safety

Singapore is a safe country with a very low crime rate. "Low crime doesn't mean no crime", though, warns a police poster. So, it's prudent to watch out for pickpockets and snatch thieves. There is occasional youth gang activity but it seldom – if at all – involves visitors. For police assistance call 999.

Customs Regulations

Visitors carrying more than the equivalent of S$30,000 in cash or cheques have to report this fact to the customs authorities upon entering Singapore. Duty-free allowance per adult is 1 litre of spirits, 1 litre of wine or port and 1 litre of beer, stout or ale. No duty-free cigarettes are allowed into Singapore, although they may be purchased on the way out.

Duty-free purchases can be made both upon arrival and departure, except when returning to Singapore within 48 hours. This is to prevent Singaporeans from making a day trip out of the country to stock up on duty-free goods. In addition, passengers arriving from Malaysia are not allowed duty-free concessions.

The list of prohibited items includes drugs (the penalty for even small amounts can be death); firecrackers; obscene or seditious publications, video tapes and software; reproduction of copyright publications, video tapes or discs, records or cassettes; seditious and treasonable materials; endangered wildlife or their by-products; chewing

tobacco and imitation tobacco products; and chewing gum other than for personal use. A complete list of prohibited, restricted and dutiable goods is available from the airport's **Customs Duty Officer**, tel: 6542-7058 (Terminal 1), tel: 6546-4656 (Terminal 2), tel: 6542-0519 (Terminal 3), tel: 6546-3090 (Budget Terminal), or check the **Singapore Customs** website at: www.customs.gov.sg.

D isabled Travellers

The **National Council for Social Services** (tel: 6210-2500; www.ncss.org.sg) is a good information source. The **Disabled People's Association of Singapore** (DPA; tel: 6899-1220; www.dpa.org.sg) has a booklet titled *Access Singapore*, which gives details of facilities for the disabled.

Some of the newer buildings are designed with the disabled in mind, but generally if one is confined to a wheelchair, getting around by public transport might be a problem. Only selected buses can accommodate wheelchairs. The good news is most taxi operators take advance bookings for wheelchair-friendly taxis.

E lectricity

Electrical supply is 220–240 volts, 50 Hz. Most hotels will

supply transformers for 110–120 volt, 60 Hz appliances.

Embassies & Consulates

Office hours of foreign missions vary and locations may change. Call to confirm before visiting. For a full listing, check the STB website at: www.visitsingapore.com.
Australia: 25 Napier Road, tel: 6836-4100; www.australia.org.sg
Canada: 11-01, 1 George Street, tel: 6854-5900; www.canada international.gc.ca
New Zealand: 15-06 Ngee Ann City Tower A, 391A Orchard Road, tel: 6235-9966; www.nzembassy.com/singapore
UK: 100 Tanglin Road, tel: 6424-4200; http://ukinsingapore.fco.gov.uk.
USA: 27 Napier Road, tel: 6476-9100; http://singapore.usembassy.gov

Singapore embassies in other countries:
Australia: 17 Forster Crescent, Yarralumla, ACT 2600; tel: (61) 2 6273-9823; www.mfa.gov.sg/canberra
New Zealand: 17 Kabul Street Khandallah, Wellington 6440; tel: (64) 4 470-0850; www.mfa.gov.sg/wellington
UK: 9 Wilton Crescent, Belgravia, London SW1X 8SP; tel: (44) 20 7235-8315; www.mfa.gov.sg/london
USA: 3501 International Place, NW Washington DC 20008; tel: (1) 202 537-3100; www.mfa.gov.sg/washington

Emergencies

Fire, Ambulance: 995
Police: 999
Police Hotline (non-emergency): 1800-255-0000
Ministry of Health Hotline: 1800-333-9999

Etiquette

Some local customs and habits recall inherited traditions and a familiarity with local mores, but, generally, with everyday etiquette being relaxed and fairly cosmopolitan, visitors behaving courteously stand little chance of

BELOW: remove shoes before entering mosques.

Above: praying at Kong Meng San.

unintentionally giving offence. For deeper insights on local traditions though, read JoAnn Meriwether Craig's *Culture Shock! Singapore* (see page 264).

In Public

What is more obvious, however, are law-enforced rules governing public behaviour, some of which carry hefty fines. There are usually clear signs explaining what you can or cannot do. In general be mindful of the following:

Road Crossing – Pedestrians must use a designated crossing if one is available within 50 metres (165ft), or else risk a fine of up to S$1,000 for jaywalking. Designated crossings are zebra crossings, overhead bridges, underpasses, and traffic-light junctions fitted with red and green pedestrian signal lights.

Littering – The government has taken great pains, not only to keep Singapore's streets clean, but also to inculcate civic-conscious habits in its citizens. Litter bins are found everywhere and make it inexcusable to litter. First-time offenders are fined S$300 (be it a bus ticket, a cigarette butt or a sweet wrapper). Repeat offenders are also sentenced to participate in a corrective work order programme, where they have to collect rubbish in a public place for a period of time, or up to S$5,000 in fines.

Toilets – Failure to flush urinals and water closets after use in public toilets (hotels, shopping complexes, etc.) can result in a S$150 fine. It is interesting to note, however, that to date no one has ever been convicted of this offence. Still, take no chances.

Smoking – Smoking is banned in all public covered areas. The only exceptions to this rule are the designated smoking areas in pubs, bars, clubs and similar nightspots. If you have to light up in a restaurant, choose one that has an outdoor dining terrace. There is a fine of S$200 if you're caught smoking in a prohibited place and, if convicted in court, the fine could go up to S$1,000. Signboards that serve as reminders are on display in such places. Youths under 18 years are prohibited from buying cigarettes and smoke in public.

Chewing Gum – Contrary to belief, you won't go to jail for chewing gum. The ban – imposed in 1992 because the authorities got fed up with people sticking wads of used gum on train and cinema seats – covers only the sale and importation of chewing gum, not the actual act of gum-chewing. Remember only to chew the gum, not hawk it at street corners or stick it under seats when no one is looking.

Note: A new law passed in 2003 allows the sale of gum with therapeutic value, for instance, nicotine-laced gum to help smokers kick the habit. These items can only be bought from the pharmacist, not off the shelves.

Public Transport – No eating, drinking or smoking is allowed aboard buses and MRT trains. And passengers are banned from carrying smelly durians on board MRT trains too!

Private Homes

If you are invited to the home of a local, it is customary to take a small gift along – whether some cakes or pastries, fruit, chocolates or flowers. Never bring alcohol, wine or beer to the home of a Muslim though.

Most Singaporeans remove their shoes at the door so as not to bring dirt into the house. No host would insist that visitors do the same, but it is only polite to follow this custom.

Asian meals are usually served family-style in large bowls or plates placed in the centre of the table, with diners helping themselves to a little from each bowl or plate. Piling up your plate with food is impolite.

Temples and Mosques

Removing one's shoes before entering a mosque or an Indian temple has been a tradition for centuries. Inside, devotees do not smoke, yet neither of these customs generally apply to Chinese temples, where more informal styles prevail. Visitors are most welcome to look around at their leisure and stay for religious rituals, except in some mosques. While people pray, it is understood that those not participating in the service will stand aside. A polite gesture would be to ask permission before taking photographs: the request is seldom, if ever, refused. Modest clothing is appropriate for a visit. Most temples and mosques have a donation box for funds to help maintain the building. It is customary for visitors to contribute a token amount before leaving.

G ay & Lesbian Travellers

Engaging in homosexual activity is an offence – which doesn't mean it is non-existent. In fact, several establishments now attract a gay crowd (see page 247 for gay and lesbian nightlife venues). In general, Singapore society is still fairly conservative when it comes to gay public displays of affection, and these actions are likely to draw stares. But that's as much reaction as you'll get, as Singaporeans do not usually react aggressively to homosexuality *(see also text box on page 66).*

The local gay rights advocacy group **People Like Us** (www.plu.sg) has not been allowed to register as a legitimate society and only operates as an online portal. Some useful websites on Singapore's gay scene are found at www.fridae.com and www.utopia-asia.com.

H ealth and Medical Care

Most of Singapore is as sparkling clean as advertised. Safe drinking water and strict government control of all food outlets make dining out a great experience.

Singapore is malaria-free, although dengue fever, spread by daytime mosquitoes, occurs occasionally in the older residential neighbourhoods. However, there is no cause for alarm, as these are not areas usually frequented by tourists.

Yellow fever vaccinations are unnecessary unless arriving from infected areas.

If you are travelling to less developed countries in the region, the **Travellers' Health & Vaccination Clinic** (tel: 6357-2222) at Tan Tock Seng Hospital (Moulmein Road) is an excellent place for vaccinations and booster shots against tropical diseases.

Hospitals

Singapore has the best healthcare facilities in the region. Medical services in both government and private institutions are excellent. Government and private hospitals are found all over the island. They compare favourably with those in the West. The hospitals here are advanced and well equipped to cope with the most complicated and difficult procedures. Most of their services are available to non-citizens but at substantially higher rates. For this reason, ensure that you have bought adequate travel insurance.

Singapore General Hospital
7 Outram Road
Tel: 6222-3322
www.sgh.com.sg
Excellent public hospital with the best facilities in the city.

Mount Elizabeth Hospital
3 Mount Elizabeth
Tel: 6737-2666
www.pgh.com.sg
Private hospital close to Orchard Road. Has both a walk-in clinic and emergency services.

KK Women & Children's Hospital
100 Bukit Timah Road
Tel: 6225-5554
www.kkh.com.sg
Specialises in obstetrics, gynaecology, children and infant care. It

has a 24-hour women's clinic and a children's emergency department.

Raffles Hospital
585 North Bridge Road
Tel: 6311-1111
www.raffleshospital.com
Has a 24-hour walk-in clinic; it also provides a 24-hour house, hotel and ship-call service.

Clinics

There is no shortage of private clinics in Singapore. All doctors speak English and at least one other language. They are professionally trained either here or abroad. The average cost per visit varies between S$30–55 for a practitioner and S$100–150 for a first consultation by a specialist. Ask your embassy or hotel reception to recommend a private practitioner or specialist.

Pharmacies

In Singapore, most clinics can dispense medication, but there are also numerous registered pharmacies with a qualified pharmacist on duty. The largest ones include **Guardian Pharmacy** and **NTUC Healthcare Pharmacy**, found in most shopping centres in town. A pharmacist is usually on duty daily from 9am to 6pm; purchasing a controlled medication will require a doctor's prescription. Most pharmacies also stock personal care items, baby products, toiletries, cosmetics, vitamins, nutritional supplements and even unrelated sundries like gift cards and sweets.

I nternet

The following cyber-cafés are centrally located in the city.
Blue Chip
02-10 Midpoint Orchard,
220 Orchard Road
Tel: 6100-7873
www.bluechipgroup.com.sg
Open daily 10am–10.30pm.
Cyberia
545 Orchard Road
Tel: 6732-1309
Open daily 9am–11pm.

BELOW: Singapore's healthcare is the best in the region.

Hotels catering to a business clientele also offer internet access, albeit at higher rates. **Wireless@ SG** is a scheme that provides free wireless connection at selected hotspots. You will need a mobile device with Wi-fi facility, and you have to register online with a service provider: **iCELL** (tel: 6309-4525; www.icellnetwork.com), **QMax** (tel: 6895-4833; www.qmax.com.sg) or **SingTel** (tel: 1610; www.singtel.com). Check the Infocomm Development Authority website (www.ida.gov.sg) for locations of hotspots.

L eft Luggage

Baggage storage services are available 24 hours daily at Changi Airport's Terminal 1 (tel: 6214-0628), Terminal 2 (tel: 6214-1683) and Terminal 3 (tel: 6242-8936).

Lost Property

The loss of your passport or valuables should be reported immediately to the local police. Call 1800 255-0000 or head to the police headquarters at 391 New Bridge Road, Police Cantonment Complex. For loss of items in taxis, buses and MRT trains, contact the respective transport service operator *(see page 233)*.

M aps

Excellent Singapore maps, with areas of interest to the visitor shown in detail, are freely available at Changi Airport's arrival hall and throughout the city.

Most bookshops also stock maps of Singapore and the region. Particularly good is the **Insight Fleximap Singapore**, laminated for durability and easy folding. For a comprehensive street atlas, get a copy of the **Mighty Minds Singapore Street Directory** (2011 edition).

Media
Television

The range of programming is

diverse, and free-to-air television runs for most of the day and night, some even for 24 hours. The local programming is not very exciting, though, given the fact that it is a virtual monopoly operated by Mediacorp.

There are seven channels, of which **Channel 5**, **Okto** and **Channel NewsAsia** broadcast in English. **Channel 8** and **Channel U** broadcast in Mandarin, **Suria** in Malay and **Vasantham** in Tamil. Check the daily papers or *8 Days* (a weekly entertainment magazine) for schedules.

Many Singapore homes are wired up and cable-access-ready. Pay TV is available through **Starhub Cable Vision** (SCV), which offers over 100 TV channels to subscribers 24 hours a day. Singapore is a hub for several foreign broadcasters, which beam their programmes out of Singapore via satellite to regional and worldwide audiences.

Radio

The most popular English radio stations are: **Gold 90FM** (90.5 FM), featuring contemporary music; **Symphony 92.4** (92.4 FM), airing mostly classical and jazz; **938Live** (93.8 FM) for news; **987FM** (98.7 FM) for contemporary hits and Top 40 music; and **Class 95** (95 FM), which is easy listening. SAFRA's (Singapore Armed Forces

Reservist Association) radio station, **Power 98**, plays the usual mainstream hits.

There is also the 24-hour **BBC World Service** (88.9 FM) to keep you up to date on international news events.

Newspapers and Magazines

The Straits Times and *Business Times* are good English-language dailies for domestic and foreign news and a very active letters-to-the-editor forum. There is also the tabloid *The New Paper*, sold in the afternoons. In addition there is a free English daily, *Today*, available free from MRT stations. Pick up free *I-S* and *Where* magazines, with the latest on dining and clubbing, at some eateries and bars.

A business and investment weekly, *The Edge Singapore* provides in-depth financial-related news on Singapore. For wider coverage of the region, on both politics and business news, pick up a copy of the daily *Wall Street Journal Asia*.

The *International Herald Tribune* and *Wall Street Journal* are available on the day of publication. American, British, European and Asian newspapers and current affairs magazines are available at hotel news-stands and bookstores such as MPH, Times, and Kinokuniya.

ABOVE: Vesak Day parade.

Money

The country's currency is the Singapore dollar (S$). It is divided into 100 cents. Banknotes are available in $1, $2, $5, $10, $20, $50, $100, $500, $1,000 and $10,000. The $1 note, although still in circulation, has largely been replaced by the $1 coin. Other coins are in denominations of 5, 10, 20 and 50 cents.

At the time of press, £1 was roughly equivalent to S$2, US$1 was worth S$1.3, and €1 was worth S$1.8.

ATMs

ATMs are found in banks, shopping malls and MRT stations; many feature the Cirrus and PLUS systems.

Changing Money

Licensed money-changers in shopping malls along Orchard Road (Lucky Plaza), Scotts Road (Far East Plaza) and North Bridge Road (Peninsula Shopping Centre and Peninsula Plaza) offer better rates than banks. Hotels and department stores offer the least attractive rates.

Money-changers trade in most of the world's major currencies and all of the Southeast Asian ones. They are also open for business seven days a week, usually from 9–10am until about 9pm. Exchange rates are not necessarily uniform, so don't be bashful in asking for better deals. Generally, you enjoy a better rate if you are changing a large sum of money.

If you are unable to change your leftover Singapore currency before leaving the country, don't despair: you can change it elsewhere in the region, as the Singapore dollar is widely accepted.

Credit Cards

Major credit cards are accepted at airline offices, hotels and most restaurants and upmarket stores. Some small travel agencies, camera and electronic goods stores tend to add a surcharge of between 2 and 4 percent. Be sure to ask before making payment.
Amex: 1800 296-0220
Diners: 6416-0800
MasterCard: 800 110-0113
Visa: 800 448-1250

Emergency Money

Cash advances can also be obtained at banks using major credit cards. Credit cards with a personal identification number and certain bank cards can also be used to withdraw money from ATMs found all over the island (at some MRT stations, in shopping centres and outside banks).

Tipping

Hotels, larger restaurants, and many clubs and bars usually levy a 10 percent service charge, which is added to your bill along with the standard 7 percent GST. There is no need to tip unless the staff have gone out of their way to provide exceptional service.

Porters and bellboys receive S$1 upwards, depending upon the number of bags carried or the complexity of the errand. Beyond that, tipping is the exception rather than the rule. In small local restaurants, food stalls and taxis, there is no service charge and no tipping – a smile with a simple thank you (*terima kasih* in Malay or *xie xie* in Mandarin) is more than sufficient.

Travellers' Cheques

Singapore is a major financial centre, and travellers' cheques can easily be cashed in most banks. Many shops also accept travellers' cheques in lieu of cash after conversion at the prevailing rate of exchange.

Opening Hours

Business hours are generally from 9am until 5pm. Government offices are open Monday to Friday and on Saturday mornings; hours vary between 8–9am and 5–6pm, and until 1pm on Saturdays.

Department stores and shops open from about 10–11am until about 9pm. Most are also open on Sundays, including those in Little India and Chinatown. Some shopping malls in Orchard Road open until 11pm on Fridays and Saturdays.

Banks are open from 10am until 3pm on weekdays, and 9.30–11am on Saturdays.

Photography

In a tropical place like Singapore, it is best to protect cameras from excessive heat and humidity. Do not leave your camera in the sun or in a hot car. If you have an SLR camera, use a UV filter to protect your lenses or a polarisation filter to reduce glare and to enhance the blue of the sky. Best times for outdoor photography are the earlier part of the day and later in the afternoon when the sun is lower in the sky.

Digital processing can be completed within the hour at any of the photo stores found in malls and tourist areas.

Postal Services

Singapore Post is very efficient and mailboxes can be found near every MRT station. An aerogramme or airmail postcard to anywhere costs just 50 cents. Letters weighing not more than 20 grams to North and South America, Europe, Africa, Middle East, Australia, New Zealand and Japan cost S$1.10. For all other countries in Asia and the Pacific, it costs 65 cents. The fee for a registered item is S$2.20 (plus postage).

Apart from postal services, Singapore Post provides other services, such as parcel delivery, issuing travellers' cheques, local and foreign money orders and bank drafts, philatelic sales, postbox mail collection, and a variety of other services.

Singapore Post's main branches are at listed below. Most other branches are open from Mon–Fri 8.30am–5pm (Wed until 8pm), and Sat 8.30am–1pm.

For more information, call 1605 for postal enquiries or check www.singpost.com.sg:
Change Alley
02-02 Hitachi Tower, 16 Collyer Quay
Tel: 6538-6899
Open Mon–Fri 8.30am–6.30pm, Sat 8.30am–1pm; closed Sun and public holidays.
1 Killiney Road
Tel: 6734-7899
Open Mon–Fri 9.30am–9pm, Sat 9.30am–4pm, Sun and public holidays 10.30am–4pm.
Changi Airport
Terminal 2
tel: 6542-7899
Open daily 8am–9.30pm.

Courier Services

Singapore Post has a courier service called **Speedpost**, which services more than 200 countries at fairly reasonable rates. Call tel: 1800 225-5777 or check www.speedpost.com.sg for more information and rates.

Several air-cargo carriers including **Federal Express** (tel: 1800 743-2626), **Cargolux** (tel: 6543-0006) and **UPS** (United Parcel Service, tel: 1800 738-3388) have offices at Changi Airport.

Public Holidays

New Year's Day: 1 Jan
Chinese New Year: Jan/Feb (two days)*
Good Friday: Mar/Apr*
Labour Day: 1 May
Vesak Day: May*
National Day: 9 Aug
Deepavali: Oct/Nov*
Christmas: 25 Dec
Hari Raya Puasa: *
Hari Raya Haji: *
*Precise dates vary. Check the Singapore Tourist Board (STB) website or any of its Visitors Centres (see page 263).

R eligious Services

Buddhism and Taoism are most commonly practised by the Chinese, among whom about 17 percent are Christians. Malays are Muslim and Singaporeans of Indian descent are either Hindu, Sikh or Christian. The Eurasians are largely Christians, either Roman Catholic or Protestants.

In multiracial, multi-religious Singapore, most major religions have their adherents. Call the relevant place of worship directly for prayer times or ask your hotel reception desk.

In the city area, services in English are held at the following churches:

Anglican
St Andrew's Cathedral
11 St Andrew's Road
Tel: 6337-6104
www.livingstreams.org.sg/sac
Sunday services at 7am, 8am, 9am, 11.15am and 5pm.

Roman Catholic
Cathedral of the Good Shepherd
Queen Street
Tel: 6337-2036
www.veritas.org.sg
Saturday sunset mass at 6.30pm; Sunday masses at 8am, 10am and 6pm.

Methodist
Wesley Methodist Church
5 Fort Canning Road
Tel: 6336-1433
www.wesleymc.org
Sunday services at 7.30am, 9.30am, 11.30am and 5pm.

T axes

A **Goods and Services Tax** (GST) of 7 percent is levied. In addition to GST, most hotels, restaurants, bars and nightclubs add a service charge of 10 percent.

As a visitor, you can have the GST refunded on goods purchased through the **Global Refund Tax Free Shopping** scheme. To qualify, you must spend at least S$100 in a single receipt from stores which participate in the **Global Refund Tax Free Shopping** or the **Premier Tax Free** schemes. Note: refunds are only given for visitors who depart Singapore by air. Designated stores will display a Tax Free Shopping sticker. The goods purchased must be for export only. The refund may be made either by cash, cheque or through your credit card.

Claim forms and the correct procedure on how to make a claim can be obtained at all participating retailers.

Accumulated shopping cheques can be cashed at Changi

Above: a Singapore Visitors Centre.

Airport's **Global Refund Counter** (tel: 6546-5089) or the **Premier Tax Free Scheme Counter** (tel: 6546-4353). Please note that the purchased goods have to be presented so head for the Refund Counter *before* checking in bulky purchases. Hand-carried items can be verified at the Refund Counters located after the immigration checkpoint.

Telephones

Most hotel rooms have phones that allow you to make **International Direct Dial** (IDD) calls. Charges are reasonable compared to many other countries.
• Singapore's **country code** is 65. There are no area codes.
• To call overseas from Singapore, dial the **international access code** 001 followed by the country code, area code and local telephone number. Alternatively you can dial 013 or 019 for cheaper IDD rates, although the lines may be weaker.
• For **international directory assistance**, operator-assisted, collect or person-to-person calls, dial 104.
• For **local directory assistance**, dial 100; each enquiry is charged at 63 cents.

Public Phones

There are three types of **public pay phone** commonly found at shopping centres and MRT stations: coin-operated pay phones for local calls (increasingly rare these days), card phones using phonecards and credit card phones for local and IDD calls.

Phonecards are available in S$2, S$5, S$10, S$20 and S$50 denominations and can be used for both local and overseas calls. Local calls cost 10 cents for the first 3 minutes and 10 cents for every subsequent 3 minutes, up to a maximum of 9 minutes. Phonecards may be purchased from all post offices *(see Postal Services, page 261)* and convenience stores like 7 Eleven shops.

Mobile Phones

Only users of **GSM mobile phones** with global roaming service can connect automatically with Singapore's networks. Check with your service provider at home if not sure, especially if coming from Japan or the US. Mobile phone reception is good to excellent throughout the island.

If you're planning to be in Singapore for any length of time, it's more economical to buy a local SIM card from one of the three

service providers: **SingTel** (tel: 1626 or 6738-0123; www.singtel. com), **M1** (tel: 1627 or 1800 843-8383; www.m1shop.com.sg) or **Starhub** (tel: 1633 or 6825-5000; www.starhub.com). These cards cost a minimum of S$20 and can be topped up when the value falls. You will be given a local mobile number to use.

Note: all local mobile numbers start with an 8 or 9.

Time Zone

Singapore is 8 hours ahead of Greenwich Mean Time (GMT).

Toilets

When nature calls, you can easily dash into any shopping centre, hotel, bus interchange or hawker centre, where there are always public toilets available. What may come as a surprise, however, is that the use of such toilets isn't always free. Some public toilets have attendants who charge 10 to 20 cents per entry – which is preposterous considering that some of these toilets are less than hygienic. There are usually one or two toilet stalls which have Asian-style squat toilet bowls – best avoided if you have wobbly knees.

Tourist Information

The **Singapore Tourism Board** (STB; www.stb.gov.sg) is highly respected for the crisp efficiency so characteristic of the place it represents. The board also approves tour operators and travel agents, and monitors them to make sure their services rank high by international standards. For more information, log on to www.yoursingapore.com.

Singapore Visitors Centres

Singapore Visitors Centre @ Orchard
Junction of Cairnhill Road and Orchard Road
Open daily 9.30am–10.30pm.
Singapore Visitors Centre @ ION Orchard
ION Orchard Level 1 Concierge
Open daily 10am–10pm.
Singapore Visitors Centre @ Bugis Street
Along Cheng Yan Place, next to Iluma shopping centre
Open daily 11am–10pm.
Singapore Visitors Centre @ Changi Airport
Arrivals halls, Terminals 1, 2 and 3
Open daily 6am–2am.

STB Offices Overseas

Australia
Sydney
Level 11, AWA Building,

BELOW: visitor centre staff.

47 York Street, Sydney,
NSW 2000, Australia
Tel: 61-2 9290-2888

Europe/United Kingdom
Frankfurt
Hochstrasse 35-37,
60313 Frankfurt, Germany
Tel: 49-69 9207-7018
London
Grand Buildings,
1–3 The Strand, London
WC2N 5HR,
United Kingdom
Tel: 44-20 7484-2710

United States
Los Angeles
5670 Wilshire Boulevard,
Suite 1550, Los Angeles,
CA 90036, USA
Tel: 1-323 677-0808
New York
1156 Avenue of the Americas,
Suite 702, New York,
NY 10036 USA
Tel: 1-212 302-4861

V isas and Passports

Visitors need to satisfy the following requirements before they are allowed to enter:
• Passport valid for at least six months;
• Confirmed onward or return tickets;
• Sufficient funds to maintain themselves during their stay in Singapore;
• Visa, if applicable.
Citizens of British Commonwealth countries (except India, Bangladesh and Pakistan), UK, European Union, Canada and the USA do not require visas. Such visitors will automatically be given a 30-day social visit pass when arriving at the airport, in the form of a stamp in their passports.

Check with your local Singapore embassy or consulate if you need a visa for entry, the rules of which are regularly subject to change, or look up the Singapore **Immigration and Checkpoint Authority** (ICA) website at: www.ica.gov.sg.

In addition, the visitor must hand in a completed disembarkation/embarkation card to the immigration officer. Upon immigration clearance, the disembarkation portion will be retained while the embarkation card is returned to the visitor. When the visitor leaves Singapore, the embarkation portion must be handed to the immigration officer.

Visa Extensions

Your social visit pass can be extended by another 30–90 days by submitting an online application on the ICA website at www.ica.gov.sg. Alternatively, apply in person by submitting the requisite form at ICA's **Visitor Services Centre** (4th Storey, ICA Building, 10 Kallang Road, tel: 6391-6100). Forms may be downloaded directly from the ICA website. Note: a local sponsor is required in order to apply for an extension of the social visit pass. An easier way to extend your stay is to leave the country, say to Johor Bahru across the border in Malaysia, for a day and have your passport re-stamped on entry into Singapore.

W eights and Measures

Most transactions in Singapore are metric, although the old imperial system is still occasionally used at the market.

Women Travellers

Women in Singapore enjoy equality and more freedom compared to other countries in the region. Because of this, there is little or no sexual harassment – a fact foreign women will appreciate. Women travellers can also expect to walk safely in Singapore's streets even when alone and late at night. Although shorts and sleeveless T-shirts are generally acceptable, women travellers should still exercise common sense when it comes to dressing. Topless bathing is not permitted at the beaches.

FURTHER READING

General

Singapore: State of the Art by Ian Lloyd and Joseph R. Yogerst. A hard-cover book filled with photographs that capture the spirit of Singapore.
Singapore: The Encyclopedia by various authors. Everything you've always wanted to know about Singapore is found in here.

History and Culture

The Air-Conditioned Nation: Essays on the Politics of Comfort and Control by Cherian George. Keen insights into what makes Singapore tick, by a former journalist.
From Third World To First: The Singapore Story: 1965–2000 by Lee Kuan Yew. In this memoir, the man who was responsible for the Singapore miracle tells his story.
Sinister Twilight: The Fall of Singapore by Noel Barber. Fascinating account of the fall of Singapore.
There is Only One Raffles: the Story of a Grand Hotel by Ilsa Sharp. Recounts the history of the grand Raffles Hotel.
Conversations with Lee Kuan Yew by Tom Plate. This candid, one-on-one conversation with the internationally respected political leader is startling and even humorous at times.
Singapore's Greatest Disasters: The Untold Stories by Malcolm Oei. Some of Singapore's most talked-about disasters – such as the collapse of the Hotel New World and the hijacking of a Singapore Airlines flight – are told through fictitious eyes.

Fiction

Foreign Bodies by Hwee Hwee Tan. A ripping bestseller by a home-grown writer.
Island Voices: A Collection of Short Stories from Singapore by Angelia Poon and Sim Wai Chew. A collection of stories about Singapore society by some of the best local writers.
One Fierce Hour by Alfian Sa'at. Highly charged poems about life in Singapore by one of the city's best poets and playwrights.
The Song of Silver Frond by Catherine Lim. A tale of love between a rich old man and a beautiful village girl by a well-known local writer.
Tanamera: A Novel of Singapore by Noel Barber. A romantic novel capturing the splendour of the colonial period.
Walk Like a Dragon by Goh Sin Tub. A local writer's collection of the personal stories of Singaporeans who relive the bygone years.

Natural History

Birds: An Illustrated Field Guide to the Birds of Singapore by Lim Kim Seng and Michael Rands. Comprehensive sourcebook for both expert and amateur bird-watchers, filled with illustrations.

Architecture

Pastel Portraits by Gretchen Liu. Focuses on Singapore's traditional shophouse architecture. Beautifully illustrated.
Singapore: Architecture of a Global City by Robert Powell, Albert K.S. Lim and Li Lian Chee. Focuses on the city's modern architecture and skyline.

Singapore Houses by Robert Powell. Featuring the best of sophisticated residential architecture in Singapore.

Food

The New Mrs Lee's Cookbook Vol. 1 and 2 by Shermay Lee. A delightful introduction to Peranakan cuisine and culture.
Makansutra Singapore 2011 by K.F. Seetoh. A guide to no-frills hawker food in Singapore by Singapore's well-known foodie.
Shiok!: Exciting Tropical Asian Flavours by Terry Tan and Christopher Tan. One of the best books on Singaporean cuisine.

Miscellaneous

Complete Notes from Singapore: The Omnibus Edition by Neil Humphreys. A British humorist weighs in on the idiosyncrasies of Singaporeans.
The Coxford Singlish Dictionary by TalkingCock.com. Can't understand what Singaporeans are saying? This hilarious "dictionary" on Singlish will help.
Culture Shock! Singapore by JoAnn Meriwether Craig. Insights into Singapore customs as seen through the eyes of the wife of an expatriate.

Other Insight Guides

Titles in the acclaimed *Insight Guides* series highlighting destinations in the region include guides to *Malaysia*, *Indonesia* and *Bali and Lombok*.

The *Insight Step by Step Guide Singapore* features an itinerary-based approach designed to assist the traveller with limited time.

SINGAPORE STREET ATLAS

The key map shows the area of Singapore covered by the atlas section. An index of street names and places of interest shown on the maps can be found on the following pages. For each entry there is a page number and grid reference

Map Legend

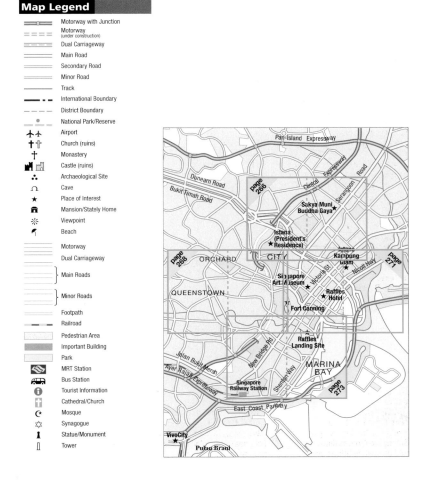

	Motorway with Junction
	Motorway (under construction)
	Dual Carriageway
	Main Road
	Secondary Road
	Minor Road
	Track
	International Boundary
	District Boundary
	National Park/Reserve
✈	Airport
✝	Church (ruins)
†	Monastery
⌂	Castle (ruins)
∴	Archaeological Site
∩	Cave
★	Place of Interest
⌂	Mansion/Stately Home
※	Viewpoint
▀	Beach
	Motorway
	Dual Carriageway
	Main Roads
	Minor Roads
	Footpath
	Railroad
	Pedestrian Area
	Important Building
	Park
◈	MRT Station
⌷	Bus Station
❶	Tourist Information
✝	Cathedral/Church
☾	Mosque
✡	Synagogue
⚑	Statue/Monument
⧠	Tower

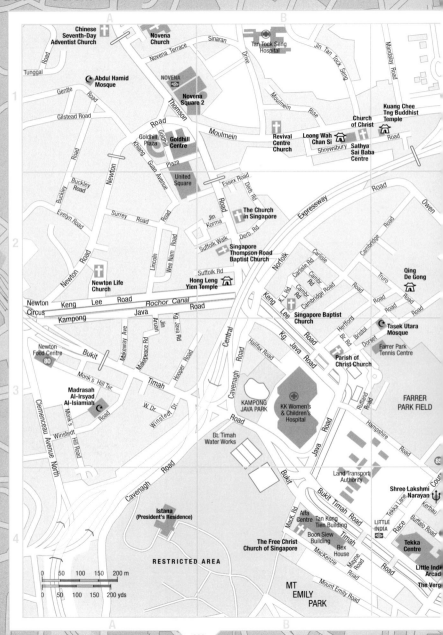

Restaurants ❶

Orchard Road and Surrounds
80 Newton Circus A3

Little India & Kampung Glam
84 Ananda Bhavan C4
85 Banana Leaf Apolo C4
86 Kashmir C4
87 Komala Vilas C4
88 Muthu's Curry C3

Hotels ❶

Little India & Kampung Glam
56 Moon @ 23 Dickson C/D4
58 Parkroyal on Kitchener Road D3
59 Wanderlust Hotel D4

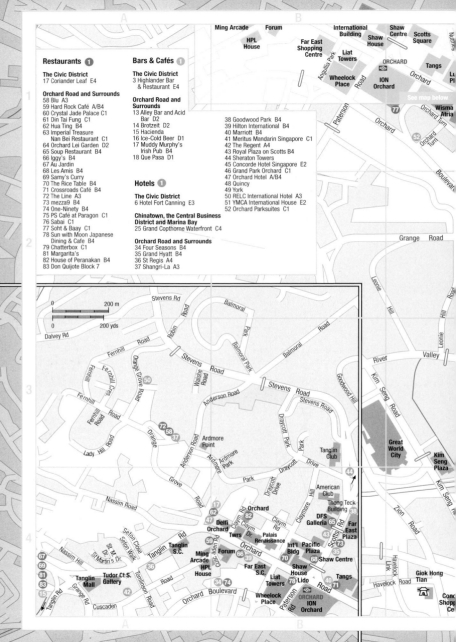

Restaurants ❶

The Civic District
17 Coriander Leaf E4

Orchard Road and Surrounds
58 Blu A3
59 Hard Rock Café A/B4
60 Crystal Jade Palace C1
61 Din Tai Fung C1
62 Hua Ting B4
63 Imperial Treasure
Nan Bei Restaurant C1
64 Orchard Lei Garden D2
65 Soup Restaurant B4
66 Iggy's B4
67 Au Jardin
68 Les Amis B4
69 Samy's Curry
70 The Rice Table B4
71 Crossroads Café B4
72 The Line A3
73 mezza9 B4
74 One-Ninety B4
75 PS Café at Paragon C1
76 Sabai C1
77 Soht & Baay C1
78 Sun with Moon Japanese
Dining & Cafe B4
79 Chatterbox C1
81 Margarita's
82 House of Peranakan B4
83 Don Quijote Block 7

Bars & Cafés ❶

The Civic District
3 Highlander Bar
& Restaurant E4

Orchard Road and Surrounds
13 Alley Bar and Acid
Bar D2
14 Brotzeit D2
15 Hacienda
16 Ice-Cold Beer D1
17 Muddy Murphy's
Irish Pub B4
18 Que Pasa D1

Hotels ❶

The Civic District
6 Hotel Fort Canning E3

**Chinatown, the Central Business
District and Marina Bay**
25 Grand Copthorne Waterfront C4

Orchard Road and Surrounds
34 Four Seasons B4
35 Grand Hyatt B4
36 St Regis A4
37 Shangri-La A3

38 Goodwood Park B4
39 Hilton International B4
40 Marriott B4
41 Meritus Mandarin Singapore C1
42 The Regent A4
43 Royal Plaza on Scotts B4
44 Sheraton Towers
45 Concorde Hotel Singapore E2
46 Grand Park Orchard C1
47 Orchard Hotel A/B4
48 Quincy
49 York
50 RELC International Hotel A3
51 YMCA International House E2
52 Orchard Parksuites C1

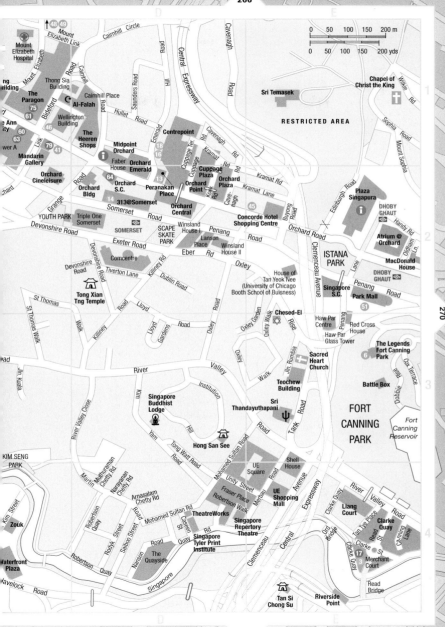

MT EMILY PARK
Mount Emily Road
Upper Wilkie Road
Wilkie Road
15
Sophia Road
Adis Road
Peace Mansion
Full Gospel Assembly
Mount Sophia
Cathay Building PictureHouse
MacDonald House
14

Church of Christ of Malaya

BRAS BASAH PARK
Orchard Rd
Bras Basah
Kirk Terrace
Bencoolen Mosque
17

Little India Arcade
Tekka Mall
Golden Wall Centre
Emmaus Baptist Church
Tamil Methodist Church
Prinsep Street Presbyterian Church
Peace Centre
Parklane Shopping Lane
Paradiz Centre

Hastings Road
Clive St
Dunlop St
Dalhousie Lane
Madras Street
Lasalle College of the Arts
McNally St
Short Street
Middle Road
Selegie Road
Niven Road
Selegie St
Prinsep

Sungei Road
Rochor Canal Rd
Canal Rd
Rochor Canal Rd
Bencoolen Centre
Bencoolen Link
Kwan Im Tong Hood Cho Temple
Sri Krishnan
Sculpture Square
Selegie Arts Centre

60
Abdul Gaffoor Mosque
Mayo St
Sim Lim Tower
Sungei
Our Lady of Lourdes
Sim Lim Square
Albert Complex
Rochor Centre
Fu Lu Shou Complex
Albert Centre
Bugis Street Market
New Bugis Street
Stamford Arts Centre
Midlink Plaza
Iluma at Bugis
Bugis Junction

Sungei Market (Thieves' Market)
Weld Road
Pasar Rd
Larut Rd
Old Male Cemeter
Kampong Gla
MUSLIM CEMETERY
Victoria Lane
Canal Rd
Queen Street Bus Terminal
Victoria Street Wholesale Centre
Jalan Pinang
Victoria St
90
89
Su Mos
55
BUGIS
Raffles Hospital
Parkview Square
Fraser Street

MACKenzie Road
Mount Emily Road

Church of Christ of Malaya

Bencoolen Street
Bras
Lor Payah
Waterloo
Maghain Aboth Synagogue
Church of St Peter & Paul
St Joseph's Church

Bras Basah
Fort Canning Road
Wesley Methodist
Fort Canning
Percival Rd
National Museum
Fort Canning Centre & Black Box
Keramat Iskandar Shah
The Substation
Peranakan Museum
28
National Archives
Philatelic Museum
Central Fire Station
13
Civil Defence Heritage Gallery
Funan DigitaLife Mall
MICA
High St Plaza
High St Centre
Coleman Bridge
CLARKE QUAY
Eu Tong Sen St
New Bridge Rd
Upper Circular Road
The Riverwalk
Elgin Bridge
Boat Quay
Parliament House
The Arts House

Plaza by the Park
Singapore Art Museum
Singapore Management University
11
MPH Building
Stamford Centre
Stamford House
Armenian Church
Burhani Mosque
Capitol Building
Peninsula Plaza
The Treasury
The Adelphi
New Supreme Court
Old Supreme Court
Parliament Place
Victoria Concert Hall & Theatre

Cathedral of the Good Shepherd
12
Chijmes
23
6
Raffles Hotel Shopping Centre
22
Raffles City
CITY HALL
6
26 11
10
St Andrew's Cathedral
City Hall
Colombo Ct
St Andrew's Road
Singapore Cricket Club
Lim Bo Seng Memorial

National Library
North Bridge Centre
Bras Basah Complex
29
20
Mint Museum of Toys
9
Beach Centre
25
14
3

53
Middle Road
Purvis St
Talin
Bain Street
Middle
Millg
Carver
Cashin
North
Carlton Towers
Bras Basah
Beach Road

Prince Theatre
Shaw Towers
Jade Theatre
Nicoll Highway
Suntec C Mall
Twr r
Twr 5

Suntec City
Singapore International Convention & Exhibition Centre
ESPLANADE
Temasek
i
Raffles Link
21
8
One Raffles Link
Marina Bay Front
2
Marina Square
4
19 24
10
Raffles Ave
Esplanade Drive

WAR MEMORIAL PARK
Civilian War Memorial
Singapore Recreation Club
Tan Kim Seng Fountain
PADANG
ESPLANADE PARK
Cenotaph
Connaught Drive
Queen Elizabeth Walk
Esplanade – Theatres on the Bay
7
Esplanade Mall
MARINA
Marina Seating Gal
The Floa Marina

Central Police Station
Fountain Wealth
3
2

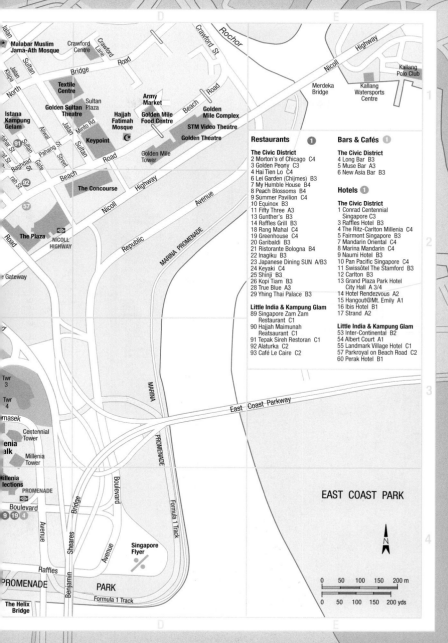

★ Malabar Muslim
Jama-Ath Mosque
Crawford Centre
Jalan Sultan
Jalan Kaya
North

Bridge

Crawford Lane
Crawford Road
Crawford St.
Rochor
Nicoll Highway

Merdeka Bridge
Kallang Watersports Centre
Kallang Polo Club

Textile Centre
Sultan Plaza
Army Market

Golden Sultan Theatre
Istana Kampung Gelam
Hajjah Fatimah Mosque
Golden Mile Food Centre
Golden Mile Complex

Alwar St.
Jalan Sultan
Minto Rd
Pahang St.
Baghdad St.
91
92
57
Sultan Gate
Beach Road
STM Video Theatre
Golden Theatre

Keypoint
Golden Mile Tower

The Concourse
Beach Road
Highway

Republic Avenue

The Plaza
NICOLL HIGHWAY
Nicoll Highway

MARINA PROMENADE

Gateway

Twr 3
Twr 4
masek

Centennial Tower
Millenia Tower

East Coast Parkway

MARINA PROMENADE

enia alk

Millenia lections
PROMENADE
9 19 4
Boulevard
Boulevard

EAST COAST PARK

Boulevard
Bridge
Sheares
Avenue
Formula 1 Track

Raffles
PROMENADE
The Helix Bridge
Benjamin
PARK
Singapore Flyer
Formula 1 Track

N

0   50   100 150 200 m
0   50   100 150 200 yds

Restaurants ➊

The Civic District
2 Morton's of Chicago C4
3 Golden Peony C3
4 Hai Tien Lo C4
6 Lei Garden (Chijmes) B3
7 My Humble House B4
8 Peach Blossoms B4
9 Summer Pavilion C4
10 Equinox B3
11 Fifty Three A3
13 Gunther's B3
14 Raffles Grill B3
18 Rang Mahal C4
19 Greenhouse C4
20 Garibaldi B3
21 Ristorante Bologna B4
22 Inagiku B3
23 Japanese Dining SUN A/B3
24 Keyaki C4
25 Shinji B3
26 Kopi Tiam B3
28 True Blue A3
29 Yhing Thai Palace B3

Little India & Kampung Glam
89 Singapore Zam Zam
    Restaurant C1
90 Hajjah Maimunah
    Reatsaurant C1
91 Tepak Sireh Restoran C1
92 Alaturka C2
93 Café Le Caire C2

Bars & Cafés ➊

The Civic District
4 Long Bar B3
5 Muse Bar A3
6 New Asia Bar B3

Hotels ➊

The Civic District
1 Conrad Centennial
    Singapore C3
3 Raffles Hotel B3
4 The Ritz-Carlton Millenia C4
5 Fairmont Singapore B3
7 Mandarin Oriental C4
8 Marina Mandarin C4
9 Naumi Hotel B3
10 Pan Pacific Singapore C4
11 Swissôtel The Stamford B3
12 Carlton B3
13 Grand Plaza Park Hotel
    City Hall A 3/4
14 Hotel Rendezvous A2
15 Hangout@Mt. Emily A1
16 Ibis Hotel B1
17 Strand A2

Little India & Kampung Glam
53 Inter-Continental B2
54 Albert Court A1
55 Landmark Village Hotel C1
57 Parkroyal on Beach Road C2
60 Perak Hotel B1

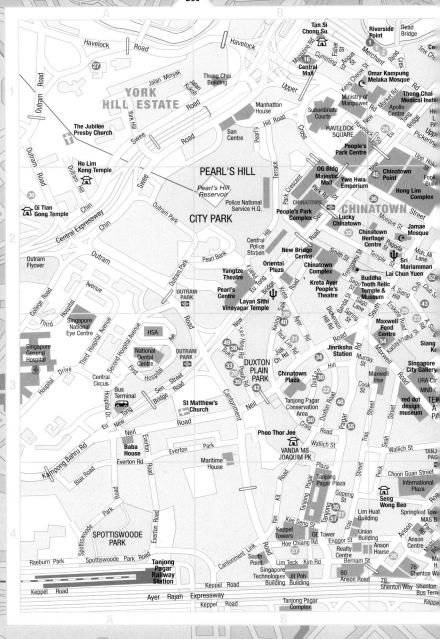

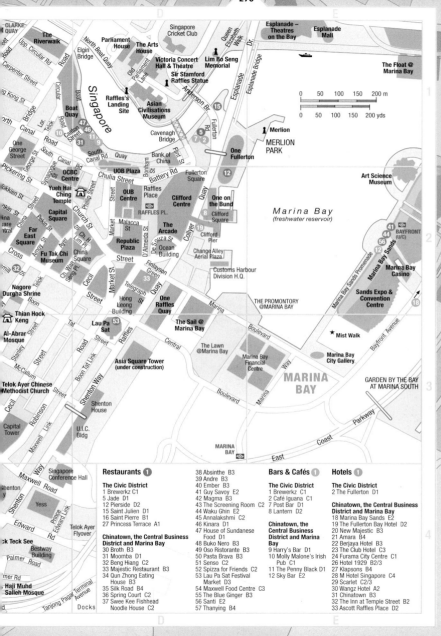

Restaurants ❶

The Civic District
1 Brewerkz C1
5 Jade D1
12 Pierside D2
15 Saint Julien D1
16 Saint Pierre B1
27 Princess Terrace A1

**Chinatown, the Central Business
District and Marina Bay**
30 Broth B3
31 Moomba D1
32 Beng Hiang C2
33 Majestic Restaurant B3
34 Qun Zhong Eating
   House B3
35 Silk Road B4
36 Spring Court C2
37 Swee Kee Fishhead
   Noodle House C2

38 Absinthe B3
39 Andre B3
40 Ember B3
41 Guy Savoy E2
42 Magma B3
43 The Screening Room C2
44 Waku Ghin E2
45 Annalakshmi C2
46 Kinara D1
47 House of Sundanese
   Food D1
48 Buko Nero B3
49 Oso Ristorante B3
50 Pasta Brava B3
51 Senso C2
52 Spizza for Friends C2
53 Lau Pa Sat Festival
   Market D3
54 Maxwell Food Centre C3
55 The Blue Ginger B3
56 Santi E2
57 Thanying B4

Bars & Cafés ❶

The Civic District
1 Brewerkz C1
2 Café Iguana C1
7 Post Bar D1
8 Lantern D2

**Chinatown, the
Central Business
District and Marina
Bay**
9 Harry's Bar D1
10 Molly Malone's Irish
   Pub C1
11 The Penny Black D1
12 Sky Bar E2

Hotels ❶

The Civic District
2 The Fullerton D1

**Chinatown, the Central Business
District and Marina Bay**
18 Marina Bay Sands E2
19 The Fullerton Bay Hotel D2
20 New Majestic B3
21 Amara B4
22 Berjaya Hotel B3
23 The Club Hotel C3
24 Furama City Centre C1
26 Hotel 1929 B2/3
27 Klapsons B4
28 M Hotel Singapore C4
29 Scarlet C2/3
30 Wangz Hotel A2
31 Chinatown B3
32 The Inn at Temple Street B2
33 Ascott Raffles Place D2

STREET INDEX

ART AND PHOTO CREDITS

General Index

RESTAURANTS

BARS

INSIGHT GUIDE
SINGAPORE

ABOUT THIS BOOK

Project Editors
Tom Le Bas, Rachel Lawrence
Art Director
Steven Lawrence
Senior Picture Researcher
Tom Smyth
Series Manager
Rachel Lawrence
Publishing Manager
Rachel Fox

Distribution

UK & Ireland
GeoCenter International Ltd
Meridian House, Churchill Way West
Basingstoke, Hampshire RG21 6YR
sales@geocenter.co.uk

United States
Ingram Publisher Services
1 Ingram Boulevard, PO Box 3006,
La Vergne, TN 37086-1986
customer.service@ingrampublisher
services.com

Australia
Universal Publishers
PO Box 307
St. Leonards NSW 1590
sales@universalpublishers.com.au

Worldwide
**Apa Publications GmbH & Co.
Verlag KG (Singapore branch)**
7030 Ang Mo Kio Ave 5
08-65 Northstar @ AMK
Singapore 569880
apasin@signet.com.sg

Printing

CTPS-China

©2011 Apa Publications GmbH & Co.
Verlag KG (Singapore branch)
All Rights Reserved

First Edition 1972
Twelfth Edition 2011

What makes an Insight Guide different? Since our first book pioneered the use of creative full-colour photography in travel guides in 1970, we have aimed to provide not only reliable information but also the key to a real understanding of a destination and its people.

Now, when the internet can supply inexhaustible (but not always reliable) facts, our books marry text and pictures to provide that more elusive quality: knowledge. To achieve this, they rely on the authority of locally based writers and photographers.

This new edition of *City Guide Singapore* was comprehensively updated by Malaysian-born journalist and writer **Amy Van**. Amy has lived in Singapore for more than 12 years and calls this city state her home. With more than a decade of editorial experience, she contributes to a variety of food, travel and lifestyle publications in the region as well as international travel guides. She has also worked on numerous book projects as writer and editor.

The book was copy-edited by **Stephanie Smith** and the project managed by **Rachel Lawrence** and **Tom Le Bas**.

Earlier editions of the guide were the work of Singapore-based managing editor **Francis Dorai** with the assistance of Singapore lifestyle writer **Joan Koh**. Joan wrote several of the insightful features chapters including those covering shopping, food, nightlife and the government's social campaigns. Other former contributors include **Wyn-Lyn Tan, James Gomez, Sylvia Toh, Tan Chung Lee, Chua Chong Jin, Tisa Ng, Robert Powell, Shamira Bhanu, Kenneth Wong, Joseph Yogerst, Rachel Farnay, Ilsa Sharp, David Pickell, Julia Clerk, Marcus Brooke, Star Black** and **Eric Oey**.

Most of the striking images that bring the city to life were taken by **Vincent Ng**, winner of Insight Guides' photography competition.

The book was proofread by **Neil Titman** and indexed by **Helen Peters**.

SEND US YOUR THOUGHTS

We do our best to ensure the information in our books is as accurate and up-to-date as possible. The books are updated on a regular basis using local contacts, who painstakingly add, amend, and correct as required. However, some details (such as telephone numbers and opening times) are liable to change, and we are ultimately reliant on our readers to put us in the picture.

We welcome your feedback, especially your experience of using the book "on the road". Maybe we recommended a hotel that you liked (or another that you didn't), or you came across a great bar or new attraction that we missed.

We will acknowledge all contributions, and we'll offer an Insight Guide to the best letters received.

Please write to us at:
**Insight Guides
PO Box 7910, London SE1 1WE**
Or email us at:
insight@apaguide.co.uk

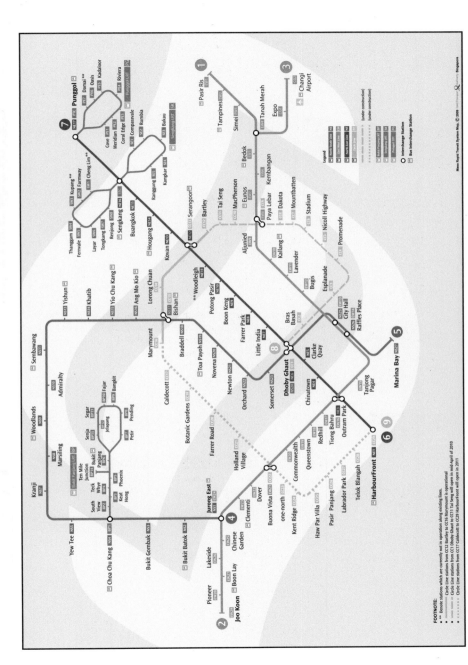

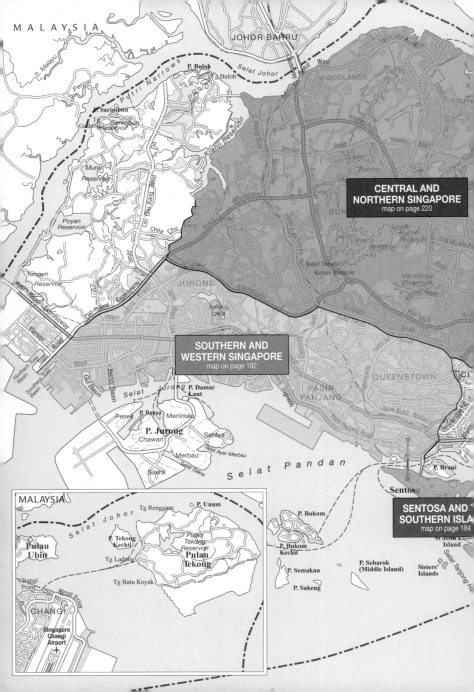